A Guide to the World of Drea

In *A Guide to the World of Dreams,* Ole Vedfelt presents an in-depth look at dreams in psychotherapy, counselling and self-help and offers an overview of current clinical knowledge and scientific research, including contemporary neuroscience. This book describes essential aspects of Jungian, psychoanalytic, existential, experiential and cognitive approaches to dreams and dreaming, and explores dreams in sleep laboratories, neuroscience and contemporary theories of dream cognition.

Vedfelt clearly and effectively describes ten core qualities of dreams, and delineates a resource-oriented step-by-step manual for dreamwork at varying levels of expertise. For each core quality, key learning outcomes are clarified and resource-oriented; creative and motivating exercises for practical dreamwork are spelled out, providing clear and manageable methods. *A Guide to the World of Dreams* also introduces a new cybernetic theory of dreams as intelligent, unconscious information processing, and integrates contemporary clinical research into this theory. The book even includes a wealth of engaging examples from the author's lifelong practical experience with all levels and facets of dreamwork.

Vedfelt's seminal work will be essential reading for Jungian analysts, psychotherapists, psychologists, counsellors, and psychiatrists. The book's clear method and real-life examples will inspire readers of all backgrounds, encouraging them to explore how increasing their understanding of dreams can stimulate everyday creativity and enhance their professional life.

Ole Vedfelt is leader of the Institute for Integrated Psychotherapy and Cybernetic Psychology, Denmark, and supervisor for the Danish Psychologist's Association. He is certified as a Jungian analyst, gestalt therapist, body psychotherapist, and meditation teacher. Ole has 45 years of professional experience with dreamwork.

A Guide to the World of Dreams

An Integrative Approach to Dreamwork

Ole Vedfelt

Routledge
Taylor & Francis Group
LONDON AND NEW YORK

First published 2017
by Routledge
2 Park Square, Milton Park, Abingdon, Oxon OX14 4RN

and by Routledge
711 Third Avenue, New York, NY 10017

Routledge is an imprint of the Taylor & Francis Group, an informa business.

British Library Cataloguing in Publication Data

A catalogue record for this book is available from the British Library.

Library of Congress Cataloging in Publication Data
Names: Vedfelt, Ole, author.
Title: A guide to the world of dreams: an integrative approach to dreamwork/Ole Vedfelt.
Description: Abingdon, Oxon; New York, NY : Routledge, 2017. | Includes bibliographical references.
Identifiers: LCCN 2016055046| ISBN 9781138948075 (hardback : alk. paper) | ISBN 9781138948082 (pbk. : alk. paper) | ISBN 9781315669717 (ebook)
Subjects: | MESH: Dreams–psychology | Psychotherapy–methods | Psychoanalytic Interpretation
Classification: LCC BF175.5.D74 | NLM WM 460.5.D8 | DDC 154.6/3–dc23
LC record available at https://lccn.loc.gov/2016055046

ISBN: 978-1-138-94807-5 (hbk)
ISBN: 978-1-138-94808-2 (pbk)
ISBN: 978-1-315-66971-7 (ebk)

Typeset in Times New Roman
by Cenveo Publisher Services

Contents

Preface

All human beings dream and all cultures have found meaning in dreams. Dreams have created the foundations for theories reaching deeply into the human psyche. Today we know that we dream for approximately two hours every night and that our dreams are vital to our mental health.

For more than 40 years I have studied and worked practically with dreams. Throughout that time dreams have fascinated and challenged me with their boundless creativity, their ability to spotlight what is most important to us and their never-failing enrichment of anyone who approaches them with serious intent.

As a scientist, psychotherapist, workshop leader, teacher and supervisor, I have scrutinized and worked with all the most important dream theories and methods. I have examined and analyzed approximately 35,000 dreams – my own, my clients' and the dreams of both professionals and laypeople who have participated in my workshops. This has continually provided practical opportunities for testing theories and techniques, and also for sharing my knowledge.

My objectives with *A Guide to the World of Dreams* are to create a clear and current framework for the understanding of dreams and to bestow the necessary practical techniques and tools on people who are interested in working with dreams.

In Part I of this book I summarize the essential knowledge of the most prominent psychological dream schools. Further, I highlight research from modern dream laboratories and the latest knowledge about the dreaming brain. The various dream schools do, however, have differing fundamental values, personality theories and cognitive interests that rather complicate the clear application of their potentials. This challenges us to expand our understanding of dreams to a more flexible, multifaceted and integrated perception of the mind firmly planted in the twenty-first century.

Part II describes how a new understanding of consciousness and our own unconscious intelligence can creatively integrate the poetic polysemy and complexity of dreams in a practical manner. I describe the ten Core Qualities of Dreams, supported by our valid knowledge about dreams without being confined by older, theoretical frameworks.

The Core Qualities can be viewed as responses to a series of fundamental inquiries pertinent to dreaming life. Why should we pay attention to our dreams? Can the oddness of dream language be translated into something we can better understand? What do the figures and characters in our dreams mean? How can dreams help us to act more constructively when we are awake? Can we immerse ourselves in our dreams in ways other than through rational understanding? How do dreams respond when we pay attention to them? Numerous other questions are also discussed.

In Part III of the book I expound upon the principles for practical dreamwork and provide tangible exercises for dreamwork in accordance with each of the ten Core Qualities.

There are also many examples of how dreams can be enlisted to enhance the lives and develop the personalities of people at all ages. Hence, a step-by-step and transparent model helps elevate novices to more advanced stages, employing methods that can be followed by anyone who wants to learn to work with dreams.

Below, I give a more detailed overview of the three parts of the book and all 17 chapters.

Part I – Knowledge of Dreams

In the first chapter I summarize the essential knowledge of the psychoanalytic, Jungian, existential, experiential, relational and cognitive schools of psychotherapeutic dreamwork. Further, I provide an overview of varieties of contemporary dreamwork for counselling, personal development groups, self-help or even social functions.

Chapter 2, on dreams and the natural sciences, discusses the results from the dream laboratories. It describes the activity of the dreaming brain and details dream theories based on natural science.

Chapter 3 presents my overriding and integrative view: we dream because we are complex beings who process information in multiple ways that provide us with differing perspectives on our lives. I postulate that our unconscious mind contains complex intelligent systems that process information on high levels of personality organization and that this work is reflected in our dreams. I present fundamental principles for dealing with complex phenomena and describe human personality as a multileveled, cybernetic network where multiple parts simultaneously process information in parallel to each other.

Part II – The Ten Core Qualities of Dreams

In Chapters 4–13 I describe the ten Core Qualities of Dreams. The overriding paradigm for this integration is the theory of information processing in complex networks. Based on this background, I show how these ten Core Qualities are based on valid knowledge from the psychotherapeutic dream schools and from natural scientific research, including contemporary neuroscience. Each of the core qualities is exemplified by individual dreams and dream series. These dreamwork examples from men, women and children of all ages cover a large variety of important life issues. For each core quality, key learning outcomes are clarified. The step-by-step descriptions of the core qualities carry dreamwork to increasingly complex levels.

Core Quality 1 substantiates the idea that dreams deal with matters important to us. The dreaming mind is self-organizing and has the necessary complexity for processing information at higher levels of personality organization than normal waking consciousness, which is mostly preoccupied with everyday issues. Clinical and neuroscientific research suggests that dreams are activated by motivation and reward-seeking systems in the brain and psyche. The first steps in dreamwork are to find resources and motivate dreamers to tune in to the spirit of searching behind all dreams.

Core Quality 2 looks at the symbolic language of dreams as a way of expressing important experiences that cannot be represented verbally or by linear logic. The creation and intuitive understanding of symbols, as well as clarification, amplification and dynamic dreamwork with symbols, are elaborated.

Core Quality 3 describes how dreams personify important complex subsystems in the dreamer and the interaction between these subsystems. Personifications in dreams reveal a dreamer's conceptions of others, as well as more or less unknown aspects of the dreamer's own personality. The chapter deals with the continuities between the dream self and waking self at all ages, with the objective (exterior) and subjective (interior) levels of interpretation, as well as with the significance of gender in dreams.

Core Quality 4 examines dreams as test runs of future possibilities. Dream narratives are seen as virtual reality simulations. Understanding various types of storylines and dramatic structures provides important tools for dreamwork.

Core Quality 5 dreams are online to unconscious intelligence, introduces concepts of levels and states of consciousness to describe various degrees of immersion in the creative matrix of dreams through experiential dreamwork. Methods such as association, drawing, role-play, imagination and bodywork are presented. Further, the chapter explains how to approach the dynamic powers of dreams in regulated and graduated ways.

Core Quality 6 develops the concept of practical intelligence and pattern recognition as a useful tool for dealing with the complexity of dreams. It shows how past and present, as well as future, experiences are possible meaningful contexts for the understanding of dreams. Further, it introduces the concept of searching for 'goodness of fit' patterns that match the context of dreamers' lives.

Core Quality 7 views dreams as forms of high-level communication. Dreams strive proactively to optimize dreamers' personalities and relations to the world. Our dreams respond to any serious endeavor by our waking consciousness to understand them and to realize their optimizing tendencies. Such mutual feedback loops are found in the day-to-day work with dreams, as well as in long-term dream series. They affect the personality by bringing it into greater balance.

Core Quality 8 deals with the experience of dreams as condensed information. These condensations are not random mixtures of thoughts left over from waking consciousness but rather syntheses of important information that can be unfolded in creative dreamwork.

Core Quality 9 describes dreamwork with all the experiential modalities in dreams – thought, imagery, body sensing, emotion, feeling and movement – all meaningful channels for information processing. Methodically combining multiple modalities may improve the efficiency and control of dreamwork.

Core Quality 10 provides deeper insights into the psychological energy landscapes of dreams. Their dynamics are described in accordance with information processing in parallel distributed networks. This makes it possible to evaluate the intensity and information density of various parts of dreams and guide dreamwork along the creative edge between order and chaos, until harmonization occurs between conflicting energies and contents. This chapter places a special focus on how to understand and process further peak experience dreams which mark turning points in dreamers' lives.

Chapter 14 concerns traumatic dreams and presents research and psychological theories relevant to this issue. I provide ample examples, plus dream series describing how traumatic dreams can be processed based on an understanding of the ten Core Qualities.

Part III – Principles and Exercises for Practical Dreamwork

Chapters 15 and 16 present principles and exercises for practical dreamwork related to the core qualities. These recommendations can be used in psychotherapy and counselling, as well as for self-help and in groups for personal development.

Chapter 15, Working with Core Qualities 1–5, elaborates fundamental ethical principles for dreamwork. It shows how to work with dreams in a safe, resource-oriented and motivating way while respecting the age and readiness of the dreamer for dreamwork. Tools are provided for unfolding the meaning and power of dream symbols and to communicate about dreams verbally and nonverbally. Progressive steps for interpretation are outlined. I describe exercises for working with the dream characters and the dream narratives of dreamers of all ages. Further, I provide a detailed model for the composition of comprehensive dreamwork encompassing experiential, analytical and cognitive behavioral dimensions.

Chapter 16, Working with Core Qualities 6–10, outlines a schematic model for relating dreams to the contexts of dreamers' lives. This chapter summarizes how to respond to the self-organizing capacity of dreams and to their active feedback on any serious considerations of the dreamer. It further expands the understanding of levels of communicating in groups, depending on the setting, as well as the skills of dreamers and the participants. Practical exercises for using imagery, bodily aspects and emotion in dreamwork are detailed, as well as the principles for advanced dreamwork skills. I explain the principles for identifying and relating to peak experience dreams, lucid dreams and parapsychological experiences in dreams. Finally, inspiration for practical work with dream series is provided and related to the sequence of the ten Core Qualities.

The epilogue highlights how Dreamwork with The Ten Core Qualities can stimulate social skills and innovative abilities for the benefit of society and the future of humankind.

A Guide to the World of Dreams offers readers a multilevel experience. This book provides an updated and integrative description of dreams, dream science and dreamwork that can be utilized by psychotherapists, counselors, teachers and students of psychology as a basic textbook or sourcebook. Yet the themes and examples in the book still remain universal and firmly adapted to modern human life. Thus the book also reaches out to anyone who wishes to gain knowledge about the fascinating world of dreams and employ their own dreams in improving their lives, their relationships and their personal development.

Acknowledgements

I would like to thank my many clients, workshop participants and students who have contributed to deepening my understanding and pedagogical presentation of the subject through their feedback on my work.

Special thanks to my wife, Lene Vedfelt, who is a psychotherapist and educational supervisor of the Vedfelt Institute, and who has backed me up and supported my working processes. Lene and I have enjoyed many valuable and inspiring conversations about this book's theme. Special thanks to my translator Paul Englar for his empathic and never-faltering work with the translation of this book into English. Also, great thanks to Henriette Løvdal who, besides being a psychotherapist and having an MA degree in the literary sciences, also has extensive experience in publishing. Henriette has provided valuable and inspiring feedback in the early stages of developing this book.

Ole Vedfelt
September 2016
www.vedfelt.dk

Part I

Knowledge of Dreams

Chapter 1

The Dream Schools

The discovery of the healing powers of dreamwork on the mind has played a decisive role in our modern comprehension of dreams. Starting with Freud and Jung, and continuing until today, psychotherapeutic consultation has functioned as a kind of laboratory for the exploration of dreams and their meanings to the dreamers. This has provided the basis for a number of schools of dream interpretation that, each in their own way, have contributed to our understanding of the nature and function of our dreams.

Freud and the Unconscious

Sigmund Freud's publication of *The Interpretation of Dreams* in the year 1900 was a breakthrough for psychotherapeutic research. His declared purpose was to describe a psychological technique that could explain any dream as "a psychological structure full of significance" (Freud, 1900 p. 1). For Freud, dreaming was the "royal road to the unconscious" (Laplanche and Pontalis 1973, p. 475).

In *The Interpretation of Dreams*, Freud sketched the outlines of multiple issues that have occupied dream research ever since. He provided the foundation for the utilization of dreams in practical therapeutic purpose and he developed a model for unconscious processes.

Consciousness and the unconscious

Freud described the mind in *The Interpretation of Dreams* as being organized in layers with consciousness on top and unconscious layers beneath. The deeper you delve into the unconscious, the more fundamental and early-formed character traits and experiences you uncover. During the day, consciousness is occupied with outer impressions that are converted into action and thought activity. During the dreaming process contact to the outer world is partially disconnected. A surplus of mental energy thus appears that activates primitive, unconscious urges and floods consciousness with memories.

According to Freud, the deeper layers of the unconscious contain childish and often sexual wishes that are unacceptable to consciousness (Freud, 1900 p. 1).

Between consciousness and the unconscious is a layer that he calls 'precon-scious'. In principle, it is accessible to consciousness, but it is separated by a censorship function that disguises impulses from the unconscious (Laplanche and Pontalis 1973, p. 325). In the dreaming state, this censorship is somewhat weak-ened, yet it still manages to disguise these wishes to such an extent that they do not waken the dreamer. Thus, dreams have two functions – a safety valve for forbidden desires and sleep preservation (Nagera 1969, p. 56 ff).

Freud called the original, uncensored dreams 'latent dreams'. They provide an illusion of the satisfaction of suppressed wishes. Dreams that are experienced after being censored he called 'manifest dreams'.

Besides memories from childhood, "the material and sources of dreams" are impressions from the preceding day – day-residues – which contribute to our dreams. Day-residues may be insignificant impressions that are used as the build-ing blocks for manifest dreams. Impressions deriving from emotionally signifi-cant events are more important, yet, according to Freud, the dream-censor disguises these impressions (Freud 1900).

Less common sources of dreams are bodily conditions and states during sleep, such as fever, poor digestion, cold, heat and pain, etc.

Freud described four 'dream mechanisms' that he believed created dreams out of unconscious raw material.

- 'Condensation' means that the individual elements in dreams are connecting points for several dream-thoughts at a time.
- 'Displacement' refers to those forbidden thoughts and feelings that are moved from one object to another such as, for instance, in a waking state when we dump our anger on a less dangerous person than the one who is the true object of our aggression.
- Later, the dream takes on a clarifying form by allowing abstract thought to be depicted as images, symbols and cohesive stories. Freud called this 'consid-erations for representability'.
- Finally, Freud believed that our dreams, very cleverly, receive one final 'secondary revision' to appear less strange to our waking consciousness. According to Freud, this is a superficial phenomenon that does not provide deeper access to the meanings of dreams (Nagera 1969, p. 52).

Freud developed a therapeutic method he called 'free association' that provided oppor-tunities to get behind the camouflage of manifest dreams. The dreamer is brought into a relaxed, introverted state and tells all thoughts and imaginings for each part of the dream that spontaneously occur in his or her consciousness, no matter how strange, illogical or unpleasant they may seem (Freud, 1900 p. 56). From the material produced in this manner, Freud primarily focused on sexual symbolism and childhood experi-ences that seemed relevant to his psychoanalytical theory.

The 'ego', 'id' and 'superego' are all terms contained in a model of the psyche that Freud developed later in life. The ego is the source of the will – the individual's image of him/herself. The ego in dreams, connected to our sense of identity, represents the dream-ego. The superego represents society's demands on the individual – conscience and morality. In dreams, parental figures, other authority figures and institutions that make demands on the individual belong to this category. The id is representative of unconscious drives – everything in dreams that is wild, animalistic, uncontrolled and forbidden (Freud, 1920).

Freud also believed that the early developmental phases in childhood were very important to the understanding of dreams. According to Freud, a small child goes through several developmental phases in the course of the first three years of life: an 'oral' phase, where urges and feelings of pleasure are focused around the child's mouth; an 'anal' phase, centered on the rectum and a 'phallic' phase where focus is on the genitals (Freud, 1905). A child's experiences during these phases become the prototypes for personality traits that may last a lifetime. Through their symbolism, dreams may refer to these phases (Hall, 1954).

Freud has taught us that dreams contain important knowledge of unconscious childhood experiences. He contributed to the understanding of the sexual symbolism of dreams and created a method of free association.

C. G. Jung's Depth Psychology

Carl Gustav Jung, the Swiss psychiatrist, has been as equally important to dream research as Freud. Jung perceived dreams and the unconscious as forms of creative activity that contain age-old wisdom.

He acknowledged portions of Freud's work, yet did not believe that dreams were disguising forbidden – largely sexual – wishes. While Freud paid particular attention to what dreams could tell us about the past, Jung mainly focused on future developmental potential.

In *Man and His Symbols*, Jung (1964) provides an excellent, accessible image of his understanding of dreams. Other good sources are articles entitled 'General Aspects of Dream Psychology' (1948), 'On the Nature of Dreams' (1948a) and his book, *Memories, Dreams, Reflections* (1961).

Jung agrees with Freud that the psyche is layered. Consciousness is found on top and beneath this is the 'personal unconscious' that somehow corresponds to Freud's understanding of the unconscious. However, according to Jung, beneath this personal layer is found a much older layer which he called the 'collective unconscious'.

The collective unconscious is made up of universal patterns of experience and behavior – the so-called archetypes. Archetypes can be universal models for motherliness, fatherliness or other important roles in life. They can also be models for common human life situations or typical patterns of personality development. To Jung, archetypes are the most important sources in our dreams. Dreams are, according to Jung, created by the unconscious. The deeper and more archetypical the layers they derive from, the more meaningful and intense they are (Jung 1964a).

The function of dreams is to "complement" consciousness with unconscious knowledge and "compensate" for narrow-mindedness (Franz 1985, p. 14).

One central concept for Jung is that every human being contains a potential developmental plan that gives each personality uniqueness. Jung called the realization of this plan the "process of individuation". In dreams, symbols are created that support this process. This is especially evident during vital transitional phases in life where dreams can be very intense and loaded with archetypal symbols.

Jung was especially interested in human development at a mature age after adaption to society and consolidation with the external world are more complete. His model of the individuation process, as reflected in dreams, is as follows: adaptation to society leads to the identification with a social 'mask' (persona), which typically appears as human figures or sceneries in dreams that are conventional, established and petit bourgeois. When awareness of the persona is achieved, the dreamer is confronted with what Jung called the "shadow-side", – the dark sides of the personality. Jungians also often use the concept of the shadow in a narrower sense, for example as murky personality traits represented in dreams by figures of the same gender.

The next step in the process of individuation is achieving awareness of the innate qualities of the opposite sex. For men, these are female qualities called the 'anima' (Latin for soul). For women, male qualities are called 'animus' (Latin for spirit). When these aspects of the opposite gender have been recognized and integrated, symbols appear in dreams that reflect the wholeness and unity of the personality. Jung called this the "Self" (Jung 1928). These steps in the process of development appear in dream series.

Even if Jung primarily explored dreams in relationship to the process of individuation, he also considered the dreamer's particular life situation and entire life history.

Jung (1938/1939) supplemented dream interpretation with a method he called "amplification". In amplification, the meaning of a dream element is expanded by drawing parallels to symbolic material from mythology, religion, and the initiation rites of tribal peoples, etc. He devoted a great deal of his life to the study of the symbolism in alchemical texts, which he found shed light on the dreams and inner developments of modern human beings (Jung 1944).

Jung also employed an experiential method which he called 'active imagination'. Through this method the dreamer relives their dream in their imagination and can therefore enter into dialogue with dream figures. This is done with the understanding that these figures reflect sides of the dreamer that can be explored more deeply and developed further. Joan Chodorow (1997) has collected and presented Jung's key writings on active imagination.

Jung explored the universal symbolism in dreams. He found that dreams stimulate the development of the personality at a mature age. He called this personality development "the process of individuation".

Focus on the Dream-Ego and the Waking Lifestyle

Freud was especially interested in dream revelations about events in childhood. Jung explored the potential for self-development that pointed the way forward in the course of each individual's life.

Other dream theorists like Alfred Adler, Erich Fromm and, later, Calvin Hall focused on how dreams help us manage our current, everyday lives. They emphasized the connection between dreams and waking lifestyles and found that dreams are problem solving and prepare us for the upcoming day. Among these theorists, Hall has had the greatest influence. He was dissatisfied with the fact that dream theories were primarily built on the clinical experiences of individuals in therapy. He classified the content and compared it to information about the dreamers' ages, genders and personality profiles, etc. This research demonstrated a clear connection between the manifest dream content and the dreamers' waking personalities. Hall discovered that dreams contain a great deal of material from our everyday lives. Hall presented his viewpoints and research in his book *The Meaning of Dreams* (Hall 1953a).

Hall has also demonstrated that, viewed over long timespans, people have a high degree of consistency and continuity in their dreams, to the extent that certain types of relationships, psychological and behavioral reactions, and even objects and issues, are constantly repeated (Hall and Nordby 1972).

According to Hall, dreams are created by the ego and its defense mechanisms and not the deeper unconscious layers as Freud and Jung described. Dreams give precise pictures of how individuals see themselves and reality. If you dream about something, you must have thought about it. In his descriptions, he is mostly interested in the dream-ego.

For Hall, symbols were not disguises, they were "a kind of mental stenography." Even if a pistol might symbolize male genitalia, as a symbol it suggests much more. It is a precise and condensed description of an aggressive perception of the dreamer's sexuality (Hall 1953a).

Hall based his individual interpretations on dream series, which he believed could provide an accurate image of the personality. This can be done by comparison with statistically normal material. Just as knowledge about the dreamer can be harvested from what has been dreamed, it can also be interesting to look at what has not been dreamed.

The task of dreams, according to Hall, is problem solving – they are the result of hard, creative thinking work in a sleeping state (Hall 1953 p. 233–34). He found Freud's and Jung's theories useful, yet insufficient.

Hall's methods have since been developed and modified: as practical tools for working with individual dreams; as sociological methods for investigating dreams and lifestyles of larger groups; and also as a means to confirm dream theories statistically. There are, for instance, studies that suggest that universal dream themes exist and that dreams reflect gender differences, gender roles, age and political attitudes.

According to Hall, we often repeat certain themes and symbols in dreams that, when seen as a whole, provide a picture of our personalities and waking lifestyles.

Existential Dream Interpretations

Inspired by existential psychology, a wide range of psychotherapeutic schools work with dreams. Existentialists are critical of Freud's and Jung's theory systems which they believe lead to an over-interpretation of dreams. The existentialists recommend a 'phenomenological method' with a greater openness to the immediate experience of the reality beyond theoretical abstractions and preconceived ideas (Boss 1977).

In connection with dreams, these viewpoints are most consistently described by French psychiatrist Medard Boss. Boss views human beings as creatures who are open from the outset but whose openness often takes a beating until we become alienated from ourselves and our own spontaneous experiences. This openness is expressed in our dreams that give poetic, condensed images of our life situations. They must be allowed 'free expression' to 'tell their own stories' and thereby provide dreamers with a more immediate, emotional contact with their own existence (Stern 1977).

Instead of analyzing dreams to determine which troublesome, unconscious motives the dreamer may be harboring, Boss uses a more appreciative form of communication. He highlights what dreams might be saying about an individual's resources and how that reflects non-realized life potential.

Some existential therapists, such as Irwin Yalom, place the main emphasis on what they call the ultimate concerns. Relevant in connection with dreams are themes such as the relationship to death, isolation, freedom and meaninglessness, etc. (Yalom 1980).

The fact that phenomenology is concerned with experiencing the notion of 'interpretation' with the greatest immediacy is already a stumbling block. Phenomenological dream theorists have described the therapist's role as that of an 'illuminator' who gets the dreamer to see what actually takes place in dreams. Therapists help by shedding light on overlooked nuances and 'draw attention to' or make suggestions. Emphasis is placed on spontaneity and creativity as opposed to intellectualizing experiences. It is a matter of 'lifting out' aspects of dreams and seeing what sets them in motion, and then letting this process determine the next step in the interpretation (Knapp 1979; Gendlin 1977).

The existentialists have suggested various ways of immersion in subjective experiences. Being more attentive to feelings and body sensations or telling the dream out loud several times in the present tense helps to make it more visceral (Spinelli 1989).

Existential and phenomenological dream interpreters highlight the value of being open to the direct effects of dreams on the psyche and of respect for the dreamer's own subjective experience.

Freud and Jung's Successors

After Freud and Jung, many outstanding therapists continued to develop and expand the understanding of the unconscious psyche and offered their contributions to a broader understanding of the many things dreams could do.

While classical psychoanalysis has primarily focused on inner life and unconscious drives, after Freud interest in exploring the relationships between people has continually increased. The so-called 'object relations theory' has been the most influential, in which the word 'object' actually refers to people. According to this theory, the personality is built up in the first years of life based on the ability to create lasting relationships with certain people. In the course of this development, inner expectations are created within the child, first in relationship to the mother, then the father, siblings and other close people (Rycroft 1968). The 'inner objects' are fantasies that control the individual from within. They also influence relationships in adult life, so that we constantly try to bring these old patterns into play through the interaction with other people.

The interaction between dream figures often reflects how we relate to others in unconscious ways. This is especially applicable to the relationships we have with people to whom we attribute parental qualities, such as supervisors and therapists. This is why dreams can provide important information about the course of therapeutic processes.

The research and experience of many clinicians are involved in object relations theory. The most well-known are English psychoanalysts Melanie Klein, Donald Winnicott and Wilfred Bion, as well as Hungarian-American child psychiatrist Margaret Mahler.

Other well-known Freudian successors, such as the American Erik Erikson, have been interested in the connection between dreams and psychosocial development (Erikson 1954). His fellow countryman Donald Meltzer found acclaim with his descriptions and particularly nuanced thinking about feelings and relationships in dreams (Meltzer 1983).

The further development of these theories has been called *The Relational Turn* (Mitchell and Lewis 1999). This movement has been criticized, however, for the loss of some of the original insights of the classical schools, and it has been suggested that the relational skills of the therapists can be masking authoritarian attitudes (Carmeli and Blass 2010).

Jungian James Hillman states that dreams contain something of such a different nature from consciousness that it cannot fundamentally be translated into rational language. Instead, he suggests that consciousness learns from dream language (Hillman 1979) – it thinks and expresses itself in symbols and metaphors.

Erich Neumann, a successor of Jung, has demonstrated how the magic and mythological forms of experience of earlier cultural stages are paralleled in the developmental stages of children and their inner world. He has also shown how this provides new perspectives on the understanding of dreams (Neumann 1963; Neumann 1973).

For Jung's successors – despite differences of opinion – the consensus is still that dreams are creative products. The lives of individuals can be seen as a myths or stories reflected in dreams.

Freud and Jung's successors have explored what our dreams can tell us about our relationships to others and have also emphasized the creative qualities of dreams.

Experiential Work with Dreams

For Freud, Jung and Calvin Hall the primary focus in dreamwork was on analysis and comprehension, and this was also true of the existentialists to a certain extent. Other schools with points of departure in phenomenology and existential philosophy have concentrated on enhancing dream experiences through creative expression, dramatization and emotional catharsis. The most well-known of these was Fritz Perls' Gestalt Therapy. He sees all dream elements as projections of dreamers' own egos. Perls brings to life individual dream elements through role-playing by playing birds, persons or even a riding path, etc. Anything in a dream that is experienced as important can be explored through role-playing. This Gestalt therapeutic method is intended to guide dreamers beyond cliché-imbued self-regard to create space for a renewed joy of life and immediacy of experience through the processing of suppressed and perhaps painful emotions. Perls' dreamwork is vividly described in his book *Gestalt Therapy Verbatim* (Perls 1969).

In Perls' method, therapist and client, encircled by the group, work in tandem to play all possible roles. Often a single dream scene is worked on, one that seems to be emotionally charged or is in other ways particularly significant. Using psychodrama techniques, a dream can be staged so that – potentially – all participants in a group get a chance to immerse themselves in the roles the dream suggests (Vedfelt 2002). In body dreamwork particular emphasis is placed on the dreamer's bodily experiences or elements within the dream are examined that can tell something about the body (Boadella 1987).

American psychologist and dreamworker Eugene Gendlin has consistently developed methods of using bodily associations to disclose dreamers' subjective experiences of dreams instead of relying on theoretical concepts (Gendlin 1986). According to Gendlin, "Freud's free association and Jung's daydream was to engender something to break through directly from the 'unconscious'." Working with the body is a further development of their methods (Gendlin 2012).

Meditation and immersion are also often employed in dreamwork and dream images can be tied to diverse theories about states of consciousness and mediation systems. It is particularly those mediation schools that work with 'chakra symbols' that have shown interest in dreams (Vedfelt 2002).

Upon closer examination, these methods do not need to be seen in opposition to those of their predecessors. Freud's free association technique is experiential and the same is true of Jung's active imagination. The difference lies in where the greatest emphasis is placed – on experience or on understanding.

Experiential therapies expand the dream experience through dramatization, role-playing, drawing, visualization, body awareness and meditation.

Cognitive Therapy

One of the most popular therapy forms of our times is Cognitive Therapy. It was created by American psychologist Aaron Beck in the early 1960s, primarily as a treatment for depression.

Beck discovered that depressive people have more manifest dreams about loss, defeat, obstacles and force than other people. Yet he did not believe, as Freud did, that the unpleasant dreams of depressed individuals are covering up masochistic 'wishes', but rather that they are negative thinking patterns also found in waking life.

According to Beck's cognitive dream theory, inappropriate thinking patterns of the waking state muddle input from the outside world. When outer stimuli are eliminated during sleep, and the brain reaches a certain level of activity, these thinking patterns appear quite clearly in dreams.

Beck was interested in dreams during periods of mental disorder and he used them to crystallize specific problems and also as diagnostic tools. As mentioned, according to Beck, depressed patients tend to dream about defeat, obstacles and coercion. Paranoid patients dream more often about being pursued and unfairly attacked. The dreams of manic patients have more expansive themes. Anxiety neurotics particularly dream about danger (Beck 1971).

Beck's successors toned down the focus on dreams for a period, but cognitive dreamwork has been developed further since the 1990s. The focus is on symptoms and what the dreams can tell about specific problems needing treatment, rather than on the meaning of a dream as a whole. In cognitive therapy, the therapist is educating and actively structuring (Ablon and Jones 1998).

Younger cognitive therapists have designed techniques to restructure negative thinking patterns in ways that are extensions of Jung's active imagination (Hill and Rochlen 2004). Individual authors describe studies of the integration of cognitive dreamwork with various forms of experience and body-oriented therapies (Leijssen 2004). The idea is to move away from seeing dreams as reflections of psychological flaws and toward using them as sources of inspiration for problem solving (Rosner et al. 2004).

Cognitive therapy employs dreams in the treatment of mental disorders such as compulsion, depression and low self-esteem, yet is also moving toward a more creative understanding of dreams.

Varieties of Contemporary Dreamwork

Therapeutic settings are vital laboratories for developing principles for practical dreamwork. The classic methods target long-term processes. Each method has its own particular framework for ensuring safe integration of unconscious material in the self and the sphere of consciousness, and for extracting information about dreams that could not otherwise be acquired.

Today, work is done with dreams in shorter and more limited contexts. Related to cognitive therapy, 'focus-oriented therapy' has been described by American psychologist and dream researcher Deirdre Barrett, among others. Barrett explains how modern psychologists often limit their interests in a dream to one particular psychological problem and make the solution of that problem the goal of therapy. While Freud saw dreams as a "royal road" to the unconscious, Barrett calls them "a shrewd shortcut" to a patient's symptoms (Barrett 2004). This work covers, for instance, psychological counselling, couples' relations, sorrow groups, and traumatized people, etc.

Even existential psychology and the experiential therapies have embraced a far wider spectrum of dreamwork concerned with personal and spiritual development.

The American Association for the Study of Dreams was founded in 1983 and later became the International Association for the Study of Dreams. This organization publishes the scientific periodical *Dreaming,* in cooperation with the American Psychological Association, and also the periodical *Dreamtime,* aimed at bringing broader information about dreams to a more general population.

James Hillman (1990) described the emergence of "a grassroots dreamwork movement" which has moved dreamwork away from a psychotherapeutic framework. A popular, non-therapeutic group method was created by Montague Ullman and described in cooperation with Nan Zimmerman (Ullman and Zimmerman 1979). These groups have leaders who need not have expertise in dreams but instead guide the groups and help maintain certain rules of group dynamics. Dreams are not interpreted. When a participant recounts a dream other members of the group have an opportunity to immerse themselves in it and then provide feedback on how they experience various aspects of the dream as if it was one of their own. Thus, dreamwork becomes a group event. Dreamers are still free to be inspired by any offered feedback and dismiss anything that does not touch them. The leader summarizes any contributions from the participants and ensures that everyone stays within the method framework.

This method has been employed in many community-based dream groups and is professed to "cut across socioeconomic, racial, gender, and age boundaries" (Krippner *et al.* 1994). Swedish psychologist Binnie Kristal-Andersson (2001) has utilized the method in groups for victims of torture.

Various authors, including Kelly Bulkeley (2001), have researched the use of dreams in religious and spiritual traditions and have found inspiration for modern dream understanding and dreamwork. Others, such as Stanley Krippner and his co-workers (2002), have systematically studied "extraordinary dreams," i.e. dreams that were experienced as particularly powerful, often related to altered states of consciousness, initiation into spiritual contexts or even accompanied by parapsychological experiences.

Angel Morgan (2014) compared healing experiences reported by members of indigenous dream groups with reports from American grassroots dream-appreciation groups. She found that fear and safety concerns, and simply a lack of interest, have affected the paucity of dream sharing in Western societies.

Dreams that are shared and dealt with in a gathering of people may be referred to as social dreaming. In these situations, dreamwork may have an explicitly non-individual purpose because dreams and the associations to them are used to explore possible social and political meanings (Armstrong 1998). This type of dreamwork might focus on the activities of a group or broader societal matters and even global issues.

Gordon Lawrence from the Tavistock Clinic pioneered such groups in the early 1980s. He was inspired by Charlotte Beradt's studies of dreams (1966) in Germany between 1933 and 1939, which clearly reflected the social and political climate of The Third Reich.

Lawrence's method is called a 'social dream matrix'. The word matrix refers to "a place out of which something grows." The method can be viewed as an expansion of relational psychoanalysis, since dreams not only testify to the relationship between therapists and clients, they also refer to larger units such as groups (Lawrence 1998).

Social dreaming is also experienced as compatible with Jung's theory of the collective unconscious, which refers to a common human fount of archetypal patterns and experiences. According to Misser Berg (2001) from the Jung Institute of Copenhagen, many dreams recounted to a dream matrix are so called 'big dreams' that contain much content from what Jung called the collective unconscious. These dreams are not individually interpreted yet may be used to explore collective trends in society or the world at large. In my experience, the matrix can also provide inspiration to further the understanding of the hidden dynamics within a group.

References

Ablon, J. S. and Jones, E. E. (1998) 'How expert clinicians' prototypes of an ideal treatment correlate with outcome in psychodynamic and cognitive-behavioral therapy.' *Psychotherapy Research*, 8, pp. 71–83

Armstrong, D. (1998) 'Introduction' in G. W. Lawrence, *Social Dreaming @ Work.* (London: Karnac Books) pp. xvii–xxi

Barrett, D. (2004) 'The "Royal Road" becomes a shrewd shortcut' in R. Rosner, W. Lyddon, *et al.*, *Cognitive Therapy and Dreams.* (New York: Springer Publishing), pp. 113–123

Beck, A. (1971) 'Cognitive patterns in dreams and daydreams' in R. Rosner, W. Lyddon, *et al.*, *Cognitive Therapy and Dreams.* (New York: Springer Publishing), pp. 27–32

Beradt, C. (1966/1985) *The Third Reich of Dreams.* (London: The Aquarian Press)

Berg, M. (2001) 'A dream matrix for a new millennium' in P. Skogemam, *Symbol, Analysis, Reality. A Jungian Approach.* (Copenhagen: Lindhardt & Ringhof)

Boadella, D. (1987) *Lifestreams. An Introduction to Biosynthesis.* (Abingdon, UK: Routledge and Kegan Paul)

Boss, M. (1977) *"I Dreamt Last Night..."*. (New York: Gardener Press)

Bulkeley, K. (Ed.) (2001) *Dreams – A Reader on Religious, Cultural, and Psychological Dimensions of Dreaming*. (London: Palgrave Macmillan)

Carmeli, Z. and Blass, R. (2010) 'The relational turn in psychoanalysis: revolution or regression?' *European Journal of Psychotherapy & Counselling*, Vol. 12, Issue 3, pp. 217–244

Chodorow, J. (1997) *Jung on Active Imagination*. (London: Routledge)

Erikson, E. H. (1954) 'The dream specimen of psychoanalysis'. *Journal of the American Psychoanalytic Association*, Vol. 2(1), pp. 5–56

Franz, M.-L. von (1985) *Träume*. (Zürich: Daimon)

Freud, S. (1900/2013) *The Interpretation of Dreams*. (Sunderland, UK: Dead Dodo Vintage), Kindle edition

Freud, S. (1905/1974) 'Three essays on the theory of sexuality' in *The Standard Edition of the Complete Psychological Works of Sigmund Freud* Vol. 7. (New York: Hogarth Press), pp. 125–244

Freud, S. (1920/1974) 'Beyond the pleasure principle' in *The Standard Edition of the Complete Psychological Works of Sigmund Freud* Vol. 18. (New York: Hogarth Press), pp. 3–69

Freud, S. (1923/1974) 'The ego and the id' in *The Standard Edition of the Complete Psychological Works of Sigmund Freud* Vol. 19. (New York: Hogarth Press), pp. 3–69

Gendlin, E. (1977) 'Phenomenological concept vs. phenomenological method' in C. I. Scott, *On Dreaming – An Encounter with Medard Boss*. (Chico, CA: Scholars' Press), pp. 57–72

Gendlin, E. (1986) *Let Your Body Interpret Your Dreams*. (Asheville, NC: Chiron Publications)

Gendlin, E. (2012) 'Body dreamwork' in D. Barrett and P. McNamara, *Encyclopedia of Sleep and Dreams*. (Westport, CT: Greenwood Publishing), Kindle edition, location 2535–2712

Hall, C. S. (1953) 'A cognitive theory of dream symbolism.' *Journal General Psychology*, Vol. 48, pp. 169–186

Hall, C. S. (1953a) *The Meaning of Dreams*. (New York: McGraw-Hill)

Hall, C. S. (1954) *A Primer of Freudian Psychology*. (New York: The World Publishing Company)

Hall, C. S. and Nordby, V. J. (1972) *The Individual and His Dreams*. (New York: New American Library)

Hill, C. and Rochlen, A. (2004) 'The Hill Cognitive-Experiential Model of Dream Interpretation' in R. Rosner, W. Lyddon, *et al.*, *Cognitive Therapy and Dreams*. (New York: Springer Publishing), pp. 161–178

Hillman, J. (1979) *The Dream and the Underworld*. (New York: Harper & Row)

Hillman, J. (1990) 'The emergence of the grassroots dreamwork movement' in S. Krippner (Ed.) *Dreamtime & Dreamwork: Decoding the Language of the Night*. (New York: Jeremy P. Tarcher Inc.), pp. 13–20

Jung, C. G. (1928/1981) 'The relation between the ego and the unconscious' in *The Collected Works of C.G. Jung: Two Essays on Analytical Psychology*, Vol. 7. (Abingdon, UK: Routledge and Kegan Paul)

Jung, C. G. (1938/1939) *Kinderträume I og II* (Zürich: Eidgenossische Hochschule)

Jung, C. G. (Author), Adler, G., Fordham, M. and Read, Sir H. (Eds) (1944) *The Collected Works of C.G. Jung: Psychology and Alchemy*, Vol. 12. (Abingdon, UK: Routledge and Kegan Paul)

Jung, C. G. (1948/1981) 'On the nature of dreams' in G. Adler, M. Fordham and Sir H. Read (Eds) *The Collected Works of C.G. Jung: The Structure and Dynamics of the Psyche*, Vol. 8. (Abingdon, UK: Routledge and Kegan Paul), pp. 443–529

Jung, C. G. (1948a/1981) 'On the nature of dreams' in G. Adler, M. Fordham and Sir H. Read (Eds) *The Collected Works of C.G. Jung: The Structure and Dynamics of the Psyche*, Vol. 8. (Abingdon, UK: Routledge and Kegan Paul), pp. 530–569

Jung, C. G. (1961) *Memories, Dreams, Reflections.* (New York: Random House)

Jung, C. G. (1964): *Man and His Symbols.* (London: Aldus Books)

Jung, C. G. (1964a) 'Approaching the unconscious' in *Man and His Symbols.* (London: Aldus Books), pp. 18–103

Knapp, Susan (1979) 'Dreaming: Horney, Kelmann and Shamberg' in B. Wolman, *Handbook of Dreams.* (New York: Van Nostrand Reinhold Company), pp. 351–352

Krippner, S. *et al.* (1994) 'Community applications of an experiential group approach to teaching dreamwork.' *Dreaming*, 1994, Vol. 4(4), pp. 215–222

Krippner, S. *et al.* (2002) *Extraordinary Dreams and How to Work with Them.* (Albany, NY: State University of New York Press)

Kristal-Andersson, B. (2001) 'From wound to scar – easing the pain of trauma and torture experiences through dreamwork.' *Drömdialog* (Membership journal for Drömgruppsforum) nr. 1, pp. 9–17

Laplanche, J. and Pontalis, J. (1973/2006) *The Language of Psychoanalysis.* (London: Karnac Books)

Lawrence, G. W. (1998) *Social Dreaming @ Work.* (London: Karnac Books)

Leijssen, M. (2004) 'Focusing-oriented dream work' in R. Rosner, W. Lyddon, *et al.*, *Cognitive Therapy and Dreams.* (New York: Springer Publishing), pp. 137–160

Meltzer, D. (1983) *Dream-Life – A Re-examination of the Psychoanalytical Theory and Technique.* (Strathclyde: Cluney Press)

Mitchell, S. A. and Lewis, A. (1999) *Relational Psychoanalysis: The Emergence of a Tradition.* (Hillsdale, NJ: The Analytic Press)

Morgan, A. K. (2014): *Dream Sharing as a Healing Method: Tropical Roots and Contemporary Community Potential.* IN: *Journal of Tropical Psychology*, Vol. 4, Cambridge Journals Online, UK., 2014.

Nagera, H. (1969/1981) *Basic Psychoanalytic Concepts on the Theory of Dreams.* (London: Maresfield Reprints)

Neumann, E. (1963) *The Great Mother.* (Princeton, NJ: Princeton University Press)

Neumann, E. (1973) *The Child.* (New York: Putnam's Sons)

Perls, F. (1969/2013) *Gestalt Therapy Verbatim.* (Gouldsboro, ME: The Gestalt Journal Press), Kindle edition

Rosner, R., Lyddon, W. and Freeman, A. (2004) 'To dream, perchance to sleep: awakening the potential of dream work for cognitive therapy' in R. Rosner, W. Lyddon, *et al.*, *Cognitive Therapy and Dreams.* (New York: Springer Publishing), pp. 181–191

Rumelhart, D., *et al.* (1986) 'Schemata and sequential thought' in J. L. McClelland and D. Rumelhart, *Parallel Distributed Processing Vol 2 – Explorations in the Microstructure of Cognition: Psychological and Biological Models.* (Cambridge, MA: The MIT Press), pp. 7–57

Rycroft, C. (1968/1979) *A Critical Dictionary of Psychoanalysis.* (London: Penguin Books)

Spinelli, E. (1989) *The Interpreted World.* (London: Sage Publications)

Stern, P. J. (1977) 'Foreword' in M. Boss, "*I Dreamt Last Night...*". (New York: Gardner Press), p. xiii

Ullman, M. and Zimmerman, N. (1979) *Working with Dreams*. (New York: Delacorte Press)

Vedfelt, O. (2002) *The Dimensions of Dreams*. (London: Jessica Kingsley Publishers)

Yalom, I. D. (1980) *Existential Psychotherapy*. (New York: Basic Books)

Chapter 2

Dreams and Natural Science

REM Sleep and NREM Sleep

When we sleep, we make rapid eye movements at regular intervals. These sleep periods are called Rapid Eye Movement (REM) stages. If we are awoken during these stages, we can usually recall our dreams.

Adult humans dream for an average of two hours every night, though a bit more for the youngest of us and a bit less for the eldest. Measurement of brain activity has demonstrated that our brains are at least as active when we are dreaming as when we are awake. From sleep initiation to deep sleep we move through four stages, descending to the depths and then ascending again, until we are almost in a waking state. This takes 90 minutes. Our brain activity varies depending on which phase we are in. Every night we are led through this 90-minute cycle four to six times, depending upon how long we sleep. REM sleep is always 'stage one' sleep, i.e. we dream when we are closest to the waking state. REM periods grow longer and longer as the night progresses and dreams become more intense and imaginative (Cartwright 1977) (Figure 2.1).

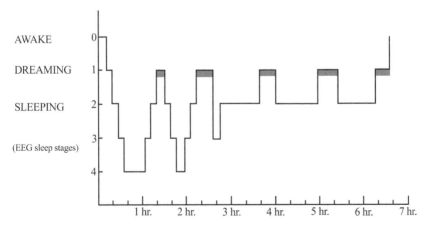

Figure 2.1 Typical pattern of sleep stages in the course of the night. The dark plateaus are dream stages. These become longer as night progresses

The periods between REM stages are called non-REM (NREM). During NREM sleep, the mental activity is reminiscent of fragmented waking thought and transient imagery. This activity does not have the same intensity and dramatic form as our dreams, yet 20 percent of dreaming still occurs during NREM sleep. NREM sleep does not enhance creativity, but it does strengthen learning by memory (Lewin and Glaubmann 1975). REM sleep and NREM sleep also show slightly different sides of our personalities. We are generally kinder towards others during NREM sleep than during REM sleep (McNamara *et al.* 2005).

The sleep initiation stages – when we fall asleep – are special because we often swing between dreaming and waking states. This is called a hypnagogic state and typically lasts five to ten minutes.

The first real dreaming takes place slightly less than 90 minutes after sleep initiation. It lasts a little longer than the hypnagogic state. The next dream lasts even longer and so forth until the last dream of the night can be 30 to 40 minutes long. When we dream, our outer sensing and muscle activity are partially disconnected, so we are cut off from relating to the world at large (Cartwright 1977).

Mechanisms for regulating sleeping and waking states are already developed approximately 6–7 months into pregnancy. REM sleep accounts for 50 percent of infants' sleep and even more for premature babies. The amount of REM sleep reduces slightly over the years. For young people, the average is 24 percent of their sleep – a level that is maintained until mid-life, after which the amount of dreaming begins to decrease somewhat. The variation for REM time for adults is between 18 percent and 33 percent of sleeping time yet, individually, the REM level is remarkably stable from night to night, no matter what takes place during the course of the day (excepting illness and medication use). The lion's share of our dreams are in color (Cartwright 1977, p.10).

NREM activity was found in primitive species of mammals that evolved 200 million years ago, while REM sleep appeared in more highly evolved animals and has a history of approximately 150 million years.

Beneficial REM Sleep

The discovery of REM sleep initiated a new scientific epoch in dream research, making it possible to get closer to the nature of dreaming.

It has been demonstrated that outer influences during sleep do not, as a rule, directly affect dreams. Calvin Hall and his co-workers studied this in dream laboratories. When outer influences do affect dreams, they are transformed to fit into dream stories in symbolic ways. For example: a ringing alarm clock becomes church bells or the clanging of a fire engine; a car starting may be heard as pistol shots or an earthquake; a cold wind or cold arm might be experienced as a dogsled ride in the arctic north. In Hall's studies, the symbols arising could be interpreted into the entire dream in a meaningful way and in accordance with the comprehensive image of the individual derived by psychological testing (Hall 1953, pp. 6–7).

Dreams are real phenomena and not fantasies we invent while awake. When outer stimuli are incorporated at regular intervals during REM sleep, they coincide well with the timeline presented in the waking recounting of the dream (Dement and Wolpert 1958). Changes in blood pressure, breathing and heart rhythm during REM sleep reflect changes of emotional intensity when the dreamer is recounting the dream (Kramer 1993). Finally, experiments with hypnosis and lucid dreaming (where dreamers are aware they are dreaming and can respond with finger signals) confirm that the dreams truly take place while asleep (LaBerge *et al*. 1986).

Since many people only occasionally remember their dreams, we could ask ourselves what good are forgotten dreams? To answer this question extensive studies have been done where people are awakened every time they enter REM sleep. They were thus deprived of their dreams without a reduction in their sleep. In other words, they dreamed less than people sleeping normally who are not awakened while dreaming. It has been demonstrated afterwards that such a lack of dreaming creates emotional imbalance, behavioral problems and also disturbances in creative thinking and problem solving (Hartmann 1973; Greenberg and Pearlman 1993).

Animal studies show that the need for REM sleep increases when faced with learning difficult tasks. Even studies done on humans during exam situations point to the importance of REM sleep for efficient learning (Smith 1993). For instance, REM sleep increases the ability to solve tests of creativity (Lewin and Glaubmann 1975). Immediately after a REM phase, we are intellectually more flexible, more capable of associating easily and better at spotting the contexts of meanings than in normal waking states (Kahn and Hobson 2003).

A common perception is that it can be 'a good idea to sleep on it', when stumped in problem solving. As an example, author John Steinbeck said "the committee of sleep has worked on it" after a good night's sleep. American Milton Kramer and his co-workers found the atmosphere in dreams to be generally more positive the later in the morning that the dreams occurred. Dreams also had a more defined problem-solving character, and the more people who appeared the better the mood upon waking. This applied irrespective of gender, age, individual variations in temperament, and social situations. We are discussing statistical probabilities here. Significant exceptions to this pattern appear for depressed (Vogel *et al*. 1968; Vogel *et al*. 1977) and traumatized (Punamäki 1999) people whose REM/NREM rhythm can be disturbed.

Other laboratory studies, combined with brain research, suggest that REM sleep has a positive effect on mastering stress (Germaine *et al*. 2003).

On average, we dream for two hours every night. Whether we remember our dreams or not, they still have a positive effect on our moods and stress levels, as well as on emotional and social balance.

The Dreaming Brain

In recent years, advances in scanning methods, research in brain chemistry and studies of people with brain injuries have expanded our knowledge of the dreaming brain. The study of the human brain is also based on experimental data and comparisons with animal brains – called cross-species comparisons – where similarities and differences can be observed (Panksepp 1998).

Since the brain is so complex, it is not possible to give a complete graphic illustration in a single picture of the multitude of neural networks that are active while dreaming. Figure 2.2 is a schematic rendition of the brain where some structures are depicted on the same plane, even though they overlap or even hide each other. I will provide short descriptions of various areas, then connect these to the newer dream theories and, later in the book, provide more in-depth explanations that are relevant for understanding dreamwork. Researchers who have contributed to the knowledge of dreaming will be referenced and named in the following sections and chapters.

In dream study literature, networks involved in dreaming are either named by their anatomical locations (in Latin) or sometimes by their shape. Some of these names are so long that abbreviations are often used.

The evolutionary model of the brain structure proposed by American neuroscientist Paul MacLean divides the human brain into three strata (MacLean, 1990). The lower portion of the brain, including the brainstem and the cerebellum, is called the "reptilian brain." It regulates innate behavioral knowledge – basic, instinctual action tendencies and habits related to primitive survival issues.

Above the reptilian brain is the old mammalian brain, also called the limbic system or the emotional brain. It contains affective knowledge: subjective feelings and emotional responses to world events interacting with innate motivational value systems.At the top is the highly expanded neomammalian brain or neocortex which generates higher cognitive functions, reasoning and logical thought employed in sensing the exterior world and for executive functions (Panksepp, 1998 loc. 1746 ff.).

Through evolution, newer emerging systems have conserved, modified, and expanded components of preexisting systems thus linking together these three layers in complex vertical neural networks which allow the entire brain to coordinate everything from simple motor movements to complex abstract function (Cozolino, 2014 loc. 470 ff.).

When we dream, a multitude of connections between the top, middle and lower parts of the brain are reinforced and regulated by mutual feedback processes. Below, I will provide a more detailed description of the complexity of the dreaming brain from the base to the crown, i.e. from the brainstem to the emotional brain and the dream-active areas of the neocortex.

The white areas on Figure 2.2 illustrate the most active parts of the brain during dreaming, while the shaded areas are the less active parts.

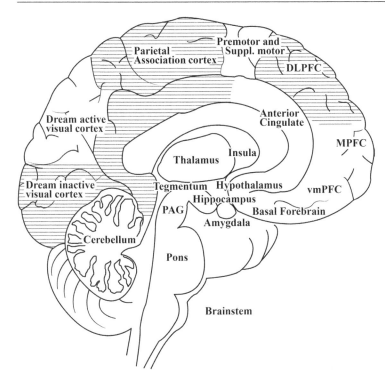

Figure 2.2 The brain networks involved in dreaming

Regions with high activity in dreaming.
Pons. Initiation of PGO waves
PAG, Tegmentum, Basal forebrain. Activation, arousal. Basic emotions. Core consciousness
Thalamus. Relaying and Synchronizing information
Amygdala. Unconscious memory. Fears. Maternal emotions
Hippocampus. Episodic memory
Hypothalamus. Hormones and chemicals
Dream active visual cortex. Dream images
mPFC & vmPFC. Imagination, self-consciousness, theory of other people's mind. Refinement of feelings. Body-mind unification
Insula. Body-mind-emotion link
Cerebellum. Premotor and suppl. motor cortex. Dream movement.

High activity while awake. Uncoupled in dreams.
DLPFC. Attention, analyzing data from surroundings, execution
Parietal association cortex. Sensory perception
Dream inactive visual cortex. Sight.

The Brainstem in Dreaming

During REM sleep, strong wave activity is found traveling at intervals from the central part of the brainstem (called the pons – Latin for 'bridge') to the image-creating areas of the occipital lobe. These ponto-geniculo-occipital (PGO) waves pass through an area called the geniculum. PGO waves were discovered in connection with electrical stimulation of certain areas of the brain (in cats) during REM sleep by French neuroscientist Michel Jouvet (1975). This discovery has been further elaborated on by Allan Hobson in relation to human dreaming (Hobson and McCarley 1977). Direct observation of PGO waves in human brains has not been possible because this would require indwelling electrodes. Moreover, current methods of brain scanning cannot detect the very brief 'spikes' that characterize PGO waves. Experiments have, however, been carried out during REM sleep that incorporate subliminal stimuli, thus activating rapid eye movements seen as an indication of PGO activity (Sammut and Russel 2012). The intensity of eye movements during dreaming is also assumed to match the intensity of PGO waves, as well as the intensity of the dream experience, including lively image-shifting and jumps in plot (Germaine *et al.* 2003).

The brainstem is also involved in the modulation of sensation, movement, and consciousness. At the top of the brainstem, an area called the ventral tegmental, involved in reward seeking, shows increased activity during dreaming.

When we dream, intense activity is also found in a network of small nuclei in the brainstem that controls our basic moods (also called background emotions), such as being calm or tense, relaxed or irritable, listless or optimistic, open or withdrawn, enthusiastic or depressed, etc. These networks connect moods to bodily sensations like well-being or discomfort (Damasio 2000). They are the seat of our fundamental sense of being: "This is me, I'm in this body and right now I feel like this (Solms and Turnbull 2002 p. 90)." Central to this process is an area called the periaqueductal grey (PAG). When we are exposed to disturbances, the PAG network registers this and develops background emotions that we must respond to in order to restore balance (Erikson 2003). These states have been especially explored in relation to dreams by South African neuropsychoanalyst Mark Solms and his colleague Oliver Turnbull (2002). Their work makes important references to Antonio Damasio's groundbreaking research into the subtle levels of feeling consciousness (Damasio 2000).

The PAG network is included in a larger system of nuclei called the reticular activation system, which is important to arousal, alertness and awareness in dreams as well as in waking life. It stretches upward to a system called the thalamus, a very important relay for circulating information between brain systems (Solms and Turnbull 2002).

When we dream, as well as when we are awake and alert, some small (intralaminar) nuclei in the thalamus regulate activity at a frequency that oscillates between 25–100 hertz, typically 40 hertz. These oscillations are called gamma waves. Their function is to synchronize the interaction between active brain networks (Gold 1999; Ratey 2001).

The image-forming areas of the cerebral cortex are absolutely necessary to our ability to dream. They are found at the rear of the brain in a transitional area between the occipital and temporal lobes that is involved in the generation of visuospatial imagery (Solms and Turnbull 2002).

The Emotional Brain in Dreaming

The limbic system, labeled the 'emotional brain' by groundbreaking brain researcher Joseph LeDoux, is active when we dream. Located just above the brainstem, it is crucial to all facets of our emotional lives and relations to others (LeDoux 1998). The emotional brain processes all our primary feelings such as joy, fear, anger, surprise, interest, and contempt, etc. This part of the brain is very active when we dream.

The Basic Emotion System

Solms and Turnbull were inspired by LeDoux, and also by Jaak Panksep's widely acknowledged studies of the phylogenetic development of the brain from animals to humans (Panksepp 1998). Solms and Turnbull describe a number of 'basic emotion command systems' related to the evolutionary emotions of exploration, feeding, nurturing, aggressive dominance displays, parental care, bonding and attachment. Basic emotion command systems both respond to various inputs and are able to learn from experience to a very great extent in human beings. For example, an emotional care subsystem stores nurturing experiences in a child as well as in the child's mother, while another system is occupied with play or learning about dangers in the surrounding environment. All these systems are highly active during REM dreaming (Solms and Turnbull 2002). Solms and Turnbull claim that "Precisely because these mechanisms take so long to develop, and also because they have such potent survival value, they are deeply conserved in humans as well as in animals" (Solms and Turnbull 2002, p. 113).

Louis Cozolino, who has written extensively on the neuroscience of human relationships, emphasizes that this concerns areas and connections that refine human attachment and social relations – themes that play important roles in psychotherapy, (Cozolino 2014, loc. 468ff) often disclosed in dreams.

The emotional brain contains important separate networks that work closely together internally as well as with the rest of the brain when we dream.

The Amygdalae

The amygdalae are two almond-shaped nuclei networks located in the innermost part of the temporal lobes. Part of a fear system, LeDoux calls them a lexicon of dangerous things. Information from external stimuli reach the amygdalae along two different paths: by a short, fast, yet imprecise route, directly from the thalamus; and by a long, slow, but precise route by way of the cortex. The short, more direct route allows us to start preparing for potential danger and possibly even survival without delay (LeDoux 1998, p. 162ff).

Fast information goes directly to the PAG – the location for basic emotions and feelings of pleasure/non-pleasure. This does not necessarily mean that we react to this information. Areas in the frontal lobe can dampen or block the effect even without our knowing or feeling. The central nuclei of the amygdalae also have a high density of opioid receptors that are biochemical mechanisms for bonding and attachment behavior (Cozolino 2010).

Almost all of amygdalae connections are two-way, but the strength of the output is far greater from the amygdalae and the rest of the emotional brain towards the 'thinking brain' than in the opposite direction (Nunn, *et al.* 2008, p. 135). This gives our emotions a considerable power over our rational considerations. However, emotions and reactions may be registered in dreams and therefore can be helpful in dealing with fear and anxiety. Similarly, themes of attachment are often disclosed and processed in dreams.

The Hippocampus

The hippocampus, so called because of its resemblance to a seahorse, is located just behind the amygdalae. This region is absolutely vital to memory and is related to personal recollections of locations, situations and persons, which is called episodic memory (Nunn, *et al.* 2008). The hippocampus does not store memory. It filters new associations, deciding what is important and what to ignore or compress. Then it sorts the results and sends various packets of information to other parts of the brain (Ratey 2001). It has been called a funnel into long-term memory. The hippocampus is related to 'declarative' verbal memory accessible to consciousness. This memory is fragmented in dreams where individual elements of episodes are picked out and combined in new ways.

The Anterior Cingulate Cortexes

The anterior cingulate cortexes, which are also highly active during dreaming, are located above the bridge between the two brain hemispheres. According to neuroscientist John Ratey, a complex system of arousal, emotion, and motivation feeding the attention system appears to be coordinated by the anterior cingulate cortex. The primary emotional signal the anterior cingulate cortex receives derives from the amygdalae. "It decides which bits of sensory information are to be granted entry into the frontal lobes, and which should be dealt with for how long and with how much energy" (Ratey 2001 Loc. 1972).

Damasio's book, *Looking for Spinoza: Joy, Sorrow, and the Feeling Brain*, describes how the anterior cingulate cortexes (ACC), in connection with the vmPFC (see below) and the brainstem nuclei, are involved in such spontaneous expressions as crying and sorrow, laughter and joy. Damage to the right ACC may make it impossible to react with a "natural smile" rather than a "say cheese smile" (Damasio 2003 loc. 76). Thus the involvement of the anterior cingulate cortexes in dreaming may bring us closer to our own naturalness, which I think is an important quality of dreams.

The Insula

The insula is a large region inside the temporal lobe, which may also be highly active when we dream . In recent mindfulness research it has been found to be important to emotional attunement, not only with people in our everyday lives, but also for the attunement of our minds to the needs of the inner self (Siegel 2007). Patterns of emotional attunement that we are not aware of may be revealed in dreams.

The Hypothalamus

The hypothalamus plays an important role in the emotional brain. The hypothalamus is located near the amygdalae just above the pituitary gland. This area receives input from the amygdalae and insula, etc. and sends it on to the autonomic nervous system (ANS) in the brainstem. The hypothalamus 'reads the temperature of each situation' and cooperates with the pituitary gland in sending hormones and others chemicals to perform vital tasks. The major functions of the hypothalamus and pituitary gland are emergency responses to threat and the promotion of homeostasis, growth and reproduction (Nunn, et al. 2008). All of this adds to the unconscious information that can be brought into consciousness through dreamwork.

The Frontal Lobes in Dreaming

The medial prefrontal cortex, often abbreviated as mPFC in the literature, is an important midline structure found in front of the anterior cingulate cortexes (Pace-Schott 2012). Together with the anterior cingulate cortexes, the medial prefrontal cortex is involved in bottom-up as well as top-down regulation of emotional states. These regions are generally larger in the right hemisphere than in the left, which indicates intuitive, imaginative, and unconscious information processing. They also develop more rapidly in infancy than other parts of the cortex. They are part of the 'social brain' with important functions for attachment, relationships, affect regulation, and higher-level input into bodily homeostasis (Cozolino 2014). The medial prefrontal cortex is important for self-awareness, as well as the ability to mentalize the intentions and feelings of others (Gusnard 2006). Further, it is often suggested that it plays an important role in the creation of the dream narrative (Amodio and Frith 2006; Braun et al. 1997).

The medial prefrontal cortex is the area in the brain that has the most robust activity during REM-dreaming, while the most precipitous decreases are found in the dorsolateral prefrontal cortex situated next to the mPFC. In wakefulness, the opposite is the case (Yu 2012) – the dorsolateral prefrontal cortex (often abbreviated in literature as DLPFC) registers and coordinates data from the world at large, analyzes this data and transforms it into actions. Yet the DLPFC is more or less disconnected during dreaming processes.

The lower portion of the medial prefrontal cortex is called the ventromedial prefrontal cortex (often abbreviated as vmPFC). It is related to autobiographical memories and narratives concerning the self (Farb *et al*. 2007).

The ventromedial prefrontal cortex is connected to a system of 'somatic markers' in the brainstem, discovered by Antonio Damasio, which tag all emotions with somatic experiences (Damasio 1996). Damasio finds that the most important regions for somatosensation, required for the normal feeling of emotions, are the brainstem nuclei already mentioned, the cingulate cortex and the insula, together with the ventromedial prefrontal cortex (Damasio 2003). The somatic marker system contributes to the integration of body, emotion and mind. All of these areas have activity increases during dreaming (Pace-Schott 2012), and the integration can, as we will see, be enhanced through dreamwork. Further, the ventromedial prefrontal cortex is part of what is also called a 'default network', which is connected to creativity and fluid intelligence according to recent research (Beaty and Benedek 2014).

In dreams there is still enough rational thinking that our thoughts remain the same as they would be with the same events if they happened while awake. On the other hand, the dreamer is incapable of recognizing that the events are not actually real (Kahn and Hobson 2003).

To summarize, areas for self-esteem in the forebrain and the refinement of emotion in the central part of the frontal lobe are prerequisite for the existence of creativity, empathy and self-controlled behavior. Injury to these areas can lead to emotional blunting, a lack of ability to make plans and an odd indifference to life.

Movement, which is such a prominent attribute of dreams, is primarily initiated, executed and fine-tuned by regions in the cerebellum, the brainstem, structures called the basal ganglia, and the motor and premotor cortex – all these areas are very active during dreaming (Maquet 2000).

Areas in the brain that regulate the unconscious moods and emotions behind important decision making are active when we dream. This also applies to areas important to self-esteem, social relationships and creativity.

DREAM THEORIES BASED ON NATURAL SCIENCE

Activation Synthesis and Protoconsciousness

In 1977 American neuroscientist Allan Hobson and his colleague Robert McCarley proposed a theory of human REM sleep dreaming called *The Activation-Synthesis Hypothesis* based on French brain researcher Michel Jouvet's discovery of PGO waves. The overall generation and control of the dream state was suggested to be based on some small nuclei in the brainstem containing 'REM-on' and 'REM-off' neurons. Nuclei in the (mesopontine) tegmentum activate REM sleep, while other small nuclei – the dorsal raphe nucleus and the nucleus locus coeruleus – deactivate REM sleep and are responsible for non-REM sleep.

Hobson and McCarley (1977) suggested that "the illusion of movement in dreams ... is produced by transferring information about motor commands to the sensory systems of the brain. Since the sensory systems and motor commands are outwardly disconnected, the dreaming brain attempts to piece together randomly activated memories into a rather meaningless narrative. The dream makes the best of a bad job." This theory had a negative impact on dream interest and trust in psychotherapeutic dreamwork. It was later rebutted from many quarters and eventually modified by Hobson himself.

Recently Hobson (2014) presented a "theory of protoconsciousness," which states that consciousness and perception of self are inextricably interwoven with movement. According to Hobson, a sense of self arises hand-in-hand with the sensorimotor activation of the brain early in fetal life and with particular intensity in the third trimester where there is an abundance of REM sleep. This inner activity creates the first template for a virtual reality model of the world and makes it possible for the child to start to attune to the environment immediately after birth. This is inherent in our genetic code and a forerunner to the consciousness we develop later in life. Hobson finds his theory confirmed by the fact that newborns are able to make their needs known immediately after birth by a variety of elaborate communication signals.

Hobson still rejects the notion of any deeper psychoanalytical meaning in dreams and questions whether recollecting our dreams had any usefulness at all. However, he agrees that REM dreaming has a refreshing effect on the mind. Chemicals like serotonin or norepinephrine and histamine are unavailable during REM. According to Hobson, this has a resensitizing effect of some brain cell receptors, rendering them more effective upon awakening (Hobson 2014).

Neuropsychoanalytic Dream Theory

Mark Solms was the first to present neuroscientific documentation that the vmPFC, visual areas of the brain, as well as "core consciousness," are necessary for dreaming (Solms 1997). Solms' understanding is based on a combination of phylogenetic motivation theory, psychoanalysis and brain research. Key to Solms' theory is that "the activation of a motivationally charged seeking system, which drives our appetitive interest in the object world, appears to begin the dream process proper (Solms and Turnbull 2002 p. 211)." He finds modern neuroscience broadly consistent with Freud's psychoanalytic theory of dreams – the nature of the dream process is, according to Solms, inherently "regressive." The "latent," i.e. unconscious content of the dream has motivational impulses that parallel Freud's concept of instinctual drives. A kind of censorship distorts the material and makes "manifest dreams" appear illogical. In order to further the interpretation, "psychological techniques" are needed (Solms and Turnbull, 2002, p. 215ff). In a later paper, Calvin Kai-Ching Yu suggests that the medial prefrontal region is the neural substrate for an instinctual reservoir and describes some possible neuroanatomical correlates for dream censorship (Yu 2012).

From Cognitive to Neurocognitive Dream Theory

Cognitive dream theory is based on observations of the parallels between dreaming and waking cognition, the so-called 'continuity hypothesis'. It assumes that the same conceptual system underlying waking thought also underlies dreaming. This theory was originally based on statistical content analysis presented by Calvin Hall, and on laboratory research conducted by David Foulkes and others. William Domhoff is among the most prominent protagonists of cognitive dream theory.

According to Domhoff, most direct continuities involve the primary people in a dreamer's life and the nature of the social interactions with them. Domhoff found that "numerous studies show that the frequency with which a person, action or activity occurs in a series of dreams reveals the 'intensity' of the 'concern' with that person, action or activity in waking life ...." This continuity is not connected to day-to-day events, but to general concerns. According to his understanding, "the key issue in dream research [is] neither Freud's theory of repressed wishes, Jung's theory that dreams are compensatory, nor Hobson's theory about the activation of nuclei in the brainstem." Domhoff's primary efforts are to support his viewpoints and results of brain research, thus "making a cognitive approach neurocognitive" (Domhoff 2010).

Contemporary Theories of Dream Memory

Many studies indicate that sleep and dreaming contribute to storing and consolidating elements of memory in various systems with differing functions.

According to Patrick McNamara (2016), most researchers find that dreams are likely to process memory on a very fundamental level. McNamara himself believes dreams to be causally implicated in memories of emotionally significant experiences.

As Freud pointed out, some emotionally significant elements from events of the previous day are revisited in dreams. This observation is supported by the Jungians and most psychotherapeutic dream schools. More recent research has found that other elements appear 5–7 days after the events – the so-called 'dream lag effect'. Canadian dream researcher Tore Nielsen hypothesizes that the dream lag effect leads to newly acquired experiences being transferred from short-term to longer-term memory (Nielsen 2012).

Based on studies of brain neurotransmitters and neurohormones especially the escalation of cortisol over the course of the night's sleep, researchers Jessica Payne and Lynn Nadel assume that sleep has multiple purposes. This includes analysis of the 'residue' of recent experiences and integration of that outcome with previously stored 'knowledge'. Dreams primarily reflect the integration of knowledge people have built up over lifetimes of experience. NREM states are especially occupied with the consolidation of episodic memory. The content of the dream reflects which brain structures are active (Payne and Nadel 2004). Based on the emerging scientific data, leading sleep researchers Robert Stickgold and Matthew Walker are convinced that "a sleep-dependent memory processing system ... selects new information, in a discriminatory manner, and assimilates it into the brain's vast armamentarium of evolving knowledge, helping guide each organism through its own, unique life." They call it "memory triage" (Stickgold and Walker 2013) – a process in which things are ranked in terms of importance or priority.

In a scientific overview of recent research, Caroline Horton and Josie Malinowski (2015) conclude that dreaming has a key role in the storage of auto-biographical memory. Dreams organize memory into narratives that combine episodic recollections in new ways that are in accordance with old experience. These authors point out that narratives may be completely fundamental to the way the brain organizes and integrates experience in our understanding of our life processes and ourselves – in dreams as well as when we are awake.

Theories of Emotion Regulation During Dreaming

Many scientific dream theories attribute dreams with an emotional regulatory function, i.e. "the regular coupling of emotional surges with a problem-solving dream structure that unfolds across the night" (Nielsen and Levin 2007). Laboratory researcher Rosalind Cartwright presented a theory of dreaming as a mood regulation system (Cartwright 2005). Milton Kramer's research, as I describe above, is also an example of this.

Similarities Between Dreams and Psychotherapy

Ernest Hartmann, another important figure in the scientific dream landscape, suggests that an "emotional working through" of problems takes place in dreams, paralleling what happens in psychotherapy. Even though he recognizes the differences between dreams and psychotherapy, he still finds important similarities. He refers to Jungian analysts who call the analytic setting a sealed vessel or container within which psychological work can be done without 'acting out' inner conflicts. Such containers are secure in dreams because our bodies cannot move and because dreams are exempt from outside disturbances. Thus dreams, like psycho-therapeutic settings, function as 'safe places'. Dreams also make use of free associations in a way somewhat similar to Freud's method. According to Hartmann, this gives dreams the possibility of making new connections psycho-logically, as well as within the brain (Hartmann 1998).

Right and Left Hemisphere Differences

Robert Hoss, a former president of the International Association for the Study of Dreams, has described similarities between dream experiences and what is known as right hemisphere processing – as opposed to left hemisphere processing. The right hemisphere is attributed to be more emotional, holistic, synthetic, imaginative, intuitive and creative. On the other hand, the left hemisphere is supposed to be intellectual, verbal, linear, categorizing, analytical and rational.

Hoss also found research indicating that some influential centers in the dream state are specific to areas of the right hemisphere, such as the right inferior parietal cortex and the right hypothalamus (Hoss 2005).

A Possible Fear Extinction Function

Tore Nielsen and Ross Levin (2007) have presented a theory about a "fear extinction function" in normal dreams that breaks down in nightmares. They assume that dreams have an increased availability of elements from fearful memories. In normal dreams, these elements are reorganized and combined with non-fearful features. In nightmares, this reorganization does not take place.

The outcome is assumed to depend on a negotiation between core structures in the emotional brain that produces fear memories, and midline frontal structures that calm and reprogram these fear memories. If the midline frontal structures do not succeed, the dream will develop into a nightmare. The result depends on a particular dreamer's personality, current life situation and autobiographical memory (Nielsen and Levin 2007).

Dreaming as Model Simulation and Virtual Reality

Finnish dream researcher Antti Revonsuo has proposed a "threat simulation theory" for dreams. It suggests that dreamers are rehearsing how to handle future threats. This supposedly dates back to an era when people lived much more dangerous lives than today, when it was appropriate to simulate the many serious threats that life would present (Revonsuo 2000). Various authors have argued that, rather than a simple threat rehearsal mechanism, dreams reflect a more general virtual rehearsal mechanism in the development of human cognitive capacities (Franklin and Zyphur 2005).

The idea of dreams as virtual reality simulation is used independently by several researchers such as, for example, Hobson in his protoconsciousness model, and by Nielsen and Levin in their paper on fear extinction mentioned just above. In a recent paper entitled 'The avatars in the machine', Revonsuo and his colleagues (2015) expand upon their original theory to encompass dreaming as a simulation of social reality and human relations.

Evolutionary Dream Theories

Several modern as well as classic theories try to explain why dreams appeared at all in the history of evolution.

Freud conceptualized a fundamental opposition between untamed instinctual drives and a need for cultural adaptation. This is clearly expressed in his famous work 'Civilization and its Discontents' (Freud 1930). Freud hypothesized that dreams are an attempt to reconcile nature and culture. Dreams allow an unconscious release of instinctual energy suppressed by culture so that civilized consciousness and self-perception are not violated (Freud 1900).

Freud's evolutionary viewpoint is supported by neuropsychological discourses presented by Solms and Turnbull (2002) who underscore how the human brain continues to develop systems that have significant survival functions in animals.

Jung's theory of archetypes states that humankind developed some universal and fundamental patterns of behavior and survival through evolution, and that these patterns play important roles both for the individual and societies. According to Jung, dreams are the best point of access to this evolutionary wisdom (Mattoon 1978, p. 121).

A decade after the discovery of REM sleep, a sentinel theory was proposed by biologist Friedrich Snyder (1966). He suggests that the fact that we ascend from deep sleep and approach waking consciousness several times during the night makes it easier to respond to threats and dangers from outside and thus contributes to the evolutionary supremacy of humankind (Snyder 1966).

Montague Ullman has further developed this point of view in a "Vigilance Theory." He believes that vigilance in the human species is of "a more refined and sophisticated social nature: in the dreaming process, the organism evaluates the impact of recent disturbing events. Dreams take scans of the brain's memory layers in an attempt to tie current experiences with experiences in the past" (Tolaas and Ullman 1969).

Patrick McNamara has suggested a "Costly Signaling Theory" based on the fact that REM sleep is metabolically costly to produce, i.e. using as much energy as an alert waking state. McNamara suggests that dreams may "become valuable signaling devices for people considering cooperating with one another" (McNamara 2012).

Antti Revonsuo's above mentioned "Threat Simulation Theory" also suggests that dreaming was primarily selected during the human evolution for the anticipation of future threat in a dangerous environment.

Hartmann, in a book on *Dreams and Nightmares*, suggests that dreams have a healing function for traumatic experiences that were much more frequent for our ancestors than for most people today (Hartmann 1998).

Conclusion

Much valuable knowledge about dreams has been established within the different lines of clinical experience and scientific research with dreams. Yet there still exist significant variations in the understanding of the nature and function of dreams, as well as how to make them useful to human beings.

The various theoretical models and practical uses of dreams have been developed with differing research strategies and "knowledge interests," as German Philosopher Jürgen Habermas calls them (Habermas 1968). Behind this may be found conflicting perceptions of consciousness and unconsciousness, nature and culture, the individual and society, and even in the views of humanity.

In the following chapter I shall present a unifying theory of dreams based on a theory of complexity. In Part II of the book, I integrate and develop what I find is the most valid knowledge from these theories and methods into a cohesive model of The Ten Core Qualities for working with dreams in therapy, counseling, social contexts and self-development.

References

Amodio, D. M. and Frith, C. D. (2006) 'Meeting of minds: the medial frontal cortex and social cognition. *Nature Reviews*, 7, 268–277

Beaty, R. E., Benedek, M., *et al.* (2014) 'Creativity and the default network. A functional connectivity analysis of the creative brain at rest'. *Neuopsychologia* 64 (2014) 92–98

Braun, A., Balkin, T., *et al.* (1997) 'Regional cerebral blood flow throughout the sleep-wake cycle'. *Brain*, 120, 1173–1197

Cartwright, R. (1977) *Night Life*. (Upper Saddle River, NJ: Prentice Hall Inc.)

Cartwright, R. (2005) 'Dreaming as a mood regulation system' in M. Kryger, T. Roth and W. Dement (Eds), *Principles and Practice of Sleep Medicine* (4th Ed.). (Philadelphia, PA: Elsevier Saunders), pp. 565–72

Cozolino, L. (2010) *The Neuroscience of Psychotherapy: Healing the Social Brain* (2nd Ed.). (New York: W. W. Norton & Company), Kindle edition, location 1538–1541

Cozolino, L. (2014) *The Neuroscience of Human Relationships: Attachment and the Developing Social Brain* (2nd Ed.). (New York: W. W. Norton & Company) Kindle edition, locations 468–476, 1231–1246

Damasio, A. (1996) 'The somatic marker hypothesis and the possible functions of the prefrontal cortex'. *Philosophical Transactions of the Royal Society B*, 351, 1413–1420

Damasio, A. (2000) *The Feeling of What Happens*. (London: Vintage)

Damasio, A. (2003) *Looking for Spinoza: Joy, Sorrow, and the Feeling Brain*. (Boston, MA: Houghton Mifflin Harcourt), Kindle edition

Dement, W. and Wolpert E. (1958) 'The relation of eye movements, body motility, and external stimuli to dream content'. *The Journal of Experimental Psychology*, Vol. 55, 543

Domhoff, G. W. (2010) *The Case for a Cognitive Theory of Dreams*. Available online at: http://dreamresearch.net/Library/domhoff_2010.html (retrieved October 2015)

Erikson, H. (2003) *Neuropsykologi [Neuropsychology]*. (Copenhagen: Hans Reitzel)

Farb, N., *et al.* (2007) 'Attending to the present: mindfulness meditation reveals distinct neural modes of self-reference'. *Medicine & Health Social Cognitive & Affective Neuroscience*, Vol. 2, Issue 4, 313–322

Franklin, M. and Zyphur, M. (2005) 'The role of dreams in the evolution of the human mind'. *Evolutionary Psychology*. Vol. 3, 59–78

Freud, S. (1900/2013) *The Interpretation of Dreams*. (Sunderland, UK: Dead Dodo Vintage), Kindle edition

Freud, S. (1930/1974) 'Civilization and its discontents [Das unbehagen in der kultur]' in *The Standard Edition of the Complete Psychological Works of Sigmund Freud*. Vol. 19. (New York: Hogarth Press)

Germaine, A. *et al.* (2003) 'Psychophysiological reactivity and coping styles influence: the effects on acute stress exposure on rapid eye movement sleep'. *Psychomatic Medicine*, No. 65, 857–864

Gold, I. (1999) 'Does 40-hz oscillation play a role in visual consciousness?' *Consciousness and Cognition*, 8(2), 186–195

Greenberg, R. and Pearlman, C. (1993) 'An integrated approach to dream theory' in M. Moffitt, M. Kramer and R. Hoffmann (Eds), *The Functions of Dreaming*. (Albany, NY: State University of New York Press) pp. 368–381

Gusnard, D. (2006) 'Neural substrates of self-awareness' in J. Cacioppo, *et al.* (Eds), *Social Neuroscience: People Thinking about Thinking People*. (Cambridge MA: MIT Press), pp. 41–62

Habermas, J. (1968/2007) *Knowledge and Human Interest.* (Cambridge: Polity Press)

Hall, C. S. (1953) The Meaning of Dreams. (New York: McGraw Hill)

Hall, C. and Domhoff, B. (1963) 'A ubiquitous sex difference in dreams'. *Journal of Abnormal Psychology,* 62, 278–280

Hartmann, E. (1973) *The Functions of Sleep.* (New Haven, CT: Yale University Press)

Hartmann, E. (1998) *Dreams and Nightmares.* (New York: Plenum)

Hobson, A. (2014) *Psychodynamic Neurology: Dreams, Consciousness, and Virtual Reality.* (Abingdon, UK: CRC Press), Kindle edition

Hobson, A. and McCarley, R. W. (1977) 'The brain as a dream state generator: an activation-synthesis hypothesis of the dream process'. *American Journal of Psychiatry,* 134, 1335–1348

Horton, C. and Malinowski, J. (2015) 'Autobiographical memory and hyperassociativity in the dreaming brain: implications for memory consolidation in sleep'. *Frontiers in Psychology,* 6, 874

Hoss, R. J. (2005) *Dream Language: Self-Understanding through Imagery and Color.* (Ashland, OR: Innersource), Kindle edition

Jouvet, M. (1975) 'The function of dreaming: a neurophysiologist's point of view' in M. Gazzaniga and C. Blakemore (Eds), *Handbook of Psychobiology.* (New York: Academic Press)

Kahn, D. and Hobson, A. (2003) 'Dreaming and hypnosis as altered states of the dream mind'. *Sleep and Hypnosis,* 5(2)

Kahn, D. and Hobson, A. (2005) State dependent thinking: A comparison of waking and dreaming thought. *Consciousness and Cognition* 14 (2005) 429–438 US

Kramer, M. (1993) 'The selective mood regulatory function of dreaming' in M. Moffitt, M. Kramer and R. Hoffmann (Eds), *The Functions of Dreaming.* (Albany, NY: State University of New York Press), pp. 139–196

LaBerge, S., Leviathan, L. and Dement W. C. (1986) 'Lucid dreaming: physiological correlates of consciousness during REM-sleep'. *Journal of Mind and Behaviour,* 7(2-3), 251–8

LeDoux, J. (1998) *The Emotional Brain.* (London: Phoenix Paperback)

LeDoux, J. (1999) 'Emotion – the brain's iceberg' in R. Carter, *Mapping The Mind.* (Oakland, CA: University of California Press)

Lewin, I. and Glaubman, H. (1975) 'The effect of REM-deprivation. Is it detrimental, beneficial or neutral?' *Psychophysiology,* 12(3), 349–53

MacLean, P. (1990) *The Triune Brain in Evolution.* Plenum, NY

Maquet, P. (2000) 'Functional neuroimaging of normal human sleep by positron emission tomography'. *Journal of Sleep Research,* 9(3), 207–31

Mattoon, M-A. (1978) *Applied Dream Analysis.* (Washington, DC: H.V. Winsten & Sons)

McNamara, P. (2012) 'Philosophy of Mind and Dream Characters' in D. Barrett and P. McNamara (Eds), *Encyclopedia of Sleep and Dreams.* (Santa Barbara, CA: Greenwood Publishing), Kindle edition, location 4976–5010

McNamara, P. (2016) 'Are dreams required for memory?' *Psychology Today,* 18 February

McNamara, P. *et al.* (2005) 'A "Jekyll and Hyde" within. aggressive versus friendly interactions in REM and non-REM dreams'. *Psychological Science,* 16(2)

Nielsen, T. (2012) 'Dream-lag effect' in D. Barrett D. and P. McNamara (Eds), *Encyclopedia of Sleep and Dreams.* (Santa Barbara, CA: Greenwood Publishing), Kindle edition, location 6176–6229

Nielsen, T. and Levin, R. (2007) 'Nightmares: A New Neurocognitive Model'. *Sleep Medicine Reviews*, 11, 295–310

Nunn, K. *et al.* (2008) *Who is Who of the Brain.* (London: Jessica Kingsley Publishers)

Pace-Schott, E. (2012) 'Prefrontal cortex in dreaming' in D. Barrett D. and P. McNamara (Eds), *Encyclopedia of Sleep and Dreams.* (Santa Barbara, CA: Greenwood Publishing), Kindle edition, Location 13097–13218

Panksepp, J. (1998) *Affective Neuroscience: The Foundations of Human and Animal Emotions* (Series in Affective Science). (Oxford: Oxford University Press), Kindle edition

Payne, J. and Nadel, L. (2004) 'Sleep, dreams, and memory consolidation: the role of the stress hormone cortisol'. *Learning & Memory*, 11(6), 671–678

Punamäki, R. (1999) 'The relationship of dream content and changes in daytime mood in traumatized vs. non-traumatized children'. *Dreaming*, Vol. 9, No. 4, 213–234

Ratey J. (2001) *A User's Guide to the Brain: Perception, Attention, and the Four Theatres of the Brain.* (New York: Knopf Doubleday Publishing Group), Kindle edition

Revonsuo, A. (2000) 'The reinterpretation of dreams: an evolutionary hypothesis of the function of dreaming' in *Behavioral and Brain Sciences*, 23, 877–901

Revonsuo, A., *et al.* (2015) 'The avatars in the machine – dreaming as a simulation of social reality' in T. Metzinger and J. M. Windt (Eds). *Open MIND*: 32(T). (Frankfurt am Main: MIND Group)

Sammut, E. and Russel, C. (2012) 'Sensory stimulation as a technique to study dreaming' in D. Barrett and P. McNamara (Eds), *Encyclopedia of Sleep and Dreams.* (Santa Barbara, CA: Greenwood Publishing) Kindle edition, location 7059–7342

Siegel, D. J. (2007) *The Mindful Brain: Reflection and Attunement in the Cultivation of Well-Being.* (New York: Norton), p. 190 ff

Smith, C. (1993) 'REM sleep and learning' in M. Moffitt, M. Kramer, *et al.*, (Eds), *The Functions of Dreaming.* (Albany, NY: State University of New York Press)

Snyder, F. (1966) 'Towards an evolutionary theory of dreaming'. *The American Journal of Psychiatry*, 123, 121–42

Snyder, F. (1969/1970) 'The phenomenology of dreaming' in L. Meadow and L. Snow (Eds) *The Psychodynamic Implications of the Physiological Studies on Dreams.* (Springfield, IL: Charles Thomas Publishers)

Solms M. (1997) *The Neuropsychology of Dreams.* (Mahwah NJ: Lawrence Erlbaum Associates)

Solms, M. and Turnbull, O. (2002) *The Brain and the Inner World.* (New York: Other Press)

Stickgold, R. and Walker, M. (2013) 'Sleep-dependent memory triage: evolving generalization through selective processing' *Nature Neuroscience* 16, pp. 139–145

Tolaas, J. and Ullman, M. (1969/1979) 'Extrasensory communication and dreams' in B. Wolmann (Ed.) *Handbook of Dreams.* (New York: Van Nostrand Reinhold Co.), pp. 168–195

Vogel, G. and W. *et al.* (1968) 'Sleep reduction effects on depressive syndromes'. *Archives of General Psychiatry*, Vol. 18, 287

Vogel, G. *et al.* (1977) 'Endogenous depression improvement and REM pressure'. *Archives of General Psychiatry*, 34, 96–97

Yu, C. (2012) 'Neuroanatomical correlates of dream censorship' in D. Barrett and P. McNamara, *Encyclopedia of Sleep and Dreams.* (Santa Barbara, CA: Greenwood Publishing) Kindle edition, location 11418–11419

Chapter 3

We Dream Because We are Complex Beings

A Cybernetic Network Theory of Dreaming

Dream research has made many attempts to determine, in clear specific functions, the reasons for our dreaming life. My answer to the question, 'Why do we dream?' is that our dreams help us solve many and varied tasks. We dream because we are complex beings who need to shift between states of being that process information in different ways to provide us with differing perspectives on the lives we are living.

Dream sleep makes up a twelfth of our lives. Non-REM and REM sleep arose as our species evolved and faced more and more complex tasks. It would indeed be an odd whim of Mother Nature if this extensive biological and psychological phenomenon in such a successful species as human beings did not have a function for the organism as a whole.

As cybernetic theorist Francis Heylighen points out, evolution has a tendency to develop toward more and more complex structures. As systems evolve, their adaptiveness tends to increase and therefore also their knowledge or intelligence. Thus the general trend of evolution is a spontaneous increase of intelligent organization (Heylighen 1999).

Seen in this light, dreams can constructively be treated as natural and useful parts of the evolution of primitive organisms to higher, more developed and complex species. Conscious engagement in dreamwork may potentially increase the intelligence of humankind in innovatively rewarding ways.

The complexity of the material I have presented in the first two chapters calls for an integrative approach. Therefore, over many years of theoretical study and practical dreamwork, I have tried to filter out the most valid findings of the various fields of dreamwork to allow a comprehensive theoretical framework to emerge. This theory describes ten Core Qualities of dreams and a comprehensive understanding I call a cybernetic network theory.

My approach to dreaming is based on an understanding of the human psyche as a multilayered, self-optimizing, complex information system. This system has a spontaneous tendency to organize itself into networks of subsystems at higher or lower levels of conscious and unconscious processing. It functions as a parallel-processing neural network where many subsystems are active, simultaneously accessing differing yet overlapping memory systems. The systems are open but swing rhythmically between states more or less in contact with the surrounding world.

According to theories of complexity there may be many interactive causes to any given state – known as 'multicausality'. When a complex system like the personality is exposed to disturbances, it can find its way to a more balanced state via many paths – 'equifinality' (von Bertalanffy 1968; Gannik 2008; Cicchetti, *et al.* 1996). Using these principles, we should not only look for one but for several causes of a particular dream and acknowledge that employing a variety of dream-work methods can produce progressive and harmonizing states.

Another important characteristic of complex systems is 'emergence', i.e. the spontaneous creation of new properties by the interaction between parts. In the psychological model I present, good dreamwork tunes into the creative matrix of emergent structures.

Formulated by W. Ross Ashby, one of the basic rules of cybernetics is the law of requisite variety, which, in part, is a measure of the degree of regulation that can be achieved in a system in any given circumstance. On the basis of game theoretical considerations, he found that in a game between two systems the system that has the most variety will vanquish the one with less variety, presupposing its possibilities are fully utilized. This means that if a system is limited in its complexity, there is also a limit to how much it can regulate (Ashby 1956).

Thus waking consciousness, which is occupied with all its everyday hassles and adjustments to the outside world, must rely on alternative states and modes of conscious and unconscious information processing to deal with the complexity of life and the psyche as a whole.

Unconscious Intelligence

Since the outset of modern dream understanding, the perception that unconscious processes interact with consciousness has played a central role. By combining hermeneutic and clinical experience from the dream schools with the knowledge of dreams derived from natural science research, we see how dreamwork can supply the requisite variety needed to manage important complex issues in human life.

Intelligence is ordinarily understood as a combination of many character-istics. Intelligence encompasses problem solving, constructive reactions to external influences, interpreting large amounts of data, long-term planning, the abilities to abstract and to distinguish between what is essential and nonessential. Moreover, it involves a vast memory and a capacity for effec-tive retrieval together with rational understanding, as well as an ability to combine knowledge in creative ways. Contrary to prevalent concepts, all of these features can be demonstrated in unconscious processes (Vedfelt 2000). This constructive view of the unconscious integrates research from many different sources.

The Depth Psychological Unconscious

Freud (1900) perceived the unconscious as consisting of multiple layers – deep layers of drives and instincts with other layers on top made up of defense mechanisms that modify and channel instinctual urges to make them more palatable to consciousness. Jung also saw the unconscious as divided into layers – the deepest layers consisted of universal, archetypal patterns and, above those, layers of culturally taught forms of experience. Above these is a personal unconscious layer that contains the particular experiences of the individual (Jacoby 1959). Both authors made their discoveries by studying dreams.

The successors of Freud and Jung have increasingly differentiated these models, particularly concerning how relationships to close relatives in childhood contribute to the formation of unconscious structures. In all these theories, dreams are considered vital parts of the unconscious as well as important entrances to it.

The Cognitive Unconscious

Existential and cognitive psychologies have been critical of the psychoanalytic and Jungian concepts of the unconscious. A newer branch of research has examined a so-called 'cognitive unconscious', which is understood as the meaningful, unconscious information constantly present in our everyday lives. Experimental psychology has revealed that normal, rational consciousness can only process a very small portion of the information to which the personality as a whole can relate. American psychologist John Kihlstrom reviewed research on perceptual-cognitive and motoric skills that indicated that these skills are automatized by experience and thus rendered unconscious. In addition, a wealth of research on subliminal perception, implicit memory and hypnosis indicates that events can affect mental functions even if they cannot be consciously perceived or remembered (Kihlstrom 1987).

Unconscious sensing and non-verbal communication have been abundantly documented as intensive and meaningful activities running parallel to our waking and more conscious mental processes (Vedfelt 2000). For instance, images shown to us so briefly (at 1/100th of a second) that we cannot perceive them consciously, can still be registered unconsciously and appear in our dreams (Pötzl 1917). Leading experts in the study of this 'new unconscious' concluded that over 90 percent of our mental processing is unconscious (Bargh and Chartrand 1999; Hassin, et al. 2007).

The unconscious information we receive by reading another person's facial expressions, body language and tone of voice arrives at such a speed that consciousness cannot keep up. This affects our view of people and relationships, and our emotional states and behavior, to a great extent without our awareness. Considerable evidence pioneered by American psychologist Albert Mehrabian (1981) and others shows that approximately 90 percent of our evaluation of another person's personality and intentions is acquired through mostly uncon-scious, nonverbal perceptions. Imprints of this information – unrecognized by consciousness – can be found in dreams.

The Relational Unconscious

Neuroscientist Allan Schore uses the term "relational unconscious" for the memory traces of early relational patterns (Schore 2009), which corresponds with the 'relation turn' in psychoanalytic theories discussed in Chapter 1.

These overlapping approaches to understanding the unconscious are seemingly disparate, yet I will gather them all under the concept of unconscious intelligence and demonstrate that these approaches can support an integrated and constructive view of the complexity of dreams.

Dreams and the Borderland of Consciousness

In general, we view everyday rational consciousness as consciousness itself. Rational consciousness is obviously an extremely important part of our person-alities, yet we have a tendency to overlook that, in reality, we find ourselves in other states of consciousness for large portions of our lives.

We dream for approximately two hours every night and spend the rest of our sleep in a state which, when it comes to content, is closer to the thinking we do while awake than while dreaming. This has been demonstrated by waking subjects in sleep laboratories. Several systematic studies have shown that 20–25 percent of the waking state has a more relaxed, flowing, dreamlike and imagina-tive quality (Foulkes and Fleischer 1975; Kripke and Sonnenschein 1978). Furthermore, one aspect demonstrated in association studies is that we constantly have gaps in our flow of thoughts (Jung 1904–07). If we dissect this, we find that we spend between a third and a half of our lives in altered states of consciousness – and even more for children – so we have to assume that these states have positive functions.

One of the primary themes of this book is that we are 'online' to a network of unconscious intelligence while dreaming. To get the most out of the information flowing through our dreaming consciousness we can, while in waking states, 'go online' to networks that overlap the dreaming process.

The dream schools have utilized a variety of mental states and levels of consciousness. The most classic examples are psychoanalytic association tech-niques and therapists' free-floating attention (Freud 1912). Jungians suggest a visual and symbolic way of thinking, and experiential therapies have endeavored to stimulate emotional and creative forms of consciousness. Our understanding of altered states, levels and modes of consciousness, and their relevance to dream-work can be further developed based on contemporary neuroscience. Damasio describes various levels of feeling consciousness (Damasio 2000). Other researchers have described intuitive states like 'feeling of knowing', 'feeling of rightness' and 'feeling of meaning', which, as we will see, are all related to active areas of the dreaming brain. In dreamwork, these forms of non-verbal consciousness can be developed into progressive stages of practical intelligence called intuitive expertise. As already described, the dreaming brain is related to a creative 'default network', to networks that are active during mindfulness meditation, and to networks that play roles in empathetic states and the reading of other people's minds.

In view of this, I maintain that consciousness can function on various levels, in different states and modalities such as bodily and emotional, and through visual imagery and thinking modes of experience. All of these can be useful in understanding dreamwork (Vedfelt 2000).

A Neural Network Model

Many philosophers and modern researchers into artificial intelligence suggest that our general everyday wisdom about people and the world comes from such varied experiences that it would not be possible to make lists, with foresight, of all potential events and compile them based on rules of logic (Dreyfus and Dreyfus 1986).

From an information theoretical point of view, our experience of life is assembled through innumerable flexible patterns or 'schemata' for how the world functions in differing situations, and a similar set of manuscripts for behaviors and storylines. On top of this, a flood of information is synthesized in networks where many parts simultaneously work parallel to each other. These networks imitate the processes in the neural networks of the human brain.

The networks operate with dynamic information patterns flowing within certain boundaries. They can work with large information as a whole that cannot be reduced to single parts. The networks can learn and have new 'emergent' properties that come into being when they interact with the surrounding world or in inner processes that arise spontaneously. They are probabilistic – simulating probable models of the surroundings and/or the inner world. They are also called a neural network model; this can be used to describe psychological processes as well as physiological processes in the brain (Campbell 1989).

The dream theory I present is inspired by David Rumelhart's, James McClelland's and their co-workers' basic work on *Parallel Distributed Processing*, which primarily has psychological aims (Rumelhart and McClelland 1986; McClelland, and Rumelhart 1986).

In the network model, a mental state is described as a pattern of activation: "Alternative mental states are simply alternative patterns of activation ..." (McClelland and Rumelhart 1986, pp. 176–177). This is compatible with my model of many meaningful levels and states of consciousness.

The network organizes information in generalized experience and behavioral patterns as more trivial memories are discarded (McClelland, Rumelhart and Hinton 1986), which parallels the broadly held observation that dreams deal with the general concerns of the dreamer.

This notion of patterns is often used synonymously with the concept of schemata which, according to David Rumelhart, are the prototypes of meaning behind our understanding of the world. In memory, for instance, schemata are linked together with examples of typical situations and experiences. "The inner structure of a schema is similar to the manuscript of a stage play in many ways," Rumelhart writes. "Precisely as stage plays have characters who can be portrayed by different actors at various moments in time without changing the essential nature of the play, a schema also has variables which can be associated with differing aspects of the surroundings by various activations of the schema" (Rumelhart 1980). This perspective is useful in understanding the ever-changing patterns of dream narratives and dream characters who may personify actual relationships as well as typical inner personality traits of dreamers.

According to McClelland and Rumelhart (1986a pp. 176–7), the network has the following dynamic properties, which I find useful for the understanding of the dream process. I paraphrase the authors and compare their statement with dreams and dreamwork processes that will be exemplified in the following chapters:

- Network memory is distributed over many units and has sub-units that capture different aspects of mental state content in a manner that somehow partially overlaps, much like associations to dream elements.
- Patterns can be activated in various combinations of the sub-units depending on the context. They can be retrieved, triggered by a cue that is a fragment of the original state. In dreamwork, for example, a cue can be a subliminal impression or an emotionally salient day-residue that has been forgotten by the dreamer and then retrieved through dreamwork.
- The 'weight' of the associations – the strengths and weaknesses – between the network's elements determines what information becomes activated. Parallel to this, various dream theories use terms like 'invested energy', 'emotional charge', 'intensity of image' or 'affect load' of dream elements as important factors worth paying attention to in dreamwork.

In the following chapters, I will provide many examples of the relevance of network theory on our understanding of dreams and describe these more fully.

Based on this theoretical background, I will describe ten Core Qualities of dreams that integrate valid knowledge from the psychotherapeutic dream schools with natural scientific research, including contemporary neuroscience. I will give concrete dream examples and explain how the model facilitates the understanding of, and work with, dreams.

The Ten Core Qualities of Dreams:

1. Dreams deal with matters important to us.
2. Dreams symbolize.
3. Dreams personify.
4. Dreams are trial runs in a safe place.
5. Dreams are online to unconscious intelligence.

6. Dreams are pattern recognition.
7. Dreams are high level communication.
8. Dreams are condensed information.
9. Dreams are experiences of wholeness.
10. Dreams are psychological energy landscapes.

References

Ashby, R. (1956/1961) *An Introduction to Cybernetics*. (London: Chapman and Hall), p. 202ff

Barg, J. and Chartrand, T. (1999) 'The unbearable automaticity of being'. *American Psychologist*, 54(7), 464–479

Campbell, J. (1989) *The Improbable Machine*. (New York: Simon and Schuster)

Cicchetti, D. *et al.* (1996) 'Equifinality and multifinality in developmental psychopathology'. *Development and Psychopathology*, Vol. 8, 597–600

Damasio, A. (2000) *The Feeling of What Happens*. (London: Vintage)

Dreyfus, H. and Dreyfus, S. (1986) *Mind over Machine*. (New York: Free Press)

Foulkes, D. and Fleischer, S. (1975) *Mental Activity in Relaxed Wakefulness*. The Journal of Abnormal Psychology, Vol. 84, 66–77

Freud, S. (1900/2013) *The Interpretation of Dreams*. (Sunderland, UK: Dead Dodo Vintage). Kindle edition

Freud, S. (1912) 'Papers on technique. recommendations to physicians practising psychoanalysis' in *The Standard Edition of the Complete Psychological Works of Sigmund Freud*, Vol.12. (London, Vintage)

Gannik, D. (2008) 'Reality, theories and method in the health sciences' [Virkelighed, teorier og metode i sygdomsforskningen]. *Tidsskrift for forskning i sygdom og samfund* Årg. 5, Nr. 9, s. 33–52

Hassin, R., *et al.* (2007) *The New Unconscious*. (Oxford: Oxford University Press)

Heylighen, F. (1999) *Representation and Change: A Metarepresentational Framework for the Foundations of Physical and Cognitive Science*. (Ghent, Belgium: Communication & Cognition). Available online at: http://pcp.vub.ac.be/books/Rep&Change.pdf

Jacoby, J. (1959) *Die psychologie von C.G. Jung*. (Zürich: Rascher)

Jung, C. G. (1904–07/1973) 'The reaction time in the association experiment' in C. G. Jung, *The Collected Works of C.G. Jung*, Vol. 2. (London: Routledge and Kegan Paul), pp. 221–72

Jung, C. G. (1904/1981) 'Studies in word association' in C. G. Jung, *The Collected Works of C.G. Jung*, Vol. 2. (London: Routledge and Kegan Paul)

Kihlstrom, J. F. (1987) 'The cognitive unconscious'. *Science* 18 September, Vol. 237(4821), 1445–1452

Kripke, D. and Sonnenschein, F. (1978) 'A biological rhythm in waking fantasy' in J. S. Pope and J. L. Singer (Eds) *The Stream of Consciousness*. (New York: Plenum Press)

McClelland, J. L. and Rumelhart, D. (1986) *Parallel Distributed Processing Vol II – Explorations in the Microstructure of Cognition: Psychological and Biological Models*. (Cambridge, MA: The MIT Press)

McClelland, J. L. and Rumelhart, D. (1986a) 'A distributed model and human learning and memory' in J. L. McClelland and D. Rumelhart, *Parallel Distributed Processing*

Vol II – Explorations in the Microstructure of Cognition: Psychological and Biological Models. (Cambridge, MA: The MIT Press), pp. 170–215

McClelland, J. L., Rumelhart, D. and Hinton, G. E. (1986) 'The appeal of parallel distributed processing' in J. L. McClelland and D. Rumelhart, *Parallel Distributed Processing Vol 1 – Explorations in the Microstructure of Cognition Volume Foundations.* (Cambridge, MA: The MIT Press), pp. 3–44

Mehrabian, A. (1981) *Silent Messages.* (Belmont, CA: Wadsworth)

Pötzl, O. (1917/1960) 'The relationship between experimentally induced dream images and indirect vision'. *Psychological Issues*, Vol. II(3), pp. 41–120

Rumelhart, D. (1980) 'Schemata: the building blocks of cognition' in R. J. Spiro, *et al.* (Eds), *Theoretical Issues in Reading Comprehension.* Hillsdale, NJ: Lawrence Erlbaum. pp. 35–58

Rumelhart, D. and McClelland, J. L. (1986) *Parallel Distributed Processing Vol 1: Explorations in the Microstructure of Cognition Volume Foundations.* (Cambridge, MA: The MIT Press)

Rumelhart, D., *et al.* (1986) 'Schemata and sequential thought' in J. L. McClelland and D. Rumelhart, *Parallel Distributed Processing Vol 2 – Explorations in the Microstructure of Cognition: Psychological and Biological Models.* (Cambridge, MA: The MIT Press), pp. 7–57

Schore, A. (2009) 'Relational trauma and the developing right brain. An interface of psychoanalytic self'. *Annals of the New York Academy of Sciences*, Apr,1159, 189–203

Vedfelt, O. (2000) *Unconscious Intelligence. You Know More than You Think.* (Copenhagen: Gyldendal)

Von Bertalanffy, L. (1968) *The Organismic Psychology and Systems Theory*, Heinz Werner lectures (Worcester, MA: Clark University Press)

Part II

The Ten Core Qualities of Dreams

Chapter 4

Core Quality 1

Dreams Deal with Matters Important to Us

The collective experience of the psychotherapeutic dream schools suggests that dreams are about matters important to us. Freud was convinced that "the dream never concerns itself with trifles; we do not allow sleep to be disturbed by trivialities. The dream always contains important material if one takes the trouble to interpret them …." (Freud 1900, p. 93–97). His successors in psychoanalysis emphasize that dreams focus on central personal conflicts and important emotional relationships. Jung credited dreams with a superior wisdom (Mattoon 1978, p. 103) and stated that they support personal development by highlighting future opportunities for development. Calvin Hall concluded, based on his statistical content analyses, that dreams attempt to solve the inner problems of the person himself (Hall, 1953, pp. 233–4). Fritz Perls called dreams existential messages and treated them as visionary founts of the "wisdom of the organism" (Perls 1969, p.37). Aaron Beck, the originator of cognitive therapy, thought of dreams as core cognitive schemas (Dowd 2004).

Even William Domhoff, who was skeptical of all depth psychological dreamwork, admitted that dreams reveal the "intensity" of the "concern" of the dreamer, not only with day-to-day events, but with overriding concerns (Domhoff 2010).

It becomes clear that dreams deal with matters important to us after serious traumatic events, such as natural disasters, violent attacks and accidental fire. We know it is especially important to work through the emotions and perceptions that burden us in the wake of shock and trauma. American dream researcher Ernest Hartmann and his co-workers studied dreams after acute trauma. He demonstrated that dreams immediately following exposure to trauma contained many residuals of the traumas, and that the frequency of these dreams decreased with the individual's ability to recover from the events (Hartmann 1998).

Another example is pregnancy – the dreams of pregnant women are remarkably different from other dream material. An unusually high number of babies of all shapes and sizes appear in their dreams. These dreams are also imbued with an intense focus on their bodies and, especially during the first pregnancy, deal with inner-work of women entering their new role as mothers (Van de Castle 1994).

Neuroscience links dreams to intense brain activity that has evolved over millions of years and which, in connection with other brain systems, helps us to react rapidly, ensuring survival of both the individual and relevant social relations.

Dreams are Self-Regulating and Self-Organizing

The concept that our dreams deal with matters important to us harmonizes very well with natural science research that has documented that dreams, even when they cannot be recalled in a waking state, consolidate learning and memory, stimulate creativity and contribute to emotional balance. When we dream, brain structures are at work that belong to our common human background and that are important to our psychological existence as a whole. The activated areas motivate the satisfaction of fundamental needs. They also play a crucial role in the processing of our primary feelings and basic moods, for our social behavior and our ability to form relationships (see Chapter 2).

Neuroscientist Antonio Damasio, based on research, assumes that our whole system of emotions (which is highly active in dreams) is a self-regulating device that mostly functions outside of our awareness (Damasio 2000). Therefore, it is reasonable to view dreams as an integrated part of ongoing self-regulation that balances the personality when faced with the influences of everyday life.

Even more long-term self-organization appears to be a part of the functions of dreams. This self-organization prepares the development of the personality and important transitions from one phase in life to the next. The dream schools, and especially Jung, emphasized the long-term process of individuation, while Freud was focused more on blockages in the maturation process, which he interpreted through dreams. Erik Erikson described dreams in relation to psychosocial phases of development. The successors of psychoanalysis, and also existential psychology, primarily examined the connections in dreams between personal development and interpersonal relationships (see Chapter 1).

Self-organization is a principle that was introduced by cybernetic pioneers such as Ross Ashby (1962) and Norbert Wiener (1948), and is increasingly deemed suitable to explain the spontaneous processes of transformation where multiple variables are involved (Cicchetti and Rogosch 1996).

In self-organization, some form of overriding order emerges out of the interactions between smaller parts. The emergence of traits encompasses the system as a whole which cannot be reduced to the properties of the constituent parts.

During transitions, the system moves into a destabilizing state between chaos and order. Yet this state can be stabilized through positive feedback from the environment (Nicolis and Rouvas-Nicolis 2007). Therefore, positive feedback to resources in dreams is valuable and this is why we must pay attention to the warnings dreams give us about vulnerabilities in important transitional phases in life. This appears to apply to the early childhood phases when we are able to register them. Later, dreams anticipate, process and participate in all the great, foreseeable life transitions, for example, puberty, commitment to adult relationships, parenthood, career choices, midlife crises, retirement and other inevitable transitional periods in human life.

In various ways, these themes have been illuminated by psychoanalysts, Jungians, relations theoreticians, and in studies of human developmental phases, and they have also been seen in the study of individual dreams and dream series.

High-Level Regulation

In order to regulate the many processes constantly at work within the personality, the mind shifts between states that process information in various ways and perform varying tasks. Consciousness switches between introverted and extroverted states in a pulse-like way.

In introverted states of consciousness such as self-reflection, creativity, inspiration, relaxation therapy, imagination, free association, meditation and, not least, dreaming, we are liberated from the many practical duties of everyday life, thus creating a surplus of capacity to process information. This potentially makes space for self-organizing activities that re-establish balance between the needs of the individual and the demands of the world at large.

A parallel can be drawn with the ideas of German system theorist Niklas Luhmann, who writes about social systems making themselves unstable in order to regain stability on more abstract levels. According to Luhmann, when a system begins to turn its own properties inward on itself and not merely outward, a number of advantages are achieved. More complicated tasks and relationships can be managed. The system can "learn to learn," i.e. understand the principle of learning. Through its ability to abstract, the system can renew itself without jeopardizing identity (Luhmann 1966). It can also prepare itself for situational shifts and carry out inner trial actions that do not have direct, outer consequences (Vedfelt 2000). "If one party refuses to continue a conversation, the conversation can redefine itself around the refusal. It can abstract itself so it can perceive contradiction without breaking down" (Luhmann 1966).

Since dreams are about matters important to us, this means that they operate within our minds on a higher organizational level than in normal everyday waking consciousness.

We find a very similar understanding in neuroscientist Allan Schore's theories of the neurobiology of emotional development. He writes about "self-organizing systems that use energy to facilitate the cooperativity of simpler subsystem components into a hierarchical structured complex system" (Schore 2000, p.157).

Seen cybernetically, the personality system steps back from unresolvable conflict (in waking life) to examine whether it can be resolved on a higher level. In dreams, therefore, our minds lift above the trivialities of everyday life, sort through consciously and unconsciously received information and compare this to the more overriding patterns controlling our lives.

When we work with dreams, we move into the borderland between consciousness and unconscious intelligence. This makes it possible to connect separated memory systems to emerging novel qualities.

Approaching Dreams

In the dream schools there have been many considerations of how dreamwork could adapt to individual dreamers to avoid provoking anxiety or resistance. In psychoanalytic and Jungian therapy, this has led to an increasing interest in the transference and countertransference between therapists and dreamers. While there was a tendency earlier to select material for dreamwork that dealt with instinctual (Freudian) or archetypal (Jungian) material, dream analysis eventually became subordinate to the relationship between dreamer and therapist. Further, dreamwork was adapted to any individual vulnerabilities clients may have had in order to reduce anxiety and resistance (see Chapter 1).

Within cognitive behavioral therapies, American psychologist and dream-scientist Deirdre Barrett has described "focused-oriented therapy" where therapists limit their interest in dreams to defined psychological issues such as, for example, bereavement, depression, trauma and self-esteem, etc. In focused-oriented dream therapy, therapists often simply ask, "Have you had any dreams related to ...," i.e., issues on which agreement had already been reached (Barrett 2004).

Such methods for extracting from dreams what fits with or contributes to preconceived working methods are quite common in therapy. These methods are used when working with trauma, depression or personality disturbances and also in personal and spiritual development groups, as well as various methods of social dreaming focused on specific interests and goals.

A common feature for all the approaches is an attempt to reduce complexity in meetings about dreams in order to protect the dreamer's inner and outer balance. To some extent, these limitations may be valuable, but they also reduce possible outcomes that may be beneficial to dreamers.

My approach to dreams is intended to be as open as possible, yet maintain constant focus on resources that encourage and inspire dreamers to respond from their own perspectives. The idea is to accumulate a surplus of positive energy to meet the challenges that dreams, in all their complexity, may present. This resource-oriented approach is inspired by Robert Rosenthal's and Lenore Jacobson's study of how positive expectations of teachers enhance their students' performance – the so-called Rosenthal effect (Rosenthal and Jacobson 1992). Another inspiration is Aaron Antovsky's concept of "salutogenesis," which refers to focusing on the healing qualities that make people well, rather than what makes them ill (Antonovsky 1987).

Salutogenic methods have a considerable influence on modern healthcare professions and are presumed to enhance healing processes (Morgan 2010). When it comes to dreams, this means special attention is given to positive features rather than assumed negative ones, or reframing what seems at first sight to be negative features. Even in unpleasant dreams valuable information is to be found. One of the reasons dreamers often overlook this information is that they attempt to comprehend dreams from exactly the conscious viewpoints to which the dreams are providing alternatives.

In accordance with my resource-oriented view I hesitate to use concepts like "resistance" or "noncompliance." If a dreamer does not agree with a theoretical or methodological approach, I understand it as a breach in the relationship between myself and my client, and between waking consciousness and self-organizing variables hidden behind the dream. If this is the case, a new process of seeking must be initiated on a different level, instead of halting the creative work with a premature interpretation. The uniqueness of a complex system is that both the system and the observer can evolve through mutual feedback processes (Nicolis and Rouvas-Nicolis 2007).

Dreamwork as Information Seeking

Here in Core Quality 1, I want to especially highlight the network in the brain called the "seeking system." As described by Solms and Turnbull, this system is of major importance to dreaming. It starts in the brainstem, moves through the emotional brain (the limbic system), is connected to a reward system in the basal forebrain, amygdala and hypothalamus, and to systems in the central forebrain, the medial prefrontal cortex and the anterior cingulate (see Chapter 2). The seeking system reports important needs to the organism. It "provides the arousal and energy that something good will happen if we explore the environment or interact with objects." And further, "The seeking system is associated with terms such as 'curiosity, interest and expectancy'… When the system is activated, the subjective feeling is something along the lines of: 'What could this be? I want to know more about this'" (Solms and Turnbull 2002, p 115).

A recent study was conducted by Chinese researcher Calvin Kai-Ching Yu into the "affective valence" of dreams across the night. He found that "seeking," i.e. "feeling curious, going after or satisfying a desire," is frequent in dreams, and that exhilaration seems to be a more frequent and intense emotion in dreams than fear (Yu 2015).

Solms and Turnbull describe the seeking system as a nonspecific motivational system engaged in looking for something to satisfy needs (Solms and Turnbull 2002). Yet, during the process of dreaming, it activates various experiential and conscious contents that can be related to creativity, self-perception, empathy, social behavior and important transformational processes.

The dreamer cannot direct attention towards the outer world. The motivational energy is thus turned inward so that the system can work on itself. At the same time, inner bodily states such as thermoregulation, the endocrine systems, pulse and heart rate, etc. are poorly regulated. This lack of bodily regulation has been emphasized by Ernest Hartmann who, on the basis of this, suggests that dreaming can be considered regulation occurring chiefly at the limbic (emotional) level and the cortical (complex mental functioning) level (Hartmann 2011, p. 63).

Therefore, I suggest that motivational energy during dreaming is used on complex, high-level self-regulating and self-organizing processes including all the Core Qualities that I describe later. In accordance with this, the first task of dreamwork is connecting to the motivating powers that activate dreams and arouse the dreamer's curiosity, expectancy and interest. The next step is providing an experience in which the seeking process will be rewarded – so that something good comes out of the dreamwork.

My personal experience with many thousands of dreams confirms that behind any dream are needs that are not sufficiently valued by the individuals themselves and/or their surroundings. Recognizing this contributes to a never-ending self-optimizing process.

Resources in Pleasant Dreams

Dreams contain many positive elements and themes. Since psychotherapeutic dream schools have primarily focused on problems, they have had a tendency to overlook positive and non-conflictual content in dreams. Pleasant dreams have a purpose – they make us aware of those qualities in ourselves and our lives that we do not adequately appreciate.

For instance, a pleasant dream about being reunited with a loved one can remind us of a pleasurable sense of harmony of which we were not aware. Dreams can tell us of an urge to resume a project with which we have been passionately engaged, or even to witness the reconciliation of high-level, inner forces that have been in conflict or are fragmented. Taking a beneficial bath can underscore the importance of cleansing oneself of toxic emotions, motives and intentions, and that relief is actually possible. We can meet people who have qualities we value, or places that remind us of security, joy and freedom, etc.

When dreams highlight these positive qualities, it may be because we do not pay enough attention to them in our waking lives. Therefore, they help us to examine what is happening in our lives, what develops good feelings and states, and how we can appreciate, maintain and possibly even enhance these.

Resources in Unpleasant Dreams

William Domhoff finds it "noteworthy that about one-third of all dream reports contained 'misfortunes' that range from being lost to illness, or the death of a loved one, and that the negative emotions of sadness, anger, confusion, and apprehension, when taken as a whole, greatly outnumber the expressions of happiness" (Domhoff 2010). This kind of perception has been accepted by many researchers for a long time and is, unfortunately, a common attitude in the general population. Contemporary research suggests, however, that the number of positive emotions in dreams equals that of negative feelings (Yu 2015), and that results are often dependent on research methods.

Even if our dreams seem unpleasant, we may still find they contain resources. We have to ask ourselves what it is that dreams are trying to regulate. We can generally compare them to living organisms where balance between various subsystems is found. If one subsystem is under extreme strain, changes in other parts of the system can compensate. For instance, if you run up a flight of stairs, your breathing rate increases; if you live a long time in thin mountain air, the composition of your blood or the rhythm of your heart may actually change to compensate. Yet the greater the pressure applied to the organism, the less flexible it becomes, thus increasing the chance of breakdown. Likewise, constant psychological strain can lead to reduced mental flexibility and, at worst, psychological breakdown.

Such conditions are registered in our unconscious intelligence that can respond to these conditions with unpleasant, emotionally charged dreams. If we dream of being threatened or pursued (one of the most common dream themes) this could be reflecting feelings and thoughts that are plaguing us. We may not be aware of just how much space these tormenting thoughts and feelings are taking in our waking consciousness. Pursuit-dreams can also be expressions of long-term, self-organizing processes. As dreamers, we need to look at inner, undeveloped aspects of our personalities with which we will not find peace until they are taken seriously. If we try to enter into dialogue with those aspects of ourselves that the pursuers represent, we may find out that they are precisely the energies needed in order to move forward in our lives. This is like the fairytale in which the princess kisses the frog and transforms it into a prince.

Further, pursuit-dreams may refer to current, external experiences where we feel strain, or to undigested, traumatic memories of external pressure or abuse. Pushing dreams away or embellishing them in your imagination serves no purpose. That is like turning the smoke detector off and believing it can still save you from a fire.

Many other unpleasant themes – such as death and destruction – can also turn out to be aspects of high-level self-organization. We need to understand their symbolic meanings as elements of long-term developmental processes where outlived patterns in the personality have to die or be destroyed to make room for new developments.

In dreams following violent trauma or during severe depression, self-regulatory and self-organizing aspects may be hard to comprehend. Yet, using particular methods, these dreams can also become valuable points of departure for healing. All of this will be exemplified later.

Clarification of the Dream Content

People who are not used to working with dreams often explain them in ways that with a closer look is somewhat cursory or abbreviated to the most emotionally intense parts, thus ignoring important details that might take the understanding of the dream as a whole to another level. I call this process of unfolding the dreams in more detail, clarification. It can come about when the dreamer explains the dream a second time, going through it in a relaxed state, expressing it creatively or just by being listened to by an empathic person. In this process, a 'bad dream' can turn out to be a good dream. You will find examples of this in Chapter 6 (Sarahs dream of Nazis) Chapter 14 (Lisas Gorilla dream) and Chapter 15 (The dream of a parking lot). Thus clarification may be an important early step in the dreamwork.

Dreams focus on essential matters in our lives.
No matter whether dreams seem pleasant or unpleasant, we can still find resources in them.

References

Antonovsky, A. (1987) *Unravelling the Mystery of Health*. (San Francisco, CA: Jossey-Bass Inc.)

Ashby, W. R. (1962) 'Principles of the self-organizing system' in H. Von Foerster and G. W. Zopf Jr (Eds), *Principles of Self-Organization*. (London: Pergamon Press), pp. 255–278

Barrett, D. (2004) 'The "Royal Road" becomes a shrewd shortcut' in R. Rosner, W. Lyddon, *et al.*, *Cognitive Therapy and Dreams*. (New York: Springer Publishing), pp. 113–123

Cicchetti, D. and Rogosch, F. A. (1996) 'Equifinality and multifinality in developmental psychopathology'. *Development and Psychopathology*, 8, pp. 597–600

Damasio, A. (2000) *The Feeling of What Happens*. (London: Vintage)

Domhoff, G. W. (2010) *The Case for a Cognitive Theory of Dreams*. Available online at: http://dreamresearch.net/Library/domhoff_2010.html (retrieved 14 October 2015)

Dowd, T. E. (2004) 'Foreword' in R. Rosner, W. Lyddon, *et al.*, *Cognitive Therapy and Dreams*. (New York: Springer Publishing)

Freud, S. (1900/2013) *The Interpretation of Dreams*. (Sunderland, UK: Dead Dodo Vintage). Kindle edition

Hall, C.S. (1953) *The Meaning of Dreams*. (New York: McGraw Hill)

Hartmann, E. (1998) *Dreams and Nightmare*. (New York: Plenum)

Hartmann, E. (2011) *The Nature and Functions of Dreaming*. (Oxford, UK: Oxford University Press), Kindle edition

Luhmann, N. (1966) 'Reflexive mechanism'. *Soziale Welt*, Vol. 17, pp. 1–23

Mattoon, M. A. (1978) *Applied Dream Analysis*. (London: John Wiley)

Morgan, A. (2010) *Health Assets in a Global Context: Theory, Methods, Action*. (New York: Springer-Verlag)

Nicolis, G. and Rouvas-Nicolis, C. (2007) 'Complex Systems'. *Scholarpedia*, 2(11), 1473

Perls, F. (1969/2013) *Gestalt Therapy Verbatim*. (Gouldsboro, ME: The Gestalt Journal Press) Kindle edition

Rosenthal, R. and Jacobson, L. (1992) *Pygmalion in the Classroom* (Expanded Ed.). (Austin, TX: Holt, Rinehart & Winston, Inc.)

Rosner, R., Lyddon, W. *et al.* (2004) *Cognitive Therapy and Dreams*. (New York: Springer Publishing)

Schore, A. (2000) 'Neurobiology of emotional development' in M. Lewis and I. Granic, *Emotion, Development and Self-Organization*. (Cambridge: Cambridge University Press)

Solms, M. and Turnbull, O. (2002) *The Brain and the Inner World: An Introduction to the Neuroscience of Subjective Experience*. (London: Karnac Books), Kindle edition

Van de Castle, R. (1994) *Our Dreaming Mind*. (New York: Ballantine Books)

Vedfelt, O. (2000) 'Consciousness – Introduction to Cybernetic Psychology in Energy & Character'. *International Journal of Biosynthesis – Somatic Psychotherapy*, Part 1, April, s. 38–55; Part 2, August, s. 42–61

Wiener, N. (1948/1962) *Cybernetics, or Control and Communication in the Animal and the Machine*. (Cambridge, MA: The MIT Press)

Yu, C. (2015) 'The vicissitudes of the affective valence of dream emotions across the night. A high-density electroencephalographic study'. *Dreaming*, Vol. 25(4), pp. 274–90

Chapter 5

Core Quality 2

Dreams Symbolize

A prerequisite for all dream interpretation is an understanding that dreams live in a world of symbols where wind and weather, plants, animals and objects can all be expressions of qualities of the soul. Weather may reflect moods, animals may represent human characteristics, and objects may symbolize life processes and aspects of the personality.

The term 'symbol' is related to concepts like metaphor, allegory, sign, comparison and emblem that have been described in many ways that overlap each other. The word 'symbol' comes from Ancient Greek and means 'thrown together'. The word is generally used for clear and tangible phenomena that are perceived to be images of meanings that are not concretely tangible in themselves – for instance, when a red rose refers to love. The simplest forms of symbols are 'signs', such as the number 3 for the amount of three, a musical note for a tone, or a stop sign in traffic. These are symbols with single meanings.

Inspiration for understanding dream symbols can be found in the common metaphors of everyday language that bring abstract concepts to life and put them into contexts within our own practical intelligence and world of experience. For instance, we talk about 'dandelion children' who have grown up in difficult conditions and still have the strength to shoot up through the asphalt. Metaphors and symbols can make concepts more tangible so we can feel them in our bodies. When one grudgingly accepts something unpleasant, it is 'hard to swallow'. When the 'shoe is on the other foot' it is a good thing to know, and 'putting your shoulder to the wheel' can help get the job done. These kinds of images can appear literally in dreams and become symbols, so you actually put your shoe on the other foot or find yourself pressing your dream shoulder to a wheel.

Metaphors in Everyday Life

In their book *Metaphors We Live By*, George Lakoff and Mark Johnson (1980) have explored some of the experiential dimensions of metaphors in everyday life. They found that the dominant views of meaning in Western philosophy and linguistics are inadequate – 'meaning' in these traditions has very little to do with what people find meaningful in their lives. They also found that metaphors are key to how meaningful experiences can be expressed.

Drawing on contemporary philosophies and on a wealth of examples, they demonstrate how metaphors are systems of knowledge representation. Metaphors help people create coherent experiences – also called 'experiential gestalts'. They can highlight certain aspects of phenomena and exclude others (Lakoff and Johnson 1980, preface).

For example, we often use metaphors of war – attacking a position, indefensible, strategy, new line of attack, win, gain ground, etc. – as systematic ways of talking about the battling aspects of arguing. Or we may use time-is-money metaphors for experiences in quite different domains of life in such expressions as: 'you're wasting my time', 'how do you spend your time these days?', 'I've invested a lot of time in her', 'I don't have enough time to spare for that', 'you need to budget your time', 'he's living on borrowed time', etc. (Lakoff and Johnson 1980, pp. 7–8).

Knowledge of practical intelligence and unconscious intelligence can further expand our understanding of symbols and metaphors. For instance, if we see a person as warm, this perception may be based on observations where many details have registered subliminally through body language, a certain 'air' or other impressions, etc. Nevertheless, the metaphor 'a warm person' contributes to our overall impression, thus aiding us in navigating our relationship to that individual. This enables quicker responses without lengthy analytical examinations from where our perception/knowledge derives. In turn, this can be communicated to others and be understood in a practical and useful way.

To sum up, we can understand metaphors in waking life as natural ingredients of human concepts. They are holistic information and they contain creative potential.

Metaphors in Dreams

In waking life, we most often use metaphors without reflection, or we experience them as intuitive glimpses immediately conveyed into action. However, in dreams they may appear much more literally and visibly to the dreamer so consciousness is totally 'immersed' in the metaphors. When one can begin working with a dream in a waking state, the metaphors can be consciously tied to the life the dreamer is living.

In the following examples, I demonstrate how dreamers understood dream elements as metaphors:

- The dreamer found himself in a parking lot: *I feel my life has been parked.*
- The dream self was flying: *I am currently floating. I'm completely high.*
- The dreamer found a key: *Maybe I've found the key to a new way of doing things.*
- The dreamer walked on water: *I'd never believed I could avoid falling so deeply into it, because I was so emotionally involved.*

- The dreamer drove a car too fast: "This is probably because I am much too busy. The stress level is high these days."
- The dreamer tried to run but the air was thick: "I'm in a period where I can't seem to get moving."

Such 'aha-experiences' are always valuable. When we examine them more closely, we find that metaphors are rarely alone in a dream. Perhaps a helpful character appears in the parking lot, or the dreamer might fly into obstacles, or the key holder in the dream does not dare use it. I will return later to how individual symbols can be employed in extensive dream processes.

It may be illuminating to view symbols and metaphors as poetry – they are expressions that are very sensual and appealing to the imagination, and that open up to a much wider range of associations than dry, rational descriptions of phenomena. They interact with the receiver's intuition, which then becomes creative and makes connections to forgotten experiences, important life themes or future potential.

When I use the term 'symbol' in connection with dreams, I am also referring to a more complex and inscrutable meaning, such as when Jung (1964, p. 20) writes that symbols have "an unconscious aspect, which is never precisely defined nor fully explained."

Various Models of Symbol Interpretation

Traditional Dictionaries of Dream Symbols

In traditional dream books, interpretations are, as a rule, singular. They often refer to fixed, external conditions and predict future events. For instance, in an ancient Egyptian dream book, "crocodile meat" is a reference to greedy civil servants. In Pharaoh's dream from the Bible, "fat and lean cows" refer to future years of abundance and starvation, respectively. In Sibylle's Danish dream book from the eighteenth century, "being at an evening's supper" suggests a faithful spouse (Kaivola-Bregenhøj 1986).

This form of direct dream understanding may seem naïve from a modern viewpoint, yet could have been meaningful in societies far less complex than what we know today. Crocodiles are greedy, and civil servant corruption and exploitation might well have been everyday fare to more average Egyptians. The nutritional health of cows is vital in a society that keeps cattle, and a faithful spouse is always home at supper-time.

Freud's Method of Symbol Interpretation

Through depth psychology and the exploration of the unconscious, more hidden meanings of symbols have been found. Freud stressed that the issues we have difficulty talking about to others, or admitting to ourselves, can appear camouflaged in our dreams. He used the method of free association where the dreamer, in a relaxed state of mind, is encouraged to observe the stream of thoughts and imaginings as they spontaneously occur in consciousness. Freud was especially keen on keeping critical intellect from rejecting "freely rising ideas," thus hindering new openness to otherwise inaccessible parts of the psyche (Freud 1900, p. 56).

The separate elements in a dream were then traced back to their sources and Freud could assemble them into an interpretation. From his clients he had learned that children who witnessed the sexual intercourse of adults found it alarming and felt anxiety. In reality, Freud thought this anxiety was sexual excitation beyond the understanding and coping abilities of children, and which they rejected because their parents were involved in it. During his analyses he found that various objects in dreams could be seen as analogies of sexual thoughts and feelings. Based on his experience, Freud developed a whole catalogue of sexual dream symbols. Weapons, tools and oblong objects, for instance, referred to male sexuality, while hollow things and objects being wrought were interpreted as feminine. Climbing a ladder or stairwell symbolized increasing desire in the sexual act; falling and flying referred to other sexual sensations (Freud 1900, p. 180–91).

If you look in a dictionary of slang you will find a wealth of sexual metaphors. Also, in advertising you find a plethora of erotic symbols designed to attract attention and increase appetite for objects that are not in themselves erotic. Most dream theorists with clinical experience recognize that sexual interpretations are relevant at times. On the other hand, many theorists have purposefully expanded understandings of symbols as alternatives to Freud's method of free association.

Calvin Halls Cognitive Theory of Dream Symbols

Calvin Hall developed his own cognitive theory of dream symbolism. He suggested that symbolic processes belonged to the intellectual system of the ego (Hall 1953). Symbols are concepts translated to imagery. A pistol does not stand for the male sexual organ in itself, yet it can describe, in a very concise way, a particular man's aggressive concept of his own sexuality. Similarly, a man can dream about his mother as a cow, because a cow represents in the simplest way his perception of mother as a "nurturant" person. Symbols are not disguises but rather, "a kind of mental shorthand: my mother is a cow-like person, ergo let her appear as a cow in my dream" (Hall 1953).

As an example, Hall described the dream of a young man. *I attempted to turn on the water faucet. I then decided to call a plumber. I discovered the plumber was a lady. She turned the faucet and water flowed immediately.* At this point I awoke, having had a nocturnal emission. Hall suggested that a water faucet, which can be turned on by a female plumber, corresponded to the fact that the dreamer had a mechanical concept of sex (Hall 1953a, p. 15). Quite a different natural and sensual attitude toward sex is depicted in another 'wet dream' where the dreamer experienced: "a glorious sunrise and a climate change from cold to warm in connection with ejaculation" (Hall 1953a, p. 51).

Jungian Rules of Symbol Interpretation

Jung (1904), who did experimental research on associations at the beginning of his career, was critical of Freud's use of free association in dreams. In Freud's method, chains of associations are made to any dream element. One associates to a symbol, then associates to that association and further to new associations, and so forth. According to Jung, these Freudian zigzagging lines of associations may lead to "complexes," but they do not lead to a dream's meaning ('sinn' in German) (Jung 1938, p. 26ff). Complexes are, in Jung's understanding, more or less neurotic psychological structures – "fixed ideas" – that limit an individual's life and possible development, and conflict with the overriding psychological systems that produce dreams. In the words of Jungian analyst Michael V. Adams (2016), "The unconscious has the capacity to select an especially apt image from all those available to it, in order to serve a particular purpose. The task is to discover exactly what that purpose is."

Circling Around the Symbol

When interpreting a dream, Jung suggested that you somehow circle around each symbol and expand its meaning, rather than following lines of free associations. In other words, you remain relatively close to each symbol and integrate it into the meaning of the dream as a whole. Jung used the word "circumambulation" for this circling-around method.

These circumambulations can be divided into three approaches: personal associations, elaborations of symbols and amplifications (Mattoon 1978, p. 55).

Personal Associations

Personal associations refer to experiences the dreamer has had with a particular symbol. A dove may remind him or her of a peace dove or, on the other hand, defecate on the dreamer's balcony. A glass of wine in a dream might remind them of a glass in the childhood home, or a problem with alcohol. A certain landscape can provide associations to a holiday with a loved one, a strenuous mountain climb or many other sorts of experience.

Elaborations of Symbols

Elaborations of symbols means examining symbols carefully and clarifying their characteristics. For instance, you may explore the characteristics of a bird in a dream. Is it a migratory bird, a seabird or a forest bird? Is it a bird of prey? Domesticated or wild? Does it have a specific color? Is the gender of the bird explicit in the dream?

Amplification

Amplification means enlarging the understanding of symbols by drawing parallels to more collective material such as, for example, myths, fairytales, rituals or religious symbols. Jung found possible underlying universal – or archetypal – meanings for all of these (Franz 1978, p. 31). A woman in one of my groups dreamed that *she was cleaning an older woman's house, and then became inspired when comparing the theme of her dream with the Cinderella fairytale and with some typical experiences in her own life.* The transformation of a larva into a butterfly is a well-known symbol for spiritual transcendence. Descent into some underground space can be compared with the ancient myth of the hero's descent into the underworld to retrieve information about the past and future. This same theme is found in *The Odyssey* when Odysseus visited the realm of the dead, and the poet's descent into hell in Dante's famous *The Divine Comedy*.

Symbols of Individuation

Jung markedly employed symbol interpretation in relationship to personality development at certain stages of life. According to Jung, a bridge may be understood as an important life transition. Traveling in an unknown country can reflect an inner journey into the unconscious. Sexuality in a dream – intercourse for example – may be seen as the union of opposing energies within the personality (Jung 1946, par. 421). Jung also found parallels between motifs in old alchemical texts and the dreams of modern man. The transformation of a base metal (lead) into a precious metal (gold) can be understood as the refinement of the mind, or the transformation of impure water into the Water of Life can be seen as emotional cleansing, etc. The alchemic processing of material takes place in the alchemist's laboratory. In dreams, a kitchen, pharmacy or workshop may also refer to a mental space where the dreamwork of personality development takes place (Jung 1944). This language has a poetic and universal quality similarly to the language of dreams – it appeals to both the heart and the unconscious intelligence.

Existential and Experiential Approaches to Symbols

Medard Boss, a leading pioneer of the existential dream school, found that the most important task is to open dreamers' minds to the immediate appearance of symbols, without theoretical abstraction. He comprehends dreams as "poetically condensed images of a person's life situation at a given moment [which] also accurately reflect changes in this situation over time – hence serving as gauges of a patient's progress in therapy" (Stern 1977, p xiii).

A danger to any interpretation is that it may disturb the poetic effect contained in the dream itself. As an example of misuse of interpretation, Medard Boss mentions a dream that Freud called a beautiful dream. When analyzed however, the beauty of the dream seemed to vanish into "ugly" associations (Boss 1977, pp. 2–3). Boss suggests that, first and foremost, one should allow the images themselves to stimulate the dreamer's thoughts. Staying with these images and allowing them to impact on the dreamer's mind may provide an illuminating experience, as demonstrated by my examples with various metaphor dreams.

Fritz Perls, the founder of gestalt therapy, was even more critical of the method of free association. According to him, the associations jump "like a grasshopper from experience to experience, and none of these are ever truly experienced, but just a kind of flash, which leaves all the available material unassimilated and unused" (Perls 1969, p. 71). Perls aspired to new models of experiential dream-work that effectively evoked emotions. However, a close reading of his famous dream seminar verbatim shows that, by pursuing this intention, he misses impor-tant and stimulating imagery that pertains to dreams as wholes (Vedfelt 2000).

Also worth mentioning is Montague Ullmann who created a very popular method of dreamwork in non-therapeutic, self-help groups. Ullman claimed that, "no-one can be an expert in others' dreams." Symbols, in Ullman's theory, are entirely personal – only the dreamer can say what they really mean. "When a dream is remembered, the dreamer is ready to be confronted with the message it contains" (Ullman 1979, p. 409). I see this more as a strategy to protect the dreamer against invasive and authoritarian interpretations, than a truth about dreamwork as such.

Existential philosophy is a gateway for experiential dreamwork that, in princi-ple, allows symbols to unfold in creative ways rather than interpreting them. Be it gestalt therapy, role-playing, bodywork, or meditation, they all work. It should be added that Freud's free association method, Jung's active imagination tech-nique and his therapeutic transference work (i.e., client/therapist relations), also have experiential qualities in their own right.

As a common trait, psychoanalysts, Jungian therapists, Calvin Hall and Medard Boss all present cases in their writings where symbol or image meanings are more clearly defined by the study of an individual's series of dreams.

Utilizing the Varieties of Symbol Understanding

These varying understandings of symbols by the different dream schools may at first seem insurmountable and mutually exclusive. Their insights are, however, potentially useful if they are recognized as partial results manifested through the varied strategies of humanistic research. The most important experiences can still be integrated and nuanced using a more overriding theory of complexity and prac-tical intelligence, which will be gradually elaborated in the following chapters.

Symbol Creation and the Dreaming Brain

As described in Chapter 2, intuitive, symbolic/metaphoric thinking and visual imagination are generally more greatly attributed to the right hemisphere of the brain than the left. This corresponds well with the fact that the right side is some-what more active while dreaming than in waking life.

Further, one of the most important differences in the brain between waking life and dreams is the heightened activity in the medial and ventromedial prefrontal cortex (MPFC and vmPFC), in contrast to the dorsolateral prefrontal cortex

(DLPFC) that shuts down in very significant ways (fig 2.2). While awake, the MPFC and vmPFC are particularly active in spontaneous creative processes, connected to a so-called "default network" (Raichle *et al.* 2001).

Other important properties ascribed to the ventromedial prefrontal cortex in contemporary brain research are intuitive experiences that are called 'the feeling of knowing' and 'the feeling of rightness'. 'The feeling of knowing' is an intuitive judgment that you will be able to retrieve the knowledge required from memory. The correctness of this judgment is impaired when the right medial prefrontal has lesions (Schnyer and Verfaellie *et al.* 2004). 'The feeling of rightness' is "the ability to rapidly or intuitively determine the appropriateness and accuracy of a response which is necessary for rapid decision making in relation to current personal goals." A positive correlation between the effectiveness of the feeling of rightness and the level of activity in medial prefrontal cortex has been found when a combination of cognitive tests and brain scanning were employed (Gilboa and Alain, *et al.* 2009).

In waking life, these intuitive 'feelings' are not related to the more precise analysis and verification of that of the dorsolateral prefrontal cortex. This kind of analysis would be too time-consuming in many practical situations. Damasio found that this ability to react appropriately in an intuitive way is related to our episodic and autobiographical memory of experiences, which is relevant in decision making. This is mostly guided by emotion and partly regulated by the ventromedial prefrontal cortex. Further, the vmPFC is connected to the somatic marker system, which tags any emotion with an unconscious or consciously felt body sensation (Damasio 1996). In lay terms, this is best known as a 'gut feeling'.

The feeling of knowing, the feeling of rightness and the somatic marker system are all important aspects in my prevailing concept of "practical intelligence" (see Chapter 3). In our dreams, we are not burdened with decision making and actions needed to relate to complex incidents in the outer world. This opens up the possibility that a surplus of information capacity is available for the activation of special brain networks connecting the feelings of knowing and feelings of rightness, etc. to the active visual areas of the brain.

Thus, a vague feeling that life is stagnating may appear now and again, without any decisive effect on waking consciousness. However, dreams seem to have a capacity for creating concrete, holistic images, such as the dreamer circling aimlessly around in a parking lot, or any other of the metaphors mentioned above.

In dreams, the metaphors are not just glimpses. They literally appear to the dreamer much more visibly and tangibly.

The Power of Symbols

We know from many contexts that symbols can strongly affect our minds. They are used throughout society to motivate people to come together in community – often in extreme manners – from sport club logos to national flags, or religious images and rituals. The strong energy that symbols can activate builds up over time and is encoded into memory through the constant influence of moody, emotionally charged actions. Take national flags for instance – for generation after generation they can be connected to achievement and heroism myths that are, in turn, tied to particular symbolic treasures. Flags are raised and lowered to fanfares and national anthems, while simultaneously evoking expectations of certain types of virtues and behavior.

Symbols automatically activate heavily charged networks of imprinted emotional and behavioral patterns that have much more readily accessible energy and capacity than rational consciousness. The effect of this can be that individuals or groups – almost as if through conditioned reflex – reach a state of veneration and rapture that may then trigger broad, often incomprehensible actions.

If these driving forces are activated, they will run their own courses and attract all available energy. Even modern, internationally acclaimed scholars, eyes moist, can get choked up when their national sports team beats the drums of victory and all the prerequisite rituals are performed. To hooligans, even club logos and associated rituals are enough to excite their minds into war-like states and behaviors. These states and behaviors may then become the focal point of almost everything they do and last for days, or perhaps even weeks. Also, peaceful movements employ symbols like doves or logos against nuclear power, etc. as emotional fuel.

Dynamic Aspects of Symbols – Laura

In dreams, symbols function like strong, driving forces in internal self-regulating processes. If we pay attention to them and immerse our consciousness in the generated imagery and feelings, they will initiate a process of auto-association, intensifying the effects. They rise up like pointed peaks in psychological energy landscapes, attracting all available energy and sparking processes that will continue long after consciousness has released them (see Core Quality 10).

Such processes, whereof a great deal takes place outside consciousness, can be difficult to grasp. A therapeutic framework can create a kind of laboratory where each step in the process can be studied and further understood.

An example of this can be found in Laura who participated in a three-day dreams workshop. During a relaxation exercise, a dream came to her mind that she experienced just prior to the course: *I am standing before three doors. There is light beyond the doors. I'm afraid the doors will slam shut before I can make it into the light. Near me is a purpley-blue shadow.*

Laura drew a picture of the dream, but she had difficulty getting herself to include the purpley-blue shadow without really knowing why. When she added a chandelier to the room she was standing in, she also found the courage to add the deep, purpley-blue shadow. As she drew it, her eyes welled up with tears and a memory of her father came over her. She said that he died when she was six years old. When I quietly mirrored her and showed empathy for her sorrow, she broke down, sobbing deeply. After a while, she became more calm. It was as if she had held back her sorrow all the years since her father passed away. As I consoled her, she remembered that her mother had been very unhappy and cried all the time. Laura had to console her, yet did not cry herself.

In the evening before sleeping, she thought about the light from the chandelier she had drawn. She felt it was a protection against the sorrow. That night Laura dreamed: *the shadow is inside of me. First, I think the shadow is small, but then it is as big as me. I'm afraid it will get bigger and overwhelm me. I wish I could take a yellow color from the dream of another workshop participant, so it can light up my own dream.*

The next day, we continued to work with symbols. I told her that she could see all the elements in her dream as parts of herself, so the yellow color was actually psychic content from within her. She accepted this and used the yellow color to fill her painted room with a warm glow. This made her feel calm and she had an experience of being met with light and love. Laura said this warm, yellow light was difficult for her to receive. This made her think of her relationships to other people where she often had the opportunity to receive love and affection yet had a tendency to withdraw. We talked about this theme for a long time and made connections to concrete people and situations that came to her mind. She admitted that this was a very important theme in her life. The next night, the character of the symbols changed. Then Laura dreamed: *I was together with a teacher and I had to cross a bridge* (Vedfelt 2001).

What we witnessed that day was a process where a dreamer went into dialogue with an unconscious way of thinking, in which symbols were taken seriously. It was an inner, creative process that unfolded something new that could not have been guessed in advance. Nor could this process only be interpreted intellectually. When Laura took her symbols seriously, they gave birth to new meanings that not only focused on important themes but also showed the way forward. The continual theme of this process was summed up by an ancient symbol: the struggle, or rather, the balance between darkness and light, between warmth – the yellow color – and the fear of darkness and death.

Light typically symbolizes consciousness and illumination, darkness represents the unknown and non-conscious. Purpley-blue colors – characterized by the shadow in Laura's dream – often have spiritual, symbolic meanings. I have also often witnessed how blue and purple colors in people's drawings contribute to the activation of feelings of sorrow and grief. In Laura's work, it turned out to be a forceful and deeply meaningful expression of the suppressed sorrow connected to her father's death. It was as if the experience had been hidden in her unconscious for all those years, just waiting for a context where it could be met and allowed to unfold.

When these symbols were allowed to do their job, the quality of the symbolism changed. In her last dream, the teacher and bridge symbols are central. In that dream, Laura was together with a teacher. Metaphorically speaking, I was her teacher in self-development and thus offered, through her dream, an opportunity to be her helper during this important life transition. A benevolent, empathic male teacher is also a positive father symbol, so the dream brought hope that she might be able to replace her lost father with another father figure within herself.

The bridge might be connected – in a psychological sense – to areas in her mind that were separated from each other. Walking across the bridge could thus symbolize the transition from one state, life situation or phase to another.

We performed psychodrama in a session directed by me, employing the services of a fatherly group member of Laura's own choice as participant. She approached an imaginary bridge but her legs were hesitant to continue. Instead, she wanted to stay where she was, securely holding the hand of her fatherly figure, with the bridge in front of her as an image of hope and potential future development.

Crossing that bridge would have been a giant step. Her legs told her – via the somatic marker system – that the sudden retrieval of powerful memories produced by immersing herself into these symbols would need more work. Later, I had the opportunity to work with her individually on how to protect her vulnerability when connecting with a partner. In these sessions, the process started by her powerful symbols was completed.

A Hermeneutic Circle

In Lauras case, I have anticipated many facets of dreamwork related to other Core Qualities, just to mention a few: the use of experiential methods (Core Quality 5, Core Quality 9), the dreams reponse to the dreamwork (Core Quality 7) and the caution and security that is necessary in dealing with traumatic processes (Chapter 14). These and other themes, relevant to the case will be elaborated in more systematic ways in chapters to come.

The pendling between parts of the dream and more comprehensive wholes thus expanding the understanding is a version of what in the philosophy of interpretations is called a hermeneutic circle (Mantzavino 2016).

In cybernetic language, when activated, symbols start an auto-associative process that is more comprehensive than rational consciousness. This fits well with Laura's process and many other dreams where I have been able to follow the symbolic processes. When a certain symbol has completed its work, it makes way for new symbols.

Unconscious Memory and Laura's Brain

Although many networks seem to be involved in the dynamics of Laura's process, I especially underscore the possible complex interplay between the ventromedial prefrontal cortex, the amygdala and hippocampus. These networks are generally active during dreaming.

The ventromedial prefrontal cortex is the frontal region that is assumed to be the most involved in mnemonic functions (Gilboa and Alain et al. 2009). It is particularly related to autobiographical memories and narratives concerning the self. An increasing activation of this network in Laura's brain may parallel what happened in her mind during dreamwork.

The ventromedial prefrontal cortex is densely connected with the amygdala and the hippocampus. The relationship between the amygdala and hippocampus is extremely important to how human experience is integrated. The amygdala has a preference for storing memory in the right hemisphere and in lower parts of the brain, whereas the hippocampus plays a large role in the left hemisphere and top processing (Tsoory and Vouimba *et al.* 2008).

As Louiz Cozolino puts it in a comprehensive study of *The Social Brain*, the amygdala "has a central role in the emotional, somatic and unconscious organization of experience, whereas the hippocampus is vital for conscious, logical, and cooperative social functioning. Their relationship will have an impact on affect regulation, reality testing, resting states of arousal and anxiety, and the ability to learn emotional and more neutral information" (Cozolino 2010, loc. 1567ff).

What appeared in Laura's dreamwork, we must assume, was an increase of the ventromedial prefrontal cortex and right hemisphere activity with the use of imagery and intuitive processing of symbols. Body awareness and somatic sensing contributed to the awakening of memory traces stored in the somatic marker system.

During dreaming, there is a decreased "gamma coherence" in the hippocampus. This means that the connections that hold together detailed episodic memories when we are awake are weakened (Gottesmann 2012). The resulting relative incoherence gives the dreaming mind an opportunity to select memory elements that serve a more comprehensive self-organizing process.

In Laura's case, she was not able to express her needs as a child in logical, rational ways. She had learned from experience that her mother's needs were more important. However, her needs for mourning and consolation were still alive, waiting for something or someone to help her integrate her separate memory fragments into new coherent experience.

Making space and finding tools to create connections between diverse areas of Laura's memory helped her to reorganize her ways of experiencing. This laid the foundation for the creation of new, more extensive and coherent images of herself and her situation.

Conclusion

On the basis of what I have described so far, I propose that symbolic and metaphoric experiencing are indispensable and integral parts of human practical and intuitive intelligence. Symbols and metaphors are holistic expressions that make connections to other experiential modalities than rational thinking, such as imagery, emotions and bodily sensations, which further open other aspects of memory. Like metaphors in poetry, dream symbols are sensual expressions that interact with our imagination.

In our dreams, these capacities are reinforced because we are totally immersed in experience. Later, in waking life when we contemplate dreams, they interact with our imagination which becomes creative, playing with the symbols and creating meaning through experiential dreamwork and interpretation.

The dream schools have specialized in different aspects of the meaning of symbols.
Symbols may have comprehensive and holistic effects on the mind.

References

Adams, M. (2016) *What is Jungian Analysis?* Available online at: www.jungnewyork.com/what-is-jungian-analysis.shtml (last accessed 20 April 2016)

Boss, M. (1977) *I Dreamt Last Night.* (New York: Gardner Press Inc.)

Cozolino, L. (2010) *The Neuroscience of Psychotherapy: Healing the Social Brain* (2nd Ed.). (New York: W. W. Norton & Company), Kindle edition

Damasio, A. (1996) 'The somatic marker hypothesis and the possible functions of the prefrontal cortex'. *Philosophical Transactions of the Royal Society B*, 351, 1413–1420

Franz, M.-L. von (1978) *The Introduction to the Interpretation of Fairytales.* (Dallas, TX: Spring Publications)

Freud, S. (1900/2013) *The Interpretation of Dreams.* (Sunderland, UK: Dead Dodo Vintage), Kindle edition

Gilboa, A. and Alain, C. *et al.* (2009) 'Ventromedial prefrontal cortex lesions produce early functional alterations during remote memory retrieval'. *Journal of Neuroscience*, 15 April, 29(15), 4871–81c

Gottesmann, C. (2012) 'REM sleep properties as neurobiological endophenotypes and schizophrenia' in D. Barrett and P. McNamara (Eds), *Encyclopedia of Sleep and Dreams* (Santa Barbara, CA: Greenwood Publishing). Kindle edition, locations 14198–14219

Hall, C. (1953) 'A cognitive theory of dream symbolism'. *Journal of General Psychology*, Vol. 48, 169–186

Hall, C. (1953a/1966) *The Meaning of Dreams.* (New York: McGraw Hill)

Jung. C. (1904/1981) 'Studies in word association' in G. Adler and R. F. C. Hull (Eds, Trans), *The Collected Works of C.G. Jung: Experimental Researches*, Vol. 2. (Abingdon, UK: Routledge and Kegan Paul)

Jung, C. (1938) *Kinderträume*, Vol. I. (Zürich: Eidgenossische Hochschule)

Jung, C. (Author), Adler, G., Fordham, M. and Read, Sir H. (Eds) (1944) *The Collected Works of C.G. Jung: Psychology and Alchemy*, Vol. 12. (Abingdon, UK: Routledge and Kegan Paul)

Jung, C. (1946/1981) 'The psychology of the transference' par. 421, in G. Adler and R. F. C. Hull (Eds, Trans), *The Collected Works of C. G. Jung: Practice of Psychotherapy*, Vol. 16. (Abingdon, UK: Routledge and Keagan Paul)

Jung, C. (1964) *Man and His Symbols.* (London: Aldus Books)

Kaivola-Bregenhøj, A. (1986) *Dreams through Thousands of Years.* (Copenhagen: Hernov)

Lakoff, G. and Johnson, M. (1980/2008) *Metaphors We Live By.* (Chicago, IL: University of Chicago Press), Kindle edition

Mantzavino, C. (2016) *Hermeneutics.* In Stanford Encyclopedia of Philosophy. Available online at: https://plato.stanford.edu/entries/hermeneutics/

Mattoon, M. (1978) *Applied Dream Analysis.* (Chichester, UK: John Wiley)

Perls, F. (1969/2013) *Gestalt Therapy Verbatim*. (Gouldsboro ME: The Gestalt Journal Press), Kindle edition, pp. 143-144

Raichle, M. *et al.* (2001) 'Searching for a baseline: functional imaging and the resting human brain'. *Nature Reviews*, 2, 685–694

Schnyer, D. and Verfaellie, M., *et al.* (2004) 'A role for right medial prefrontal cortex in accurate feeling of knowing judgments: evidence from patients with lesions to frontal cortex'. *Neuropsychologia*, 42(7), 957–966

Stern, P. (1977) 'Foreword' in M. Boss (Ed.), *I Dreamt Last Night*. (New York: Gardner Press Inc.)

Tsoory, M., Vouimba, R., *et al.* (2008) 'Amygdala modulation of memory-related processes in the hippocampus'. *Progress in Brain Research*, Vol. 167, 35–49

Ullman, M. (1979) 'The Experiential Dream Group' in B. Wolmann (Ed.) *Handbook of Dreams.* (New York: Van Nostrand Reinhold Co.) pp. 406–423

Vedfelt, O. (2000) *The Dimensions of Dreams*. (London: Jessica Kingsley Publishers)

Vedfelt, O. (2001) *The Supramodal Space: A Missing Link Between Body, Soul and Spirit.* Conference paper, conference on Body-psychotherapy. (Zürich: Institute for Biosynthesis)

Chapter 6

Core Quality 3

Dreams Personify

One of the most salient features of dreams is the continual appearance of characters and the interactions between them. The concepts of unconscious and practical intelligence presented in Chapter 3 will be useful in understanding the origin and functions of dream characters.

Aspiring to simulate human reality, artificial intelligence research has found that practical intelligence does not work through logical deduction based on rules applied to separate units. It predominantly functions through recognition of holistic patterns (Dreyfus and Dreyfus 1986).

Human reality is so complex that, even in the simplest events of daily life, it is not possible to list in advance all conceivable everyday events and combine them using logical rules. If a computer is to display human-like characteristics, it has to learn these characteristics through practice. Through this practical learning, innumerable schemas or programs are built regarding how the world is constituted in different situations. Correspondingly, a set of programs or manuscripts for behavior and actions also exists (Rumelhart 1980).

Scottish infant researcher Colwyn Trevarthen has summarized a modern understanding of the inner responsiveness of infants. Even newborns have an inner motivational system that gives them remarkable abilities to not just seek out interpersonal support, nourishment and emotional bonding, but also to build human "friendship with an increasingly expanding circle of playmates and teachers" (Trevarthen and Aitken 1994).

At birth, general patterns regulating our behavior and experience begin to form groups of networks that develop through the relationships with our closest caregivers (Stern 1985). Mothers, fathers, grandparents, siblings, educators, and playmates – in that approximate order – are the most important role models. After these are colleagues, mentors, partners and individuals in other types of important relationships.

In a cybernetic network understanding these role models are personified subsystems that interacts with each other in the overall information network of the personality. The activity of the subsystems is dependent on the contexts in which they appear, and their memories overlap (McClelland and Rumelhart 1986).

Infants begin by relating to a few individuals and then expand their horizons step-by-step. As new understanding gradually increases, patterns of emotional and social skills created earlier are stored in relatively unconscious memory systems, so space in consciousness for new learning is created. The most fundamental patterns are created earliest in life and therefore are the most difficult for consciousness to access.

Personification is, as I see it a way for the mind to utilize amounts of information that are too extensive for rational consciousness to have time to digest. These personifications make it possible to relate to individuals with various types of human qualities, and to maintain, for instance, parental, collegial and partner roles. We may be bosses, employees, friends, enemies, etc. depending on what situations demand. Each of our many roles draws on certain memory systems.

In psychoanalysis and Jungian psychology the systems employed for relating to motherly, fatherly or other personified qualities are called mother complexes and father complexes, etc. Object relation theory calls such systems 'inner objects' and connections to others are 'object relations'. Based on vast clinical experience, theorists from these schools assume that inner systems appear as various characters in dreams (Vedfelt 2000b).

In John Bowlby's theory of the early attachment of children to their close caregivers, inner personifications are called "working models" of the people in the world around us (Bowlby 1969). Patrick McNamara and Andresen (2001) found that "insecure attachment styles" tend to intensify dream images, and McNamara suggests that "REM sleep and/or dream, in part, promotes attachment."

In waking life, the roles we perform depend on interactions between personified inner networks and external conditions. In dreams, these inner networks are activated based on principles that maintain a more general inner self-regulation. Personification appears as interactions between the dream self and other characters, and general patterns become more obvious than in waking life.

According to the network theory these subsystems are gathered from smaller subunits that can be combined in various ways (Smolensky 1986). On the brain level there is not a localized experience of chair or grandmother or a grandmother's chair. The global concept or image is assembled by communications between many different regions (Ratey 2001 loc. 2334 ff.). This enables flexible reactions to many different situations in waking states, and the depictions of dream characters it forms may be as varied as our self-organizing complexity demands (Vedfelt 2000a).

The Mental Skills of Dream Characters

The abilities and skills of dream characters are not simply primitive deficient versions of the waking self. According to Patrick McNamara, philosophers claim that, "a person is defined as a being who is capable of reasoning, who displays intentionality and emotion, who is self-conscious, and who has an identity that persists through time. Surprisingly, there is evidence that either the dreamer (dream ego) or other dream characters display these criteria for mentality" (McNamara 2012).

Dream characters' abilities concerning thinking, perception, emotion, relational skills, mind-reading and levels of consciousness have been thoroughly studied. Being aware of this may sharpen your attention to features in your dreams that tend to be overlooked. Comparing your individual dreams with typical dreams can also be valuable.

Thinking in Dreams

In a laboratory study, Swiss researchers Inge Strauch and Barbara Meier estimated that approximately 40 percent of dreams consist of thinking. These thoughts are not just simple ones, but include general knowledge about people and their life situations. Further, characters reflected on actions taking place in dreams and made decisions that influenced storylines. Dreamers do not puzzle at length over problems – their thoughts are primarily directed towards action-oriented dream events (Strauch and Meyer 1996).

As mentioned in Chapter 2 on the dreaming brain, David Kahn and Allan Hobson (2005) found that, *within* dream scenarios, dreamers' thoughts are generally logical and similar to those during waking cognition, but thinking *about* scenarios is usually unrealistic.

Yet Ernest Hartmann found activities we never – or at least very rarely – dream about, no matter how many hours we use on these in daily life. He calls these the "Three Rs" (reading, writing and arithmetic). He found that other activities, like "walking, talking with friends and sexual activity," were almost as prominent in dreams as in waking life. He connects this to dreams functioning much more as associative networks than as serial activities (Hartmann 2000). This understanding harmonizes well with the network theory I am proposing.

Perception in Dreams

Imagery plays an important role in dreams as well as dreamwork. Strauch and Meier estimated visual experiences make up half of all perceptions, the remaining mostly consist of auditory impressions and bodily sensations. Smell and taste only contributed to a minor part.

Emotion in Dreams

The frequency of emotions in dreams has been debated. In Strauch and Meier's laboratory investigations, emotions occupied only a small and sporadic part of dream experiences. A Canadian team of researchers found in dreamers an encyclopedia of emotions such as admiration, anger, disappointment, worry, fear, disgust, satisfaction, gratitude and happiness, etc. They recorded no less than eight feelings per dream. Most types of emotions occurred at the same rate as during important waking life events. Researchers found more negative emotions in dreams than positive. They discovered that their findings supported theories about the emotionally regulatory nature of dreams (Nielsen *et al.* 1991). Yet later laboratory investigations of emotions by Calvin Kai-Ching Yu, utilizing a different method of interviewing dreamers, gave a slight preponderance of positive emotions (Yu 2015, p. 279).

We can learn from this and general clinical experience that, while awake, dreamers must be particularly proactive if they are to become aware of their dream emotions.

Mind-reading in Dreams

Many dream characters are authentic copies of people we know regarding appearance and character traits. These characters react as if they know the dream self and know how that particular dream self typically reacts. Reciprocally, a dream self knows many other characters and also knows what they are up to. These same patterns can continue for years. This demonstrates that both dream selves and other characters have a "theory of mind," i.e. an ability to conceptualize what takes place within the minds of other characters (McNamara 2012).

Kahn and Hobson found in 94 percent of 320 dreams that feelings were evoked in dream selves by other dream characters. This 'mind-reading' can be mutual such as, for instance, when two figures in a dream can recognize that they are in love with each other, or when the dream self knows that another character is trying to lose a game just to make the dreamer feel better (Kahn and Hobson 2005a).

The incidents of 'mind-reading' by dreamers are, surprisingly, much higher than in the waking state. McNamara and his colleagues found that "REM reports were three times as likely to contain instances of mind-reading as were wake reports and 1.3 times as likely as NREM reports" (McNamara et al. 2007).

Interactions between Dream Characters

Dream character interactions are actually more frequent in dream reports than in reports of daytime experiences (Kahn et al. 2002). In about 15 out of 100 dreams, the dreamer is the sole character, according to Calvin Hall's classical content analysis. Family members often appear in dreams. Dreamers in their late teens and early twenties dream about parents more often than about other family members. For middle-aged dreamers, their mates and children play important roles. Also schoolmates and other peers often appear. Famous people are rare. Forty percent of dream characters are strangers (Hall 1953).

In a comprehensive review of the research, Tore Nielsen and co-workers observed that known, as well as unknown, dream characters are very likely to evoke emotions in the dreamer, and that feelings of caring and affection are most frequently evoked. For aggressive encounters, 68.2 percent are perpetrated by other characters – only 31.8 percent by the dream self.

Also, friendly interactions are initiated more often by other characters than by the dream self:

> Characters communicate emotional meanings through channels resembling those used by real individuals in the waking world. They display facial expressions and emotional gestures, they express concerns in speech rich

with inflection and prosody, and they touch or manipulate the dream self in provocative and intimate ways. Simulated emotional expressions of dream characters appear to be as subtle or overt, as direct or indirect, as simple or complex as expressions used daily on the social stage.

(Nielsen 2012.)

In NREM mentation, the relationships are different from REM-dreams. A study by McNamara found that the dream self never acted as aggressor in NREM dream states and was almost always the befriender in friendly interactions. Conversely, the REM-related dream self preferred aggressive encounters (McNamara *et al.* 2009). He called this the "Dr Jekyll and Mr Hyde" aspect of dreams.

Characters in Children's Dreams

We know that fetuses, infants and toddlers spend a lot of time dreaming. The regulation of sleeping and waking states begins as early as 6.5 months into pregnancy. REM sleep makes up 50 percent of an infant's sleep and even more for children born prematurely.

We also know that infants develop communication skills for their needs and interests very quickly. Studies of the earliest relations between mother and child demonstrate active infant communication directing motherly behavior (Trevarthen and Aitken 1994). Already at birth, babies can recognize their mothers' voices (Chamberlain 1988). By the age of eight months, infants clearly show joy when they hear the music played when they were in their mothers' wombs. Remembering and understanding melodies suggests abilities to analyze, predict and compare structures in cohesive linear processes (Pochmursky *et al.* 2009). So far, it has been demonstrated that children have a theory of mind as early as the age of seven months (Bryner 2010).

The many changes of personality in earliest childhood can be seen as a process of self-organization where children go through periods of crisis followed by seemingly all-encompassing changes of personality. This has been observed by most parents and has been systematically researched by Daniel Stern, among others (Stern 1985). Also, the pre-verbal emotional, visual, corporeal and intuitive forms of perception are well-documented in studies of the communicative skills of young children (Gopnik 2009; Stern 1990). These perceptions and skills are stored in sensory, motor, and affective memory systems in the brain (Cozolino 2010 loc. 1601–1620) which as described earlier are highly active during dreaming. The mutual imitative feedback loops with "corresponding dynamic brain states of caregivers" (Trevarthen and Aitgen 1994) create a neuropsychological matrix for the development of the personified patterns of experience and behavior. Particularly between one and three years of age, there is a predominance of the right brain hemisphere mainly concerned with visuospatial processing (Chiron *et al.* 1997), which is closer to the dreams processing style than the normal waking consciousness (Hoss 2005). Thus, it might be expected that numerous infant dreams are employed in the processing of the many challenges belonging to the earliest phases in life.

For many years, laboratory studies of the dreams of young children conducted by pioneer dream researcher David Foulkes have influenced how we view young children's dreams. According to Foulkes, these dreams usually depict static images, mostly of animals and body states of the dreamer. They basically lack the active representation of a self, of human characters, social interactions, dream emotions and motion imagery (Foulkes 1982).

Later studies of 4–10 year-olds in a home setting have shown that small children are able to give long, detailed reports of their dreams that are similar to those of adults in terms of length, number of characters and settings, and presence of dream bizarreness (Resnic *et al.* 1994).

This line of research has recently been followed up by Piroska Sándor and Sára Szakadát who conducted an investigation of 349 dreams of 40 four- to eight-year-old children and compared the results with the relevant research literature. The dream reports were obtained in home settings by parents who were trained in interviewing their children.

This study suggests that children of four to eight years old are likely to represent their own selves in active roles in 70 percent of their dreams. The typical dream report of a four- to five-year-old contained more than one self-initiated action by one or more of the characters. Social interactions were found in 92 percent of the dreams. Fifteen percent of the dream reports of the youngest age group contained verbs reflecting cognitive effort and metacognitive activity. This value gradually grew to 39 percent among those of seven to eight and a half years old.

As in adult research, it was necessary to explicitly ask the children about specific emotions. Positive emotions were happy, good and calm. Negative emotions were sad, scared, angry and bad. On average, there was almost one emotion per dream. More than half the dreams were experienced as positive (Sándor and Szakadát *et al.* 2015).

No systematic research of children younger than three to four years similar to the above mentioned studies appears to have been conducted. Kelly Bulkeley investigated the earliest remembered dreams of adults and found that some dreams could be dated to the age of one and a half years (Bulkeley *et al.* 2005).

Children's Dreams Examples

I have encountered many dreams from the very young children of colleagues and students in the field of psychotherapy. Other examples are referred to in the literature. Even these very early dreams show personified characters and active dream selves, as well as friendly and hostile social interactions.

The 21-month-old daughter of a trained psychotherapist dreamed: *A small animal ate my foot so I could only crawl. It has to go away.* This dream about the animal eating her foot may illustrate the fear of regressing to an earlier stage with less autonomy. Psychoanalyst Margaret Mahler has described this as typical of the rapprochement phase when a child feels challenged by a new phase of development (Mahler *et al.* 1975).

Jungian analyst Pia Skogemann recounts a dream of her 21-month-old daughter who awoke in the middle of the night crying softly. *She had dreamed that she played ball with her grandmother but was afraid of the man sleeping in the grass.*

Skogemann interprets her daughter's dream by employing a Jungian understanding of symbols. The garden – a fertile and protected place – as well as the grandmother, are seen as symbols for the Great Mother archetype that, in turn, is the source of the small girl's femininity. The man represents an archetypal masculine principle within the girl. This principle has not yet awoken, i.e. is not active, but the girl still experiences it as something threatening. In her dream there is an interaction between the dream self and the grandmother, as well as an ability to observe the awakening of the man (Skogemann 1984).

Four-year-old Freja, in connection with the birth of her family's fourth child, dreamed: *There was a mouse family with so many babies that their den exploded. So they had to leave and had no place to live. That was very sad. But then they came to our parents' house where there was enough room, and they were allowed to live here* (Vedfelt 2011). This dream can be seen as an example of emotional problem solving. Here, personification moves from the animals to Freja's realistic parents.

Dreams may reflect difficult situations in the children's surroundings in various ways. One boy had a nightmare that his home was a *"wrong" ship that had been flooded by big waves.* This dream appeared after his parents had had a terrible argument.

Sibling rivalry probably inspired the following dream by an eight-year-old boy: *Soldiers are attacking our house. We run away, but forget my big brother.* The soldiers could represent anger and running away the wish to get rid of his big brother and have his parents to himself, as suggested by therapist and dream researcher Brenda Mallon (Mallon 2002).

Yet many dreams also have pleasant activities, exciting experiences, friendships with animals, or are about receiving love and care, and performing well. Such themes are also important to pay attention to so the child can develop positive expectations about dream life. Kirstine, age seven, daughter of one of my colleagues: *I dreamed I was with Mirjam [a friend the same age] in a very pretty forest, where pieces of amber were all over the ground, up in the trees and in a small lake. We went around collecting them and it was really nice.*

Even though children's dreams bear witness to the sense of agency, intention and social interactivity of dream selves, they also reflect children's limited capacity for assertion and independence. Longitudinal studies of children's dreams show that the dreamers' ages reflect cognitive and psychosocial skills development. An increased mixture of active participation, ego strength, cognitive powers, physical capacities, and independent functioning in the world are present according to dream researcher Daniel Siegel in an overview of scientific studies of children's dreams. Freud's theory of child sexuality in dreams is rejected because of a dearth of such themes in dreams of children. Aggression levels are lower than in adults' dreams (Siegel 2005).

Friendly interactions by dreamers are relatively balanced between "giving and receiving" at the ages 9–11 years, according to a study by Inge Strauch. After that, boys aged 11–13 years and girls aged 13–15 years were less likely to be befrienders. Instead, the desire for positive attention and regard seemed to be particularly high in their dreams (Strauch 2005).

Approaching Children's Dreams

Among researchers who have especially worked with children's dreams there is a consensus that you should, first and foremost, listen and empathize with the child's experience. If a dream is frightening, then it must be taken seriously and not reduced to "It's only a dream." Dreams can – with due caution – be unfolded in drawings, or reenacted where some dream parts are played by the children or by adults in ways that are reassuring for the dreamers. Consoling and caring parents contribute to creating safe places for children. You should not give interpretations to your child, but rather look for changes in your child's life that may be causing frightening dreams such as, for example, the birth of a sibling, divorce, the presence of stress in your family, abandonment, trauma, and developmental phases (Garfield 1984; Siegel and Bulkeley 1998; Mallon 2002).

Relationship Between the Dream Self and Waking Self

The most common first word in a dream report is the word 'I'. "I am... I find myself in town X... I'm walking...," etc. In dream literature, this 'I' is referred to as the dreamer, the dreamed self, the dream self or the self-representation.

In psychoanalysis, "the self refers to the subject as he experiences himself," according to the British psychoanalyst Charles Rycroft. It is sometimes confused with the term 'ego', which "refers to his personality as a structure about which impersonal generalizations can be made" (Rycroft 1968 p. 149). Jungians have reserved the concept of 'self' for the superior regulating factors in the psyche, including all psychic contents. The ego is defined as the center of consciousness: one complex among other important complexes (Samuels *et al.* 1986).

The basic assumption in Daniel Stern's book, *The Interpersonal World of the Infant*, is that "some senses of the self do exist long prior to self-awareness and language ..." He describes this self as:

> an invariant pattern of awareness, which senses and organizes subjective experience in a preverbal way. It includes senses of agency, physical cohesion and continuity, the sense of creating organization, the sense of transmitting meaning and the ability to achieve intersubjectivity with another. The self's senses start to form at birth (if not before).

> (Stern 1985 Loc. 164ff.)

Calvin Hall coined the term "continuity hypothesis," for the contention that "the wishes and fears that determine our actions and thoughts in everyday life also determine what we will dream about" (Hall and Nordby 1972). Such continuity appears out of what I have just described. In Nielsen's investigations, the dream self's emotional reactions to other dream characters were usually judged as appropriate by the waking dreamer. Nielsen therefore suggests that dreams can be used in therapy to clarify the dreamer's relational patterns in waking life (Nielsen 2012).

Likewise, Finnish dream researcher Antti Revonsuo and his co-workers assume that "the simulation of neutral and positive social interactions in dreams serves to represent and strengthen important social connections" (Revonsuo *et al.* 2015).

In a series of dreams it is possible to follow how the self relates to specific recurring social themes and inner states for long periods of time. The absence of a self in dreams is extreme and can be found in severe mental disorders (Dieckmann 1980; Vedfelt 2017). It may however also happen to people who are trained or have a talent for contemplative activity and self-observation, or who have taken psychedelic drugs.

Examples of Coping Strategies of the Dream Self and Waking Self

In practical dreamwork it is useful to compare the dream self's coping strategies, its emotional state, relational skills and level of consciousness to the state of the waking self. It can be a surprising self-discovery for the individual. In a therapeutic setting it can be used to assess the level and depth to which the dreamwork should be taken.

The Coping Strategy of a 13-year-old Boy

Fritz, a 13-year-old boy, had a bad dream in which *he was followed by an adult man*. He lived with his divorced mother. During a conversation about his role at home, I sensed he felt responsible for his mother while, at the same time, he had no real desire to step into the adult role of her protector. His dream seemed to match an imbalance between a buried sense of emotional demands (his adult pursuer) and his desire to just be a boy (the 13-year-old dream self who wanted to flee the situation).

In therapy, I supported an age-appropriate balance between emotional responsibility and freedom to still be a boy. I also had a talk with the mother, whom I advised not to make Fritz a confident concerning her emotional problems. She complied with the advice as well as she could.

Three years later, Fritz had a "fantastic dream": *I'd been given a pistol that never missed*. At that time he was more carefree. He had found a girlfriend and was full of self-confidence. The pistol is a well-known masculine symbol tied to aggression, sexuality and, in this case, marksmanship. His dream testified to a better inner balance in this phase of his life than the previous one.

The Emotional State of the Dream Self

Sarah, a 30-year-old woman who was eight months pregnant for the first time, dreamed: *a group of people have been captured and will be executed. They are surrounded by armed guards. It seems hopeless.*

A few days later she had a dream with a radically different mood: "*she was in her mothers' support group where the atmosphere between the women was good and they were very enthusiastic. Her best girlfriends, male friends and her husband, who did not really belong to the group, were also there. She was very happy and felt safe.*"

She really wanted to know what had caused the radical shift in moods in her dreams. Was it something that she could influence or was it "just hormones"? It turned out that Sarah had received an ultrasound fetal scan just before her first dream. She immediately called her mother afterwards to get some facts and information for her journal about births in their family. Her mother answered her correctly and formally without asking about her fetus or the ultrasound and then quickly ended their conversation.

In the days preceding her second dream, Sarah and her husband had been pleased with the results of her ultrasound scan. Her girlfriends and in-laws had been in touch with her and were very interested.

Daniel Stern has described how the experience of a woman's relationship with her mother is very important to her own role as a mother, especially in the last stages of pregnancy (Stern 1995). Studies of the dreams of pregnant women have also demonstrated that this is a dominating theme, particularly in the third trimester, and that it often initiates inner conflict between the mothering style learned by the mother and the daughter's own idea of being a mother (Stukane 1985).

My experience with adult 'children' is that even when the relationships to their parents are deeply problematic, an impulse to share important experiences with the parents still exists, both when events are unfolding well and when they are not.

Sarah was at a point in any woman's life when old wounds in relationship to her mother can be most easily torn open. When we spoke of this, Sarah could easily see her own disappointment and bitterness. She said that her mother had two more children after her and therefore had no extra time and energy for Sarah. From the age of 5–6, Sarah experienced her emotional ties to her mother as broken. From that point on, Sarah had isolated herself. She moved away from home at the age of 17. After that, contact between mother and daughter was very tenuous.

The position of Sarah's self in her dream was a little unclear to me. In her first presentation of the dream she seemed to be a passive victim. When I then asked her to immerse herself in the dream again, the dream scenario reminded her of the von Trapp family in the movie and musical, *The Sound of Music*. The musical is about the unity of a family which comes together as a choir. The exciting high point of the movie is when the family escapes Nazi-occupied Austria. Thus, Sarah's dreams hinted at a quest for a solution that alluded her waking self until the dream details were later clarified. In her second dream, Sarah actively participated and had friendly interactions with all the characters.

Comparisons between the state of the dream self and actual events in her waking life allowed Sarah to get in touch with how vulnerable she was to her mother's rejections, and also how important it was for her to surround herself with people who gave her, and the arrival of her child, positive feedback.

The Mentalization and Reflection Abilities of the Dream Self

The dream self's activities are not just physical, but can also move between various levels of consciousness.

Kevin, a 45-year-old man who was studying to be a psychotherapist, dreamed:

> "I am with my supervisor. We talk of good and evil. I know I can be very inflexible but sense an atmosphere of loving acceptance from him and the place. It's very moving and helps me to allow myself to look at those attitudes within myself.
> Something falls out of the sky and into the sea with a great splash. It turns out to be several cars: my favorite toys when I was 5–7 years old."

Kevin's conversation with his supervisor testified to a high level of self-reflection and empathy. The following sequence where the toys fall from the sky seemed incomprehensible to the dreamer at first. In creative dialogue, we examined if there could be any symbolically meaningful connections between the two dream sequences.

In the second dream sequence, his toys from the age of 5–7 years and the sky (the heavens) were the central symbols. Kevin said that at that age he was plagued by the fear of the end of the world. Fuel for this anxiety came from adults talking about the Cold War and the threat of atomic weapons. At school he had a kind religion teacher who gave him an experience of heaven as a good and safe place. Kevin naturally thought that his old, favorite toys had to be up in the good heavens. He was very moved when he recalled these emotions from his childhood. This was the same quality of emotion he had experienced in the meeting with his supervisor.

Children's abilities to create imaginative and spiritual inner worlds develop dramatically between the ages of five to seven (Vedfelt 2014). Dreamwork motivated this dreamer to expand his awareness of when he could tune into an atmosphere of loving acceptance and allow it to be stimulated by memories from the period to which his dream referred.

Approaching Dreams on the Interior (Subjective) Level

The psychoanalytic and Jungian dream schools have their main interest in the inner life of the dreamer as basis for psychological transformation. Jungian analyst and dream specialist Hans Dieckmann, who has extensive clinical experience, agrees that the dream "ego" is the dream figure whose characteristics, feelings and ways of reacting are closest to the waking ego. The dream ego is that part of the dream with which the waking self can immediately identify. On the basis of this preserved "ego feeling," the dream ego appears to be very suited to creating a bridge to unconscious contents.

Dieckmann proposes at the beginning of dreamwork that concentration be focused on the dream ego's mode of experiencing and its parallels in practical living – "...the objective level." If you buttress the continuity between dream ego and waking ego, the dreamer becomes more secure in entering "the unfamiliar and incomprehensible inner world, ... the subjective level" (Dieckmann 1962).

Based on his practical experience, Jung set up some general rules for how dream characters can be viewed as expressions of psychic states and complexes in dreamers' minds (subjective interpretation) and how dreamers deal with actual individuals in the physical world (objective interpretation).

Objective interpretation, according to Jung, is most relevant if a dream character reflects an important person in a dreamer's actual life, and if that dream character appears in the dream in a realistic way.

A subjective interpretation is more relevant when it is a matter of distant relations, insignificant acquaintances or unknown persons, historical persons and fantasy figures. If dream characters also appear distorted or otherwise altered, this should encourage interpretation on the interior level (Mattoon 1978).

Jung's successors have regarded subjective interpretation as in-depth analysis leading to intra-psychic change within the individual, while objective interpretation relates to more practical everyday life (Samuels *et al.* 1986).

Practical application of this is also dependent on the individual's age, maturity, ego strength and degree of mentalization.

An Example of Objective and Subjective Levels of Interpretation

In the following dream from Pernille, a 50-year-old social worker, both the characters' social roles and their individual personalities are important to the interpretation: *My great aunt is dead. She's lying in a coffin. The Catholic priests refuse to bury her in the church. Yet my former colleague, Paul, carefully arranges her properly in her coffin and, in the end, she is buried anyway.*

The previous day, Pernille was advising a dysfunctional family. A violent drama had played out in front of her, yet she did not intervene. The intensity of the conflict had shaken her and she blamed herself for not being capable of stopping the destructiveness. She wondered if her dream was commenting on this in some way but she could not see any obvious connections. We continued dreamwork with a "clarification" the dream content and an "elaboration" of her thoughts about the dream of her thoughts about the dream characters:

- Her great aunt, according to Pernille, was a worried, insecure and rather neurotic person. She played a minor role in Pernille's childhood and she died long ago.
- Of Paul, Pernille told that he is a caring, dynamic and judicious person for whom she has great personal and professional respect. She has not had any connection to him for a long time.
- The priests remind Pernille of her strict Catholic upbringing with much emphasis on sin and moral punishment. Although she moved away from her original surroundings, her upbringing still haunted her with feelings of guilt and a guilty conscience. She worked with this in therapy and overcame depressive states due to excessive self-criticism, but she still regards this as an inhibiting force in her life.
- The dream self is present as a passive observer.

The great aunt, the priests, and Paul did not refer to any actual unfinished business in the outer world, and none of the members of this dysfunctional family from the previous had any striking likeness to the non-self dream characters. We agreed to look at these dream characters as representations of inner qualities in Pernille – to work on the subjective level.

The burial of her great aunt was not a great emotional issue for Pernille, and she did not have any recent bereavements or unfinished mourning that came to mind. This allowed for a symbolic interior level understanding of the burial as an official and respectful goodbye to an outlived attitude.

On the interior level, her dream indicates that Pernille has caring, dynamic and judicious Paul-qualities that can help her to overcome her misguided guilty conscience if energy is moved from her passive ego to this particular aspect of masculine power.

On the exterior level, she had felt powerless toward her dysfunctional family. This matched with the passive self in the dream. In her work, Pernille needed to practice a more authoritative and professional attitude. Supervision by a competent professional could be helpful to more precisely detect how her guilt issues became entangled with the problems of her dysfunctional family and with her work in general.

By this interpretation Paul, in Pernille's dream, is a constructive masculine personality part that she needed to work on more securely integrating into the sphere of her ego and self. The good outcome of her dream problem was promising for the continuous growth of Pernille's personality and professional work.

Typical Dream Characters

A number of typical dream characters are likely to appear in our dreams and they point to particular themes in our inner lives. These include friends and enemies, children, possible partners, and professionals.

Dream characters may be carriers of past memories or mirror actual social life. However, they can also be viewed as systematic, self-organizing compilations of information that the self or ego is not yet fully capable of utilizing consciously, but which emerge from within and put pressure on the personality developmentally.

In groups and societies a role is given to each individual. In development where the personality gains more latitude and depth, dreams will point to qualities we may possess ourselves that we otherwise attribute to others. We will often see friends from our youth, for instance, who continue to appear in our dreams, even if we no longer socialize with them. It may turn out that the striver or the outsider, the emotional or pensive ones, the sensual or the introverted, all represent sides of ourselves that we can choose to develop or subdue even though we have delegated these qualities to others earlier.

Enemies and competitors in dreams can be sides of ourselves with which we are in conflict. They also tell us about the conceptions we have formed about enemies.

In dreams, children can symbolize both childish sides of the personality, as well as life opportunities and creative projects (Jung 1951). Children can also refer to the objective conditions for children whom the dreamer actually knows, yet it is almost always relevant to examine what child-figures mean in an inner sense. This will be expanded on later.

Regarding parental figures in dreams, differentiating dream characters who have parental roles from those who have roles of partners/lovers/friends is often useful. Psychoanalysis has a tendency to see figures with motherly and fatherly qualities as substitutes for real childhood mothers and fathers. Dream researcher David Foulkes, in what he called *A Grammar of Dreams*, suggested the following characters refer to motherly and fatherly figures:

- Our personal mothers, as well as women with whom we have, or had, motherly, caring relationships, are important dream representatives of motherly qualities. Other representatives of motherliness are women who – because of their age, function, size or bodily appearance – seem motherly, such as nurses, teachers, female priests, queens, etc.
- Potential father figures are men who are older than the dreamer and men who have authority over or responsibility for others, such as policemen, male teachers, priests, administrators, bosses, kings, presidents, professional authorities, hosts, etc. (Foulkes 1978, pp. 225–6).

Although Jungian psychology usually views kings and queens, gods and goddesses as representatives of something much greater than the ego, in some societies they can be general representations of fatherly and motherly qualities as well. They may also represent what Jung called the "Self" – the totality of the psyche. Fatherly representations might also include male gods, heaven, and the spirit that can also be symbolized by wind or air. Impersonal mother symbols include mother church, mother nature, and mother ship, etc. Further, Jung wrote about the archetypes of the wise old man and the wise old woman (Jung 1928). Which interpretations are valid – personal or impersonal – depends on the context (Core Quality 5).

Some Salient Gender Differences in Dreams

An apparently universally widespread difference in the dreams of men and women is that, in men's dreams, an average of two men for every woman appear and, in women's dreams, one woman for every man is depicted (Hall and Domhoff 1963a). This gender division is also found in boys and girls and is already present by the age of six. Men's dreams contain more aggression toward other men than toward women, while most aggression in women's dreams is between men and women. In addition to this, men have more friendly meetings with women than with other men, while there is no distinction for women (Hall and Domhoff 1974).

Right from the earliest days of childhood men are more focused on objects and things in their dreams than people and women. Men have fewer social dream activities. Girls generally dream more about domesticated animals than boys do (Garfield 1984, pp. 39–41). Children who live in dangerous areas more often dream about aggression and being pursued than children from peaceful areas. Yet, in both cases, girls typically experience the most negative feelings in their dreams, while boys' dreams are far more likely to stage dangerous storyline events (Tartz and Krippner 2008).

The dreams of boys, and especially of young men, generally have more savagery, physical activity and struggle than those of women (Hall and Domhoff 1963a). Women as well as girls generally have a more nuanced language in dreams for relationships and feelings than men. This is typically expressed through more reflexive expressions like, "I notice, I'm aware of, I realize, I recognize," and "I understand." Furthermore, more intensive adjectives and more attention paid to body language and underlying feelings are found in the dreams of girls and women. Similarly, there are generally more considerations and observations about the nature of the contact, as well as observations of the scenery itself in their dreams (Winegar and Levin 1997).

Young men's understandings of pleasant, sexual dreams are generally more straightforward than women's. Their favorite dreams typically deal with willing uninhibited women, and their focus is more on the act itself than the atmosphere around it. In sexual dreams that are described as pleasant by young women, the main focus – to a greater extent than young men – is on romantic, sensual moods, abundance of time, emotional contact and beautiful surroundings. Some women have pleasurable dreams with gently forced sex by strong men. If dreams have aggressive or violent characters, they are generally experienced as nightmares (Delaney 1994).

While savagery in the dreams of small boys is usually symbolized by wild animals, it is often represented by more human figures as the years pass. Hostile exchanges between the dream self and other characters primarily take place between males, as opposed to hostility in the dreams of women who typically experience men as the attacking parties (Strauch and Meier 1996). Men's dreams are generally slightly more optimistic than those of women and a little less worried, and their dream selves are less frightened of making mistakes or doing something embarrassing. Young men typically have more dreams than women about sexual experiences, about flying, finding money, having magic powers or superior knowledge, about creatures that are part animal and part human, about journeying to another planet or out into the universe and about beings from outer space (Nielsen and Zadra *et al.* 2003).

From puberty onwards, a boy's maleness receives a hefty supplement of hormones and increased energies that are difficult to manage. Avoidance, confrontation and fights with male shadow figures are often seen. Prototypes of unintegrated and maladjusted masculinity in young men's dreams are bikers, punks and gang criminals. There may be a symbolic mastery of masculine objects, such as Fritz's "pistol that never misses."

Women's dreams are, of course, particularly characterized by important feminine experiences such as menstrual cycles, pregnancies and births (see Core Quality 7 and Core Quality 9).

The Opposite Gender in Dreams

The development of gender identity and our relationships to the opposite genders are key themes in all cultures and have played central roles in all dream schools.

The experience of gender can be understood as a code that helps determine the identity of the self. An experience of gender identity is formed very early in life and maintained by one's surroundings under the influence of the prevalent patterns of gender roles. In general, the opposite gender can therefore represent qualities that we also possess but do not experience and realize as intensely and consciously.

On the inner level, the male and female qualities in men and women may appear as independent parts of our personalities that make themselves known in our dreams.

In many dreams it may be relevant to view characters of the opposite sex as individual human beings and place less emphasis on gender characteristics. Yet, during important transitional phases in life and in periods of self-reflection, male and female dream characters become clearer sources of inner conflicts and symbols of overlooked unconscious potential. Thus gender may be understood in a generic way as when Freud discussed the Oedipus Complex as a universal conflict within the father/mother/child triangle, or when Jung used the terms "anima" for personifications of progressive feminine qualities in men and "animus" for personifications of male qualities in women (see Chapter 1).

In transitional phases, dream characters of the opposite sex often try to get in touch with the dream self. In men's dreams, this transforming aspect will often take the form of sexually seductive or socially and spiritually inspiring women. Likewise, in women's dreams, male characters can show useful qualities that can be integrated into the female ego (Franz 1964). From my own experience, the transformative male dream characters in the dreams of modern Western women are also often erotically attractive and display vigor, constructive initiative and spirituality.

In the beginning of the transformative process, the dream self may be in some way averse to meeting the gender-opposite character. Later, acceptance and union between the gender polarities may take place and could lead to development of psychological wholeness on a higher, more comprehensive level than earlier. The more the qualities of the opposite gender are integrated into an individual's experience and behavior, the more gender differences will be nuanced.

When working with transformative aspects of the opposite sex it is important to look at the differences between the dream figures who have parental roles and characters whose roles are those of partners/lovers/friends.

In Laura's case (Core Quality 2), I provided an example of how memories of a lost father spontaneously emerged in dreamwork, how this was associated with Laura's difficulty in relationships to possible male partners, and how her father image was substituted by the figure of a teacher. In Fritz's case, the adult male personality was probably persecuting the boy too early in life. In Pernille's dream of the burial of an old aunt, a male figure helped her to say goodbye to an outlived feminine identity. In Sarah's dream, the theme was the dreamer's attitude to her own motherliness.

References

Bowlby, J. (1969/1982) *Attachment and Loss* (2nd Ed.). (New York: Basic Books)

Bryner, J. (2010) '7-month-old babies show awareness of others' viewpoints'. *Live Science.* Available online at: www.livescience.com (last accessed October 2015)

Bulkeley, K. *et al.* (2005) 'Earliest remembered dreams'. *Dreaming*, Vol. 15(3), Sept., 205–22

Chamberlain, D. (1988) *Babies Remember Birth*. (Boston, MA: Putnam)

Chiron, C. *et al.* (1997) "The right brain hemisphere is dominant in human infants" *Brain*. Vol. 120 (Pt 6):1057–1065

Cozolino, L. (2010) The Neuroscience of Psychotherapy: Healing the Social Brain (2nd Ed.). (New York: W. W. Norton & Company), Kindle edition, location 1601–20

Delaney, G. (1994) *Sensual Dreaming: How to Understand and Interpret the Erotic Content of Your Dream.* (New York: Ballantine Books)

Dieckmann, H. (1962) 'Integration process of the ego-complex in dreams'. *Journal of Analytical Psychology*, Vol.10(1), 41–65

Dieckmann, H. (1980) 'On the methodology of dream interpretation' in I. Baker (Ed.), *Methods of Treatment in Analytical Psychology.* (Bonn: Fellbach), pp. 48–51

Dieckmann, H. (1984) *Träume als Sprache der Seele.* (Bonn: Fellbach)

Dreyfus, H. and Dreyfus S. (1986) *Mind over Machine.* (New York: Free Press)

Foulkes, D. (1978) *A Grammar of Dreams.* (New York: Basic Books)

Foulkes, D. (1982) *Children's Dreams. Longitudinal Studies.* (New York: Wiley-Interscience)

Franz, M.-L. von (1964) 'The process of individuation' in C. G. Jung, M.-L. von Franz, J. L. Henderson, J. Jacobi and A. Jaffe, *Man and His Symbols.* (pp. 158-229). (Garden City, NY: Doubleday & Company, Inc.), pp. 58–230.

Garfield, P. (1984) *Your Child's Dreams.* (New York: Ballantine Books)

Gopnik, A. (2009) *The Philosophical baby.* (London, UK: The Bodley Head)

Hall, C. (1953/1966) *The Meaning of Dreams.* (New York: McGraw Hill)

Hall, C. and Domhoff, B. (1963) 'Aggressions in Dreams'. *International Journal of Social Psychiatry*, Vol. 9, 259–267

Hall, C. and Domhoff, B. (1963a) 'A ubiquitous sex difference in dreams'. *Journal of Abnormal and Social Psychology*, Vol. 66, 278–80

Hall, C. and Domhoff, B. (1964) 'Friendliness in dreams'. *Journal of Social Psychology*, Vol. 62, 309–14

Hall, C. and Domhoff, B. (1974) 'The difference between men and women dreamers' in R. Woods and H. Greenhouse, *The New World of Dreams.* (New York: Macmillan Publishing Co.), pp. 13–21

Hall, C. S. and Nordby, V. J. (1972) *The Individual and His Dreams.* (New York: New American Library)

Hartmann, E. (2000) 'We do not dream of the three Rs: implications for the nature of dreaming mentation'. *Dreaming*, Vol. 10(2), 103–110

Hoss, R. J. (2005) *Dream Language: Self-Understanding through Imagery and Color.* (Ashland, OR: Innersource) Kindle edition, location 25

Jung, C. G. (1928) 'The relations between the ego and the unconscious' in G. Adler and R. F. C. Hull (Eds, Trans), The Collected Works of C.G. Jung: Experimental Researches, Vol. 2. (Abingdon, UK: Routledge and Kegan Paul)

Jung, C. G. (1951) 'The psychology of the child archetype' in C. G. Jung and C. Kerenyi, *Introduction to a Science of Mythology.* (Abingdon, UK: Routledge and Kegan Paul), s.95–118

Kahn, D. and Hobson, A. (2005) 'State-dependent thinking: a comparison of waking and dreaming thought'. *Consciousness and Cognition*, Sept., Vol. 14(3), 429–38

Kahn, D. and Hobson, A. (2005a) 'Theory of Mind in Dreaming'. *Dreaming*, Vol. 15(1), 48–57

Kahn, D., Pace-Schott, E. and Hobson, J. A. (2002) 'Emotion and cognition: feeling and character identification in dreaming'. *Consciousness and Cognition*, 11(1), 34–50

Mahler, M. *et al.* (1975) *The Psychological Birth of the Human Infant.* (New York: Basic Books)

Mallon, B. (2002) *Dream Time with Children.* (London: Jessica Kingsley Publishers)

Mattoon, M. A. (1978) *Applied Dream Analysis.* (Chichester, UK: John Wiley)

McClelland, J. L. and Rumelhart, D. (1986) 'A distributed model and human learning and memory' in J. L. McClelland and D. Rumelhart, *Parallel Distributed Processing Explorations in the Microstructure of Cognition, Volume II: Psychological and Biological Models.* (Cambridge, MA: The MIT Press), pp. 170–215

McNamara, P. (2012) 'Philosophy of mind and dream characters' in D. Barrett and P. McNamara (Eds), *Encyclopedia of Sleep and Dreams*. (Santa Barbara, CA: Greenwood Publishing), Kindle edition, location 12558

McNamara, P. *et al.* (2007) '"Theory of mind" in REM and NREM dreams' in D. Barrett and P. McNamara (Eds), *The New Science of Dreaming*. Vol. 1 (Westport, CT: Praeger Publishers), pp. 201–20

McNamara, P. *et al.* (2009) 'Representations of self in dreaming'. *Dreaming*, June, 17(2), 113–26

McNamara, P. and Andresen, J. (2001) 'Impact of attachment styles on dream recall and dream content: a test of the attachment hypothesis of REM sleep'. *Journal of Sleep Research*, June, 10(2), 117–27

Nielsen, T. (2012) 'Characters in dreams' in D. Barrett and P. McNamara, *Encyclopedia of Sleep and Dreams*. (Santa Barbara, CA: Greenwood Publishing), Kindle edition, location 3202–94

Nielsen, T. A. *et al.* (1991) 'Emotions in dream and waking event reports'. *Dreaming*, Vol. 1(4), 287–300

Nielsen, T. A., Zadra, A. *et al.* (2003) 'The typical dreams of Canadian University students'. *Dreaming*, Vol. 13(4)

Pochmursky, C. *et al.* (2009) *The Musical Brain*, documentary, Canadian television (CTV)

Ratey, J. (2001) A User's Guide to the Brain: Perception, Attention, and the Four Theatres of the Brain. (New York: Knopf Doubleday Publishing Group), Kindle edition location 2334ff

Resnic, J., Stickgold, R. *et al.* (1994) 'Self-representation and bizarreness in children's dream reports collected in the home setting'. *Consciousness and Cognition*, 3(1), 30–45

Revonsuo, A., Tuominen, J. and Valli, K. (2015) 'The avatars in the machine: dreaming as a simulation of social reality' in T. Metzinger and J. M. Windt (Eds), *Open MIND*, 32(T). (Frankfurt am Main: MIND Group)

Rumelhart, D. (1980) 'Schemata: the building blocks of cognition' in R. J. Spiro, B. Bruce and W. F. Brewer (Eds), *Theoretical Issues in Reading Comprehension*. (Abingdon, UK: Routledge), pp. 35–58

Rycroft, C. (1968/1979) *A Critical Dictionary of Psychoanalysis*. (London: Penguin Books)

Samuels, A. *et al.* (1986) *A Critical Dictionary of Jungian Analysis*. (New York: Routledge and Kegan Paul)

Sándor, P., Szakadát, S. *et al.* (2015) 'Content analysis of 4 to 8 year-old children's dream reports'. *Frontiers in Psychology*, 6: 534

Siegel, A. and Bulkeley K. (1998) *Dreamcatching: Every Parent's Guide to Exploring and Understanding Children's Dreams and Nightmares*. (New York: Three Rivers Press)

Siegel, A. B. (2005) 'Children's dreams and nightmares: emerging trends in research'. *Dreaming*, Vol. 15(3), s. 147–54

Skogemann, P. (1984) *Kvindelighed i vækst [Femininity in Growth]*. (Copenhagen: Lindhardt and Ringhof)

Stern, D. N. (1985) *The Interpersonal World of the Infant: A View from Psychoanalysis and Developmental Psychology* (London: Karnac Books), Kindle edition

Stern, D. N. (1995) *The Motherhood Constellation*. (London: Karnac Books)

Stern, D. N. (1990) *Diary Of A Baby: What Your Child Sees, Feels, And Experiences*. (New York. US: Basic Books)

Strauch, I. (2005) 'REM dreaming from childhood to adolescence'. *Dreaming*, Vol. 15(3), 155–69

Strauch, I. and Meier, A. (1996) *In Search of Dreams: Results of Experimental Dream Research*. (Albany, NY: New York State University Press)

Stukane, E. (1985) *The Dream Worlds of Pregnancy*. (New York: W. Morrow)

Tartz, R. S. and Krippner, S. (2008) 'Cognitive differences in dream content between Argentine males and females'. *Dreaming*, December, Vol. 18, 217–235

Trevarthen, C. and Aitken, K. (1994) 'Brain development, infant communication, and empathy disorders'. *Development and Psychopathology* 6(4), 597–633

Vedfelt, O. (2000a) *Unconscious Intelligence. You Know More Than you Think*. (Copenhagen: Gyldendal) Danish, Swedish and Polish Editions

Vedfelt, O. (2000b) 'Part personalities, object relations and cybernetic network theory' in *Psyche & Logos*, No. 2. (Copenhagen: Danish Psychological Publishers)

Vedfelt, O. (2011) Dreams selected from the children of Ole Vedfelt's colleagues

Vedfelt, O. (2014) 'The phenomenology of the spirit in childhood memories: early numinous experiences in a desacralized world' in E. Kiehl (Ed.) *Proceedings of 19th Congress of the International Association for Analytical Psychology*, (Einsiedeln Switzerland. Daimon Verlag) pp. 886–90

Vedfelt, O. (2017) *Psychosis as a Means to Individuation: A Case of Severe Psychosis Healed Through Working with Dreams, Active Imagination and Transference*. Presentation at the 20th Congress of the International Association for Analytical Psychology, Kyoto (Einsiedeln Switzerland. Daimon Verlag) (Published in spring 2017)

Winegar, R. K. and Levin, R. (1997) 'Sex Differences in the Object Representations in the Dreams of Adolescents'. *Sex Roles*, Vol. 36(7/8), s. 503–16

Yu, C. (2015) 'The vicissitudes of the affective valence of dream emotions across the night. A high-density electroencephalographic study'. *Dreaming*, Vol. 25(4), 274–290

Chapter 7

Core Quality 4

Dreams are Trial Runs in a Safe Place

It is possible to operate in a complex system with 'mental models' that allow actions to be performed completely on an interior plane and the evaluation of the consequences of possible outcomes. If a network that interprets input is connected with another that contains a model of the world in its memory, numerous situations can be tested without input and output (Rumelhart *et al.* 1986, pp. 38–44).

It would appear that, long ago, nature granted human beings such capabilities while asleep. When we dream we are cut off from doing. This makes dreams safe places where our unconscious intelligence can try out experiences and attitudes without blaming ourselves, being censored or coming to harm. In our dreams, we can make trial runs without any practical consequences.

In that sense, dreams simulate models of future possibilities in life and they may play these out on various levels. They can prepare the mind for the following day, they can be warm-up exercises for new and more extensive developmental phases, and they can keep alive old suggestions for resolutions that have never been realized. Many humanistic, clinical and natural sciences researchers assert the anticipatory and creative functions of dreams, even though they emphasize these functions in discrete realms of the human domain.

Jung suggested that a dream is "an anticipation in the unconscious of future conscious achievements, something like a preliminary sketch or plan roughed out in advance ... an anticipatory combination of probabilities not necessarily exact in every detail" (Jung 1916/1948, p. 493). He connected this to the long-term development of the personality he called the "process of individuation." Erik Erikson highlighted the appearance in dreams of life-long psychosocial developmental stages (Erikson 1954). Prominent Jungian Erich Neumann included dreams in the dynamics of the "creative unconscious," which also feeds artistic creativity (Neumann 1959). Calvin Hall found that, "Dreaming is ... essentially a creative process ... the product of good hard thought" (Hall 1953). Within psychoanalysis, Donald Meltzer described dreaming as "a creative process which generates meaning that can be deployed to life and relationships in the outside world" (Meltzer 1983). Ernest Hartmann assumed that dreams make connections in a safe place, and pointed to some similarities between dreams and psychotherapy (Hartmann 1995).

More recently, Antti Revonsuo has formulated a theory of dreams as social simulation. In another recent study, Caroline Horton and Josie Malinowski found that autobiographical memories are bound together in the holistic narrative experiences of dreams in a creative way (Horton and Malinowski 2015).

In Core Quality 4, I will highlight how creative trial runs in dreams serve self-organization and optimize psychic functioning. For practical dreamwork, it is helpful to look at how the anticipatory function expresses itself in the narrative structure of dreams in various ways.

Warnings of Emotional Complications of Consciously Planned Action

When you allow spontaneous emotion to influence your actions, some dreams provide hints of future consequences through their symbolic language.

Unexpectedly, after many years of marriage, Pia's husband left her for a younger woman. One day she decided she would contact him and "have a talk" with him. Immediately after deciding this, she dreamed that *she was with him and wanted to stab a knife in his forehead. When she did this, the knife transformed into a suction cup.* Pia and I agreed that a knife to the forehead suggested she aggressively wanted to get through to his reason. The suction cup warned that it would become even more difficult to liberate herself from him if she did so. Her hidden feelings consisted of both anger at him and missing him. She was unconsciously motivated to get him back.

Talking about the dream made Pia realize that her husband had clearly signaled he would not come back. "Having a talk" with him would not give her what she wanted. It would only bring even more humiliation and drag out the inevitable for a long time. She decided against suggesting they meet.

Understood in this way, Pia's dream offered very concrete guidance for her actions. On a higher level of self-organization, the dream was about some internal patterns within Pia that were battling each other. Her continually repeating inner dialogues moved back and forth from scolding him to surrendering to a sea of longing for what once was. This behavioral pattern could not be avoided in the external world. She had to liberate herself from these limiting thoughts and feelings because they were attacking her self-esteem. She had cried all the tears she needed. Yet there was still work to do in being 'mindful', i.e. in observing unproductive thoughts and feelings as they appeared, so she could put a stop to them. Pia quickly began to notice that this internal work proved to have an effect on improving her self-esteem and renewing her courage to meet everyday life. This was crucial to finding herself, a new life and a new man who made her happy enough that she would not wish to go back.

Since dreams are about matters important to us – i.e. core problems – test runs take place on levels other than waking consciousness. As in Pia's example, they may be warnings against action taken in the outer world because that action could be emotionally unrealistic.

In time, as you work with your dreams, trial runs begin to take place on more abstract levels. What level you choose to interpret the solutions suggested by your dreams is highly dependent on how much complexity you, as the dreamworker, can cope with. Cf: the principle of requisite variety, described in Chapter 3.

A Dramaturgical Model of Dreams

In order to analyze dream structure, Jung adapted a dramaturgic model from classical drama. I would like to present that model in the following way.

First we have the setting – time, place and characters. Then a problem may be presented and a complication appears that intensifies this problem. A turning point – some event – starts the dream action. The dream reaches a climax, called 'the point of no return' in modern dramaturgy. Finally, the story is resolved more or less satisfactorily.

The way dream stories are formed provides information about how a dreamer's psychological processes typically play out.

Tue, a 41-year-old man, is facing a crucial turning point in his career. This is his dream and its structure:

1   Setting: *I'm in my childhood home, together with my mother.* Something initiates the dream action, for example a problem presented or new figures entering the dream scenario. *Two large, lost birds flap around the rooms.*
2   Complication: *My mother is confused. She doesn't think we can do anything about it.*
3   First turning point: *I discover the big birds are trying to imitate smaller, caged birds.*
4   Climax – point of no return: *I open the window and let out the birds.*
5   New complication: *I'm worried that they have been injured.*
6   Resolution: *When they get free, I can see that one is a big, beautiful falcon, and the other is an eider. They are completely uninjured and demonstrate impressive flying abilities. They remain soaring in the wind, performing deep dives and switching between slow and quick wing strokes.*

Quite often, the setting of a dream is the childhood home. The period in which the dreamer lived there might be reminiscent of personal themes important at that time, and which may still be valuable to investigate. Tue tells that he lived at that specific place from the ages of 12–18 years.

Elaboration of the Birds

The pivotal symbols of the plot are the birds. Eiders are migratory and fly in beautiful formations, which Tue has admired when the eiders migrated along the coast. He is fascinated by the birds' ability to find their way through unknown territory, following only their instincts. He experienced this himself when he 'migrated' away from his homeland for a long period of time. He admires falcons for their swiftness and their elegant, high-soaring flights. He experiences them as strong, independent and commanding respect.

Experiential Intermezzo

Tue's spontaneous feeling of knowing and feeling of rightness is that the birds should be set free. While role-playing, he sits with his arms glued to his body as if he were trapped in a cage too small. After this, he moves about the room with his 'wings' flapping broadly. He immerses himself in this experience with ease. Tue can sense how he is forced to imitate the movements of a caged bird because the room is too narrow for the full power and speed of a large bird. This produces a very constricted feeling in his body and an intellectual experience of confusion. He opens an (imaginary) window and pretends to fly out. Tue soars up high and then dives lightning fast, enjoying the fresh air and his freedom. He takes his time, feeling the full effects of every single movement. He feels that he is not injured.

Amplification

According to *The Archive for Research in Archetypal Symbolism*, birds form a link between heaven and earth, consciousness and the unconscious. Birds are almost universally seen as symbols of the soul. Falcons are known for their extraordinary powers of sight. They are also one of the earliest images of kingship (Ronnberg and Martin 2011). Erich Neumann found in his scholarly research on the origin of human consciousness that falcons may symbolize the aspiring flights of ego-consciousness (Neumann 1973a, p. 352). This general knowledge amplifies Tue's experience and provides background reflecting general human experience.

The Hermeneutic Circle

The mutual feedback loops that makes connections to create more and more complex patterns of understanding. Now we return to the setting: Tue's childhood home from the ages of 12–18. His mother was a homemaker with no higher education. Nor did his father have any higher education – he was a totally self-made man. Tue went through important intellectual and cultural developments at school. His father was critical of all "intellectuals" and, according to Tue, envious of and competitive toward the cultural and intellectual mindset that school hatched within his son. He remembers that he had been forced to underplay himself and his knowledge to avoid conflicts at home, conflicts with which his mother had difficulty coping.

Tue does not have any unfinished business with his parents at present, so we can understand the dream on a subjective level. Tue's childhood home was not then, and is still not, the right element for wild birds of the symbolic here-and-now.

His mother was unsure of herself and Tue can sense this contagious insecurity in himself, just as his father's anti-intellectual attitude has rubbed off on him in the form of an over-critical attitude toward himself.

Tue has an exciting job with great intellectual and humanistic challenges, but has never been able to share that with his parents. Professionally, he harbors feelings of inferiority to his colleagues even though they are kind, inspiring and encourage him to unfold his talents further. His dreamwork tells us that his imagination, his intellectual sharpness and his faith in his spiritual instincts are ready to unfold.

Tue's trial run (and his dream's resolution) is his discovery of the source of his inner inhibitions that block the release of the qualities within himself that the birds represent.

In Tue's dream, we find a clearly positive solution and a model for possible changes in his attitude. He needs to provide more air under the wings of his imagination and creativity.

Pia's dream of the knife turning into a suction cup follows this dramaturgical model, albeit in a very compressed way. There was apparently no 'positive' solution, as yet, on a higher level of self-organization it inspired exploration of a possible warning in the narrative that her more or less unconscious intentions were untenable. In a metaphoric way, the dream even demonstrated why this was so, and advised her what not to do.

Chain Reaction Dreams

In another type of dream, events just get worse and worse. For instance, a young woman, Louise, dreams: *I'm running for the bus. I reach it at the last moment, but when I climb aboard, I see I don't have a ticket and have to get off. The bus drives away. I'm left behind and discover that I'm in an unknown town in an unknown country. I find out that I don't have my wallet, driver's license and passport with me. I feel lost.*

The dream's resolution is not satisfying but, in its entirety, it still has an important message for the dreamer. It uncovers a chain reaction of emotions that also occurs in her waking life when the dreamer pushes herself too hard.

A chain reaction dream can also reflect a self-destructive line of thinking in a waking state of which the dreamer is not conscious. An individual makes a minor mistake and starts reproaching him/herself. The reproach becomes more generalized ("typical me!") and goes perhaps even deeper to attack the individual's self-esteem ("I'm completely impossible!"). The structure of this process is, as a rule, not conscious to the dreamer, yet it reflects that the individual, in a waking state, can be pulled deeper and deeper into destructive thinking and behavioral patterns. Understanding dreams can make dreamers more aware of how and when these psychological processes take place in a waking state.

Cognitive therapists who work with anxiety, depression and low self-esteem often describe these kinds of dreams (Beck 1971). However, I have often seen dreams that develop from goal direction to disorientation in creative people, free-lancers and high achievers. The confusion or failure to achieve in the dream may match the stages where the solutions to a creative problem have not been found or where the skills needed to perform have been felt to reach an upper limit. The fear in the dream may match a commitment that pushes the person towards new solutions or more rehearsal. The dreamer may, of course, also ask himself if the level of ambition is unrealistically high.

Cyclical Dream Narratives

The dramatic structures in the examples above are linear processes. Dreams can also have cyclical narrative structures.

Denice, a 40-year-old mother and social worker, dreams: "I'm walking in the rain. Three owls are sitting in some trees. I find them very fascinating. Then I spot a lot of people at a shopping center. I go in – lots of wonderful and colorful clothes. It turns out that they are free. I just take what I want. But then it's just too much, I simply can't carry it all."

Associations and Amplifications to the Dream

- Walking in the rain: "The rain is mild and gentle. I'm wearing a hood so I'm protected and I have no contact with the other people. I like the rain and the protection. It provides the peace and quiet needed to keep my attention on myself."
- Owls: "They have always fascinated me. They are strong and wise."
- Shopping center: "A lot of people. For the most part, I'm with many other people. I like clothes, too. Maybe I have trouble stopping myself from being extroverted – I get a lot out of being like that. I have to try and stop myself from time to time, and get back to the state I was in with the owls."
- Amplification of Multicolored clothing: Clothes are something you show on the outside. We have a dialogue about Denice's extroverted side which has many facets.
- Amplification: The owl is the bird of the Greek goddess Athena. It has been seen as a symbol of feminine wisdom and clarity (Ronnberg and Martin 2011). Erich Neumann has described it as an expression of "matriarchal consciousness." Owls' ability to see in the dark, in this case, is related to the idea that feminine intuition goes beyond rational explanation (Neumann 1973a). Denice feels stimulated by learning about this connection to a femi-nine world community.

In the end, the dreamer Denice understood her dream as a suggestion to find more balance between her extroverted way of emotional expression and her wish for more introverted, contemplative states and knowledge seeking.

The Neuroscience of the Dream Narrative

Neuroscientist John Ratey has raised the question, where in the brain do the many data meet to create a meaningful story of an event? His answer is, "nowhere and everywhere". Yet, some small intralaminar nuclei in the Thalamus (see chapter 2) are crucial by synchronizing the inputs at a frequency around 40 hertz oscillation. "When this happens with enough networks, the oscillations become ordered. They then spread their influence, coopting more networks to join them, and consciousness arises and widens (Ratey 2001).

The dream consciousness is synchronized at the same frequency as the waking consciousness. The setting of the dream with all its elements, the mental skills of the dream persons, their actions and emotions in the dream setting are combined to a story that makes symbolic sense. The result is not random as suggested by the activation hypotheses (see chapter 2) but depending on context-sensitive self-organizing principles. To understand and utilize these dynamics in optimal ways require hermeneutic tools, psychological knowledge and dreamwork skills.

Conclusion

Among all the potential interpretations of the dramatic structures of dreams, I have emphasized four possibilities.

1   What looks like a bad dream may be a warning of the negative consequences of the actions a dreamer is considering taking, but has not yet become fully conscious of these consequences.
2   The dramatic structure of a dream may reflect important developmental directions or solutions to problems. These can be both long-term, as well as short-term, and refer to inner as well as outer developmental potentialities.
3   Chain reaction dreams demonstrates how the dream self entangles itself in experiential patterns that are counterproductive and self-destructive.
4   Cyclical Dream plots describe various stances which, each in their own way, are valuable and will benefit from being nuanced and brought into balance.

Dreams are safe places where we can test experiences and attitudes without hurting ourselves in our waking lives.

Analysis of the dramatic structures of dreams and the interaction of dream figures are important keys to interpreting dreams.

References

Barrett, D. (2001) *The Committee of Sleep.* (New York: Crown Publishers)

Beck, A. T. (1971) 'Cognitive patterns in dreams and daydreams' in R. Rosner, W. Lyddon and A. Freeman (Eds), *Cognitive Therapy and Dreams.* (New York: Springer Publishing), pp. 27–32

Erikson, E. H. (1954) 'The dream specimen of psychoanalysis'. *The Journal of the American Psychoanalytic Association*, Vol. 2, 5–56

Hall, C. (1953/1966) *The Meaning of Dreams*. (New York: McGraw Hill)

Hartmann, E. (1995) 'Making connections in a safe place: is dreaming psychotherapy? *Dreaming*, Vol. 5, 213–28

Horton C. L. and Malinowski, J. (2015) 'Autobiographical memory and hyperassociativity in the dreaming brain: implications for memory consolidation in sleep'. *Frontiers in Psychology*, Vol. 6, 874

Jung C. G. (1916/1948/1981) 'General aspects of dream psychology' in G. Adler, M. Fordham and H. Read, Sir (Eds), *The Structure and Dynamics of the Psyche: The Collected Works of C.G. Jung*, Vol. 8. (Abingdon, UK: Routledge and Kegan Paul), pp. 237–80

Meltzer, D. (1983) *Dream – Life – A Re-examination of the Psychoanalytical Theory and Technique*. (Strathclyde, UK: Clunie Press)

Neumann, E. (1959) *Art and The Creative Unconscious*. (Princeton, NJ: Princeton University Press)

Neumann, E. (1973) 'The moon and matriarchal consciousness' in P. Berry, *Fathers and Mothers*. (Zürich: Spring Publications)

Neumann, E. (1973a) *The Origins and History of Consciousness*. (Princeton, NJ: Princeton University Press)

Ratey, J. (2001) *A User's Guide to the Brain: Perception, Attention, and the Four Theatres of the Brain*. (New York: Knopf Doubleday Publishing Group), Kindle edition Loc. 2203 ff.

Ronnberg, A. and Martin, K. (2011) *The Book of Symbols: Reflections on Archetypal Images. The Archive for Research in Archetypal Symbolism*. (Cologne, Germany: Taschen)

Rumelhart, D. *et al.* (1986) 'Schemata and sequential thought' in J. L. McClelland and D. Rumelhart, *Parallel Distributed Processing Vol 2: Explorations in the Microstructure of Cognition: Psychological and Biological Models*. (Cambridge, MA: The MIT Press), pp. 7–57

Chapter 8

Core Quality 5

Dreams are Online to Unconscious Intelligence

The ways of relating to dreams I have described so far have had the main focus relatively close to rational thinking in the waking state. This applies to the understanding of the structures of dreams, amplification of their symbolic language and rules for dealing with characters that appear in them. Now I will in a more systematic way look at approaches to dreams that are more radically different from rational thinking and that bring us closer to their inner nature.

In the dreaming state, consciousness is online to unconscious intelligence (Vedfelt 2004). When we are awake, we have states of consciousness that provide certain opportunities to contact our unconscious intelligence and, in doing so, help us deeply examine the information found in dreams.

An experiential approach may be a powerful tool. It is important that the method and the dreamers personality in its totality has the requisite variety to regulate the inflow of unconscious content and energy. This chapter will explain this according to a theory of altered states of consciousness. A preliminary overview of experiential dreamwork methods will be provided, and cybernetic principles for regulation of the energy will be suggested.

American psychologist Charles Tart, a pioneer in the exploration of the states of consciousness, describes a state of consciousness as a dynamic pattern of psychological systems and subsystems. According to Tart, a specific state of consciousness is kept stable by means of four processes – loading, positive feedback, negative feedback and the limitation of activity. These processes ensure that "attention and other psychological energies are kept in habitual, desired structures …" (Tart 1983, p. 4; Vedfelt 2000a). If the state of consciousness is not constantly kept occupied, it will break down and lapse into an "altered state of consciousness".

The stability of reality-oriented waking consciousness – 'normal' consciousness – is important for carrying out purposeful tasks. Simply vital to the business of daily living, it must be loaded, receive feedback and have defined limitations in order to function, according to Tart.

Altered states of consciousness occupy close to a quarter of our waking life (Foulkes and Fleischer 1975; Kripke and Sonnenschein 1978). It can be relaxed, regenerating or creative states, or they may be filled with repetitive material such as recurring anxieties, worried thinking and ruminations.

Yet altered states of consciousness may be transformed into more contemplative and reflective states that can observe the hitherto unconscious processes and intensify the dreamwork through loading, positive or negative feedback, as well as by limiting activity.

Unconscious Cues and the Associative Network in Dreams

Unconscious intelligence does not function logically or linearly; it functions more like an associative network where knowledge is coded into memory aided by associations learned through practice. American information theoretician Paul Smolensky (Smolensky, 1986, p. 210) gives the following illustrative example of how patterns are formed in a parallel distributed network.

> A child sits reading a story about presents, party hats and a cake with candles. When asked what the story is about, the child says that the girl who is getting presents is having a birthday. Reading the story has activated the child's birthday party schema. A birthday party schema uses a knowledge structure which contains variables like 'birthday cake', 'guest of honor', 'presents' and 'location', etc.
>
> The actual word 'birthday' has not been stated in the story but the child interpolates it based on the given information, and then the child's inner, ideational world fills the scene with details which are not directly mentioned in the story.
>
> If words like 'blackboard', 'pointer' or 'teacher' had appeared, the child might think it described a school situation and not a birthday party. Yet – in a flash – once the input is evaluated and a choice made, the necessary experience and action procedures are set in motion so the child, in this given practical situation, behaves as if he or she is supposed to skip school to attend a birthday.
>
> (Smolensky 1986)

When we disconnect normal, extroverted and goal-oriented consciousness, our minds can be loaded with cues from within or by employing various dreamwork methods. We are then able to tune into associative connections that make sense on a completely different level than normal consciousness. This is somewhat like surfing the internet with a search engine presenting and arranging hits based on complex algorithms the searcher need not know.

The following very simple example of meaningful cues is from my practice, where a younger man, Waldemar, told this ultra-short dream: "Someone asks, 'Do you want coffee?' and I answer, 'No, thank you! I'd rather have tea.'" Many things can be said about coffee and tea but when the dreamer relaxed, closed his eyes and said the first thing that came to mind, he said his family only drank coffee while out with strangers. Coffee drinking was seen as something quite refined. His family drank tea at home because it was less refined.

Before his dream, the young man was very preoccupied about his boss urging him to participate in a course. He planned to say no – presumably on professional grounds. Through his dream he became aware that his resistance to the course was not professional but rather derived from feelings of inferiority around strangers (other people's coffee is more refined than his tea). He decided to participate in the course and it turned out to be an important experience for him. Thus, when the mind relaxed, we got a cue that, in dreamwork, activated a pattern of experience that was much more constructive than the biased perception of normal consciousness.

Ways of Going Online to the Dream World

By changing our states of consciousness, we can tune into the network that creates dreams. At the moment of awakening, the mind is closer to the dreaming state than it will be later. Therefore, the things you are thinking about and the recollections that pop up will be relatively close to the meaning of your dream, and may be of particular importance. As soon as you get busy with your daily routine, your consciousness becomes loaded with other programs and you have to find your way back to a more relaxed state to 're-enter' your dream again.

Techniques Using Relaxation

The traditional free association technique that Freud (1900) developed is an altered state of consciousness where normal waking consciousness is disconnected, and psychic contents, no matter how foreign or illogical they may seem, are employed in the total analysis of the dream.

Dream journeying is another technique that can be employed while lying comfortably on your back. It begins with a relaxation exercise that is followed by a small journey inward that awakens your imagination and emotions. In a relaxed state, you make a journey of discovery into your dream, trying to remember as many details as possible, checking to see if any characters have been overlooked and noticing if you can sense any other feelings than those you were aware of from the outset. Sensual qualities like fragrances, sounds or visual impressions awaken forgotten moods and bring out hitherto hidden recollections. After that, you can move on to further analytical or experiential work.

Creative Expressions

Even various forms of creative expression about a dream can inspire deeper understanding or re-affect the unconscious which then responds with new dreams. Drawings and paintings may be beneficial to increasing the wealth of associations to and empathy with your dream story. Special skills in symbol interpretation are not necessary. If you make your drawing quickly and spontaneously – without aesthetic concern and formal consideration – you give your unconscious permission to express itself.

It may be surprising how much the unconscious can tell when consciousness is not allowed to control the process. For instance, if you draw yourself unnaturally small or large in comparison with another person, it may add important symbolic information about your experience of inequality in that relationship. You may find meaningful symbolism if you draw your head too big for your body or if you do not draw your mouth, hands or feet. You can learn to hone your attention to these kinds of details. The use of color provides opportunity to spontaneously express emotional nuance. Often, figures are painted in different colors, to which various emotion or memories are associated. If you draw an object – a cabinet perhaps – the color, shape and size may suddenly awaken recollections about a particular cabinet connected to many meaningful experiences.

The way your loved ones are spatially placed in a dream may reveal patterns in your family dynamics. Thelma, a 27-year-old woman, had a dream about *conflict in her childhood family*. Thelma said that, in childhood, she had been very attached to her mother. When making a drawing of her family, she placed her mother and her siblings on the right side of the paper. The dreamer herself was near her father on the left side of the paper at a considerable distance to her mother and siblings. The size, shape and clothing of the characters she had drawn made it possible to estimate their age. She was probably 5–7 years old. Thelma's association, which surprised her, was that, to a great extent, she actually had been her father's daughter from the age of six. Reflecting on this, she realized that he had favored her in ways that had aroused jealousy in her siblings. This insight gave her a completely new perspective on her family dynamics, which had a much better fit with her dream than her first attempt at an interpretation.

The point of doing quick, spontaneous drawings is that you devote yourself to formative, unconscious forces without being inhibited by performance demands. In my practice and in my groups, I use large sheets of paper and oil pastels, and then limit the time used to make the drawings.

Naturally, it is also valuable to draw or paint a dream or a symbol with great care, skill and artistic ability. In doing so, you delve down into its mood and honor the inner dynamics that have created it.

Active Imagination and Role-play

Using Jung's method of active imagination, you can visualize your dream. You can ask questions and listen to what characters say to you in your imagination. Or you can discover new aspects of your dream, making suggestions for changes that you then imagine in the most vivid way possible (Chodorow 1997).

You can get deeper into your dream by role-playing the various figures or even phenomena appearing in it. It can be illuminating to speak or move, for instance, the way you imagine a certain dream character might. If you empathetically delve into the person behind your initial, perhaps stereotypical evaluation, you can discover unexpected sides that may open to new aspects of both your relationships to others and yourself.

Phenomena and objects – from volcanoes, oceans or winds, to riding paths, furniture and porcelain figures – can also add life and atmosphere. For example, a woman dreams about *a chest of drawers, where the drawers keep getting pulled out.* When she pretends to be the dresser and some of the participants in her dream group pretend to continually pull drawers out of her, she then discovers that this is a fitting image of her life. She has three children, a full-time job and a very demanding boss.

Role-playing can also be built up by a group into a larger psychodrama where the participants are instructed and 'warmed up' to play various roles from a dream. This also intensifies the experiences of the group members.

Meditation Bodysensing and Feeling

Meditation has become a recognized technique for becoming aware of what is taking place in your mind from moment to moment. In a loving, accepting way, you try to observe your inner life as it immediately manifests itself in your consciousness without trying to change it or analyze it. This can be quite difficult since normal awareness has a tendency to be carried away by all kinds of thoughts and emotions without being able to relate to them from a neutral stance.

In dreamwork you can choose individual symbols, feelings, moods or processes and then relate to them meditatively, or you can choose the whole dream. This is how some elements of the dream may be made clearer than others and generate more associations. The associations will not necessarily lead far from the dream, nor the individual symbols. Rather, they will orbit some possibilities of meaning that you can relate to in various ways when the meditative phase is finished.

We can also see how body awareness may be an important extension of associations and help connect your consciousness to the feelings sensed in any dream elements.

All these methods have contributed to our understanding of the balance between opening to the unconscious and limiting what the conscious self can integrate.

Employing cohesive theories, methods and skills acquired through practical training will contribute to doing justice to the complexity of dreams. My overriding view is that the more tools one has to open doors to unconscious resources, the more tools one also has to close doors and load other material if the dreamer is not able to integrate the liberated material.

Loading and Limiting Consciousness in Dreamwork

The loading and limiting of states of mind containing "psychological energies," as Tart puts it, is essential to the experiential elements in dreamwork. Freud used the concept of cathexis to designate that "a certain amount of psychic energy is attached to an idea or to a group of ideas, to a part of the body, to an object, etc." (Laplanche and Pontalis 1967, loc. 1758). Jung developed a theory of psychic energetics that describes the total psychic energy as being relatively constant and how that energy shifts between various archetypal patterns (Jung 1928). In gestalt therapy, "excitement" is a key concept for the liveliness and freedom that therapy should restore to inhibited, neurotic individuals (Perls *et al.* 1951). In cognitive psychology and neuropsychology, practitioners speak of the "degree of activation" or "arousal." Infant researcher and psychoanalyst Daniel Stern (2010) uses the term "vitality." Neuroscience, as we have seen, measures metabolic intensity to determine the degree of involvement of various brain networks in information processing (Kussé and Maquet 2012). In order to balance the amount of aroused energy and incoming information, all methods mentioned utilize not only loading but also limiting measures. As I will explain further in relation to core quality of the energy is not only mental, psychological or psychic. It may be embodied as well. Below I will describe the concept of energy change in terms of cybernetic network theory.

Balance can be implemented in, for instance, the setting in a long-term process where work with the change of emotionally charged high level personality patterns and receives continual follow-up through regular sessions typical to psychoanalytic and Jungian individual therapy. Short-term therapy can be used in focus-oriented ways to exclude that which is not relevant in dreams, thus attaining the particular objectives of therapy.

Precautions can be taken to ensure that dreamers are not 'acting out,' i.e. are not taking steps in the exterior world until the emotions and insights are integrated in responsible ways within the dreamer's waking self.

Rules regarding the relations between dreamers and their therapists, helpers and group leaders, and between members in a group, are made to ensure safe places for dreamers, whether this is in psychoanalysis, counseling and self-help groups, or the social dream matrices mentioned in Chapter 1.

Energy Charge and the Network

Network theory is a model for learning through practice. For example, advanced skills important for personification in dreams, such as recognizing faces based on network patterns, are typically built up through practical training (Wackerhausen 1998).

In a network, a mental state is a pattern of activation distributed over the units of some subset modules. If a pattern is activated it leaves memory traces that correspond to ways of interpreting the environment in a specific context. The energy charge of a certain element or module is called 'the weight.' The more weight between the connections in the network, the greater the probability that a certain pattern will emerge (McClelland and Rumelhart 1986). The weight with which an impression – for example, unconscious face recognition – is encoded depends on emotional excitement, visual intensity and bodily response.

As stated in Chapter 3, David Rumelhart suggests that the inner structure of a pattern or schema is similar to the manuscript of a stage play with characters who can be portrayed by different actors at various moments in time without changing the essential nature of the play (Rumelhart 1980). Likewise, we can understand dream narratives and dream characters as variations of more essential personality traits and relational patterns. By making dreamwork experiential – including visual, bodily, emotional and alternative thinking – we add energetic charge to the experience.

A strong charge in itself is not crucial to whether dreamwork will succeed or not. What is crucial is the quality of the information – also called the "logical depth" in information theory (Bennett 1988). You must release the emotional charge that circulates in repetitive low-level patterns and invest it on a higher level of organization. This will enable a development from less mature to more mature states or be realigned from a dysfunctional network to a functional one. Intellectualization is known to reduce the effect while, on the other hand, emotional overload may provide short-term cathartic relief without leading to any improvements in the individual's life. When it comes to traumatic experience, certain impressions can be stored in memory with such great intensity that they may be reactivated by unconscious perceptions of seemingly harmless triggers. These impressions, therefore, demand certain precautions during dreamwork (Chapter 14, Dreams and Trauma).

Cybernetic Reorganization in Dreamwork

The varying directions of knowledge and experience of the various schools of psychotherapy can be included in an overriding model for therapeutic processes where immature or conflicted patterns are transformed into more harmonious ones.

The higher the levels of organization and the stronger the energy charges between the connections in the network, the greater the chances of change that influences the entire system. Developing these states in constructive ways requires that a certain 'necessary complexity' is present. I call this "cybernetic reorganization" (Vedfelt 2000a).

Cybernetic reorganization cannot be attained by simply opening up to problematic experience or providing an individual with an experience of catharsis. Restructuring must take place on a higher level than the level where personal development or negotiations between warring factions within the mind have been arrested. Consciousness must retreat to a more abstract level where self-regulation can begin to apply pressure to create a new synthesis.

Each time an individual experiences a shift between one conflicted state to a more cohesive one, practical learning takes place and constructive healing patterns become stored in the individual's memory. Every time a pattern is stored, the more its strength increases in competition with other patterns. This creates experiential learning, increasing the ability of constructive and harmonious patterns to overcome destructive ones. The more this learning contains condensed information and takes place on a higher level, the easier it will be to attain a harmonious state.

In dreamwork – long or short-term – normal consciousness is rendered unstable in order to reorganize itself anew on a higher level. Therefore, this demands post-processing to stabilize this new state and integrate new experiential patterns.

Laura's retrieved memory of the loss of her father at the age of six, and the inadequate support from her surroundings, are examples of high-level disturbances that deeply impacted her ability to form intimate relationships. This required post-processing (see Core Quality 2).

Pregnant Sarah, who had a bad experience and a bad dream after a telephone call to her mother, is an example of an individual in an unstable state who was then stabilized by loading the psyche with positive 'mother-group' experiences, rather than disappointing 'bad mother' inputs (see Core Quality 3).

The idea of reorganisation of energy and content is implicit in all the therapeutic energy theories mentioned above, yet expressed in different terminologies. It is consistent with a parallel distributed processing thesis that "learning can occur with gradual changes in connection strength by experience (Kincaid 2017; Rumelhart and Zipser 1986)". On the brain level it is consistent with a highly acclaimed theory of 'Neuronal group selection' by Nobel laureate Edelmann: a basic tenet is that during brain development networks of nerve cells (neurons), which are often used together will be strengthened while connections between neurons not used will weakened (Edelman 1993). In our simple example in the beginning of the chapter, the birthday party schema will be strengthened by the relevant features and the school situation schema will be weakened in a process of learning.

In dreamwork, we can use altered states of consciousness to go online to the unconscious intelligence that produces dreams.

With knowledge of altered states of consciousness, we can balance the inflow of unconscious information in dreamwork and ensure a proper integration of new content into dreamers' lives.

References

Bennett, C. H. (1988) 'Logical depth and physical complexity' in R. Herken (Ed.), *The Universal Turing Machine*. (Oxford: Oxford University Press)

Chodorow, J. (1997) *Jung on Active Imagination*. (Abingdon, UK: Routledge)

Edelman, G. M. (1993) Neural Darwinism: Selection and Reentrant Signaling in Higher Brain Function – Review In Neuron, Vol. 10, 115–125, February, 1993, Copyright 1993 by Cell Press

Foulkes D. and Fleischer, S. (1975) 'Mental activity in relaxed wakefulness'. *Journal of Abnormal Psychology*, Vol. 84(1), 66–75

Freud, S. (1900/2013) *The Interpretation of Dreams*. (Sunderland, UK: Dead Dodo Vintage), Kindle edition

Jung, C. (1928/1981) 'The relation between the ego and the unconscious' in *The Collected Works of C.G. Jung: Two Essays on Analytical Psychology*, Vol. 7. (Abingdon, UK: Routledge and Kegan Paul)

Kincaid, M. (2017) 'Parallel Distributed Processing Models' in The University of Alberta's Cognitive Science Dictionary. http://penta.ufrgs.br/edu/telelab/3/paralled.htm Parallel Distributed Processing Models

Kripke, D. and Sonnenschein, F. (1978) 'A biological rhythm in waking fantasy' in J. Pope and K. Singer (Eds) *The Stream of Consciousness*. (New York: Plenum Press)

Kussé, C. and Maquet, P. (2012) 'Functional neuroimaging during human sleep' in D. Barrett and P. McNamara (Eds), *Encyclopedia of Sleep and Dreams*. (Westport, CT: Greenwood Publishing), Kindle edition, location 7789–7886

Laplanche, J. and Pontalis, J. (1967/2012) *The Language of Psychoanalysis* (Maresfield Library). (London: Karnac Books), Kindle edition

McClelland J. L. and Rumelhart, D. (1986) 'A distributed model of human learning and memory' in J. L. McClelland and D. Rumelhart, *Parallel Distributed Processing II*. (Cambridge, MA: The MIT Press), pp. 170–215

Perls, F. (1969/2013) *Gestalt Therapy Verbatim*. (Gouldsboro, ME: The Gestalt Journal Press), Kindle edition

Perls, F. *et al*. (1951) *Gestalt Therapy. Excitement and Growth in the Human Personality. Vol. I. Preface*. (New York: Julian Press)

Rumelhart, D. (1980) 'Schemata: the building blocks of cognition' in R. J. Spiro, B. C. Bruce and W. F. Brewer (Eds), *Theoretical Issues in Reading Comprehension*. (Hillsdale, NJ: Lawrence Erlbaum Associates) pp. 35–58

Rumelhart, D. and Zipser, D. (1986) 'Feature discovery by competitive learning' in D. Rumelhart and J. L. McClelland, Parallel Distributed Processing, Vol. 1: Explorations in the Microstructure of Cognition Volume Foundations. (Cambridge, MA: The MIT Press), pp. 151–194

Smolensky, P. (1986) 'Information processing in dynamical systems. Foundations of harmony theory' in J. McClelland and D. Rumelhart (Eds), *Explorations in the Microstructure of Cognition: Psychological and Biological Models*, Vol. II. (Cambridge, MA: The MIT Press), pp. 194–281

Stern, D. (2010) *Forms of Vitality*. (Oxford: Oxford University Press)

Tart, C. (1983) *States of Consciousness*. (El Cerrito, CA: Psychological Processes Inc.)

Vedfelt, O. (2000) 'Consciousness: Introduction to Cybernetic Psychology' *Energy & Character: International Journal of Biosynthesis – Somatic Psychotherapy* (Part 1, April, pp. 38–55; Part 2, August, pp. 42–61)

Vedfelt, O. (2000a) *Unconscious Intelligence. You Know More Than You Think*. (Copenhagen: Gyldendal)

Vedfelt, O. (2004) *Dreams as Unconscious Intelligence: A Cybernetic Theory*. Conference paper, invited presentation for the Annual Conference of International Association for the Study of Dreams, Copenhagen

Wackerhausen, S. (1998) *The Scholastic Paradigm and Apprenticeship*. Working paper no.2. Aarhus: Network for Non-scholastic Learning, Aarhus University, pp. 1–24

Chapter 9

Core Quality 6

Dreams are Pattern Recognition

Unconscious intelligence functions as a network of flexible patterns that reflect how the world is experienced in shifting contexts. These patterns realign many varying impressions and are models or schema for typical ways of behavior and experience. They may be developmental patterns, patterns in relationships to others, in thoughts and feelings, and in behavior. They are our unconscious theories about ourselves and the world.

In every given situation this system encounters, it seeks the inner scheme/program that best aligns with a whole picture of the situation. When a sufficient number of characteristics match, the system firmly locks in an interpretation and acts according to that pattern until something else is proven. This system thrives on incomplete information. It moves through the world with a continuous process of interpretation, and automatically fills gaps in knowledge with comprehensive experience learned by practice as to how the human world normally operates (Campbell 1989).

In practical waking life, the time needed to reason and argue logically about each decision before taking action is not available. Instead, our network seeks out patterns most likely to suit situations in our daily lives. 'Goodness-of-fit' is network-speak for the degree to which internal patterns match given situations. The degree of adaptation – 'the goodness-of-fit' – between the schema and the incoming data can be depicted as a three-dimensional rolling landscape. Taut, rigid schemas create sharp peaks in 'the goodness space', while fluid schemas produce softer hills and valleys. In rigid schemas, information coheres so closely that it is hard to activate parts of the schema without activating the whole. That is when we think we have gathered enough evidence for an interpretation. The more fluid the schema, the weaker the ties between the individual units (Smolensky 1986; McClelland *et al.* 1986). This is when we keep our minds open for alternative interpretations.

In practical life when enough features match, the psyche will latch on to an interpretation and act on this pattern until proven otherwise. The psyche is comfortable with insufficient information. It interprets its way forward and automatically fills in gaps with knowledge, which is based on extensive experience of how things normally function.

A rich variety of personal experiences, acquired cultural conventions and inherited human characteristics create a large enough probability that we will be able to function in many different contexts even though we are not truly conscious of how we do it.

The results of this work are presented to us in dreams. If we wish to benefit from them, we must align ourselves with the patterns they reveal to us. The network is 'context sensitive', (Smolensky, 1986 p. 202) that means we must look for situations that resemble dream patterns in our waking lives in the outer world (the objective level). Yet dream patterns reveal the inner criteria of the network that we are not aware of in waking life (the subjective level and interpretation).

Context of Dreams

Our inner network is closely bound to the world around us and constantly relates to the context in which it finds itself. In other words, it is 'context sensitive'.

In principle, that context encompasses the entire life history of each individual. Each of the dream schools have specialized in matching dream patterns with their own specific aspect of the context as, for example, Freud with childhood experiences, Jung with future developmental potentials, and Calvin Hall with current behavior. In all three dimensions of time, we can research whether any overlap exists between the experience of the dream and the dreamer's life. For practical reasons we can divide the various dimensions of time into the following categories:

1   close events and 'day-residues';
2   current life situations in a broader sense, including personal relationships;
3   life stories and relationship patterns in childhood;
4   the dreamer's age and life-phase;
5   future transitions and life-phases.

Day-Residues and Recent Events

Dreams usually contain two types of impressions from the day prior to the dream. Our understanding of how these impressions function has been evolving for more than 100 years.

Based on his clinical research, Freud divided day-residues into two groups: "Indifferent" impressions that recurred in manifest dreams, and "freshly experienced," significant events that could only be retrieved through painstaking analysis (Freud 1900).

German neurologist Otto Pötzl later demonstrated that individuals who were shown images so rapidly (1/100 of a second) that they could not consciously grasp them, often had dreams where the images appeared. These impressions that did not register in consciousness were likely to appear in dreams. In a systematic study Pötzl asked participants to draw pictures of dreams from the night after being exposed to these rapid images. In one example, a woman was shown an image of a train engine at a station. That night she dreamed *that a man wanted to stab her with a knife. She escaped and fled down a road into a house.* When she drew the road to the house, it looked exactly like a railroad track in perspective, placement and appearance, and the house was remarkably similar to a train engine. In this and other examples, the themes of the dreams were fundamentally different from the images. The details provided functioned more like stage props than meaningful day-residues in their own right. Therefore, Pötzl postulated that material was organized by the unconscious in other ways than by the consciousness (Pötzl 1917, pp. 48–49).

Pötzl's discoveries have been re-examined by psychoanalysts who combined laboratory experiments with psychoanalytical studies. They found that unconscious impressions are often most easily recalled when consciousness is relaxed, such as during free-association, hypnosis, visualization and in creative states. The ability to recall these impressions was found to be greatest in sensitive individuals who possessed psychological insight and empathetic ability (Shevrin *et al.* 1958; Fischer 1960).

Michael Schredl, in an overview of more recent research, emphasizes that sensitive individuals with "thin boundaries" and emotional involvement in waking experiences have increased probability of incorporating day-residues in dreams. Dreams in the latter part of the night are comprised of elements from the more distant past, while dreams of the first part of the night mostly incorporate recent, daytime experiences (Schredl 2012). Dreams are almost never intact replays of concrete waking episodes. A systematic study of 299 dream reports found that participants' sleep mentation reports reflected aspects of recent waking life experiences relatively often (65 percent), while only 1–2 percent of dreams were complete replicas of waking episodes (Fosse *et al.* 2003).

The Neuropsychological Perspective

From a neuropsychological perspective, the thalamus is the most important relay for communication between various areas of the brain. The thalamus sends some of the information we receive in waking life along a slow route to the cortex where it can be remembered consciously with relative ease. This is insignificant day-residue. Emotionally significant day-residue, we must assume, is sent along a rapid route to areas of the emotional brain (see Chapter 2). Since Freud, it has been a general experience in psychodynamic dream work that the emotionally significant day-residue can be identified and connected to the dreamer's recent emotional concerns. Yet, it may require analytical and experiential skills as well as a global understanding of the dream context before you find the goodness of fit.

As described in Chapter 2 on contemporary theories of dream memory, Dutch researcher E. van Rijn demonstrated that significant events are also incorporated into REM sleep dreams five to seven nights after these events, the so-called dream-lag effect. It has been suggested that this effect is to consolidate memory (Van Rijn and Eichenlaub 2015). The possible dream-lag effect should also be kept in mind in the dreamwork.

A generally accepted view is that this is an expression of the importance of dreams in long-term memory, especially when it comes to the dreamlag effect is of importance for the storage of emotionally significant events in long-term memory, (McNamara 2016).

Tangible External Events Consciously Recalled

In dreams, external events are used like stage props but acquire a deeper significance than they possess in waking consciousness. For instance, Michael dreams that the lights have gone out in his house. He connects this with a "mental blackout" he had during a quarrel with his wife the prior day. In fact, there had been a larger power failure in Copenhagen that previous day but none of my other clients in the area had dreamed about it.

Emotionally Important Events

These are incidents from previous days that we are not conscious of and that reveal themselves through closer examination.

Victor dreams *of a nice, finely laid table. Axel sits to the right of his usual place. He looks very hurt. A woman has taken 'his' place.* Victor says that, in waking life, Axel is known for often feeling unfairly hurt to the point of ridiculousness. Victor has had no interaction with Axel for a long time and no unfinished business with him. This makes it likely that Axel represents an aspect within Victor.

Victor cannot recall a situation where he felt hurt like that. A systematic examination of what had transpired the previous day put us on the track of a close, significant event. He visited a workplace that he often frequents in his work as a consultant. Victor occasionally meets an ex-girlfriend there, who broke up with him. He feels she treated him unfairly and tries to avoid her, even though she greets him with friendliness whenever their paths cross. Through his dream, he understands that his feelings – due to having been dumped – are more hurt than is reasonable.

Current Life Situation in a Broader Sense

As opposed to day-residues, current life situations encompass larger sections of time. For instance, I have already stated that the dreams of pregnant women focus especially on the dreamers' unique situations, and that traumatic experiences echo in dreams long after they take place. All other important events, such as starting school, getting married or changing jobs, are also commented on in dreams. Therefore, it is relevant to ask yourself, "What has especially grabbed my attention lately? What interests have I been occupied with? What do I experience as troublesome? Are there any acute crises?"

In Victor's case, it turned out that his feelings for his ex-girlfriend were referring to a current life situation in a broader sense. In a later dream Victor is: *alone in an area where I have sheltered myself, and which I am ready to defend against an unspecified threat.*

Victor does not initially understand which "unspecified threat" he has set himself against but, again, it becomes apparent that he visited the workplace where he risked running into his ex-girlfriend. During that visit he had the same emotional experience as in his dream – feeling alone and protecting himself from being hurt. His ex-girlfriend had not been there, but his expectation of her presence had activated an internal pattern of emotions and ways of reacting that were pointed out in the dream. He understood that he was not over the break-up, and that he needed to change his attitude if he was not to get caught up in his own hurt feelings.

Life History and Relational Patterns in Childhood

One of the cornerstones of the theories and fundamental understandings of the schools of psychoanalysis is that dreams contain important information about the histories of our lives and our relationship patterns in childhood. This is also recognized by Jungian therapists, existential dream researchers such as Medard Boss, and cognitive therapists with clinical experience. Objections to 'digging' into childhood histories are primarily about the regressive nature that dreamwork may take, which can pull dreamers into unproductive imaginary worlds rather than maintaining focus on themes and conflicts playing out in the here and now.

Yet I maintain that autobiographical aspects need not be in conflict with the here and now, but can, instead, be complementary. The circumstances and conditions we experience in childhood form our personalities in ways that have consequences for the rest of our lives. Dreams provide important information about our earlier relationships that may be forgotten, suppressed or have received inadequate priority.

We have already seen an example of the spontaneous retrieval of childhood memories in connection with Laura's dreamwork, and described its relation to brain networks (Core Quality 2). Just as dreams are never complete replays of waking episodes from the previous day's events, contemporary research confirms that autobiographical memory in dreams never reflects whole episodes from waking life (Horton and Malinowski 2015). Autobiographical memory seemingly integrates elements from various significant experiences into dream narratives, serving a higher purpose than simply replicating the more trivial incidences of waking life.

As an example of a clear reference to a childhood memory, I will recount a dream from 50-year-old Henrik who participated in a one-year course during weekends. Henrik dreams that *he is with his father. His father shows him a red sports car and tells him that he can have it. Henrik gets in the car, but it turns out that the key is broken, so he cannot move forward.* Henrik recalls that when he was seven years old, he ardently wished for a red toy car he had seen in a shop. His father promised to give it to him but in the end he got a small, cheap, plastic car very different from the much larger, shining and more elaborate one he had seen in the shop window.

Henrik feels this was a very emotionally significant childhood event. It somehow epitomizes his father's character. His father was a charming but unreliable man, and Henrik can look back on a long series of broken promises and disappointed expectations. He thinks this fits well with the image of having received a broken key to a cool car.

The car in Henrik's dream was an adult car. He is reminded of important occasions in his adult life where he experienced that his superiors and co-workers promised more than they could give, reflecting the same pattern he had with his father. These situations often led to dramatic breaks where Henrik had to use a great deal of time and energy on matters that could not be won, while the rest of his work life stagnated, similar to what happened when he got into the car in his dream. 'Objectively,' he can see that he is about to get mixed up in a similar situation again.

After rather extensive work with the feelings and images in his dream, Henrik admits that he may have some unrealistic expectations of what life can offer. Perhaps he is seducing himself to jump into 'cool' projects that must necessarily disappoint and thereby confirm his negative view of the world and other people.

After his dreamwork Henrik put a stop to an impending conflict and then turned his attention to more productive tasks.

Studies of Earliest Remembered Dreams

A type of dream of particular interest to our understanding of how early patterns in childhood can carry through to adult life is our earliest remembered dreams. Most adults, no matter what age we are, can remember a few dreams from childhood. Just the fact that they are imprinted on our memories with such sustainability suggests that they have special meanings.

Extensive questionnaire studies reveal that the earliest remembered dreams by adults are typically from the ages of 3–7, but some people can remember dreams from as early as ages 1–2 (Nielsen *et al*. 2003). Freud maintained that the earliest childhood dreams reveal to the greatest extent the character of the unconscious because they are not muddied by defense mechanisms. In his famous *Children's Dreams* seminar, Jung interpreted the archetypal aspects of childhood dreams recalled by adults (Jung 1938–9). A systematic Jungian study by Yehezkiel Kluger has later shown that over half the earliest remembered dreams can be classified as "archetypal," meaning they have universal themes (Kluger 1955).

An extensive study by Kelly Bulkeley suggests that these dreams are experienced, as a rule, as intense and vivid. Therefore, they are assumed to facilitate an exploration of salient aspects of the dreamer's early emotional life. Like in the Jungian study, recalled childhood dreams were found to have "an obvious symbolic connection to religious and mythological themes around the world" (Bulkeley *et al*. 2005, p. 217). Another investigation found that earliest remembered dreams were four times more likely to be nightmares and 2.6 times more likely to be recurrent dreams when compared with more recently remembered dreams (Gupta and Hill 2013).

Examples of Earliest Remembered Dreams

For many years I have paid particular attention to earliest remembered dreams and systematically explored them in therapeutic and educational groups. Under these circumstances, most people are able to find a meaning in them, thus rendering them worthy of contemplation. This process can be facilitated by training metaphorical perception and deepened through therapeutic work.

People without training will often tell about recurrent dreams in a casual way as if they are monotonously similar. Yet if you elaborate dreams and associate with them, details often appear providing meaning both in relationship to a dream's point in time and behavior patterns at that time.

During a workshop, 50-year-old Laila recounted a recurring dream from her earliest years at primary school:

> she had to cross a road between her home and school. Halfway across the street, a car came speeding towards her. She flattened herself on the ground – completely rigid – so the car could drive over without hurting her. Then she discovered the car had a metal rod that stuck down from the undercarriage. Just in the nick of time, she managed to roll up on her side, turning away from the rod and thereby avoiding it.

I suggested that she lie down and try to make herself as rigid as she was in her dream. Then she remembered how she had been scared stiff with anxiety when she had to walk from home to school because she had fallen victim to bullying. She tried turning over on her side as in her dream and this brought her a great sense of relief. She suddenly thought about how, back then, she avoided anxiety by deciding not to get involved with the other people.

Forty years later, she could recognize a lifelong pattern of anxiety and avoidance of relating to groups of people. Unnecessarily, this pattern had cut her off from available social groups.

Earliest remembered dreams contain a great variety of material. These dreams may be abstract without clearly defined settings, can totally lack recognizable characters and even lack a well-defined ego. They may, however, be close to realistic and personified life situations. Under any circumstances they can represent important patterns of past experience so fundamental that they still affect the individual.

In my dream groups I've experienced that most people can remember one or two childhood dreams when some motivation has been built up. Exercising metaphorical thinking opens up the potential and value of seeing the connection between lifelong fundamental themes and childhood dreams.

Below is a selection from these dream groups. Participants were asked to write down one or two childhood dreams, reflect on the meaning of their dreams together with another participant and then write a very brief commentary together.

A 35-year-old designer, Pauline, remembers two dreams from when she was approximately 5–10 years old. Dream one: *A large grid of squares and I'm a little figure in the corner of one square. It feels confined and I'm dizzy. I experienced the grid as all the expectations from the adults: mama, papa, my teacher at school, my aunties, uncles and cousins. I'd been kind of forced into a confined space. Now, it's more about my own expectations and demands.*

Dream two: *A figure made of sand but the sand is coming loose on the front. More sand keeps being added. There is no flesh and blood, no core: the sand figure is falling apart. When I let go of my many expectations and demands, it's important that I can sense I'm real and not a sand figure which easily dissolves – a true self, not a false self.*

Bruce musician, age 40: "I walk on the rainbow bridge that connects Midgard to Asgard. I fall off the edge but I'm caught by a black safety net. I want to get back up on the rainbow but cannot get there." [In Norse mythology Midgard is the place where the humans live and Asgard is the home of the gods.] "This dream was from when I went to school for the first time. I'd probably been living in a protected, imaginary world – I lost something playful and spiritual. The safety net could have been the support I got from home, especially my mother. Today, how I use my imagination, and creativity is important so that I don't fall back into safe routines."

Kristina, psychiatrist, chief physician in a youth psychiatric department, now 55 years' old. Dream one: *I'm lying on a table in the 'living room' and I'm a living corpse. I saw myself as Sleeping Beauty, dead on a bed. I guess I was the good girl who had to be in the 'living room'.*

Dream two: *I'm being chased by boys down a corridor in the basement. I'm scared. These threatening boys probably represent something wild and angry in me that there was no room for in my family and had to remain on a more unconscious level. It's taken many years of working with myself to bring my femininity to life and develop my wilder sides into helpers.*

Age and Approaching Life Phase

Throughout life we are unconsciously preparing for future developments. Our dreams are often a step ahead of us and seem to be providing advice for attaining inner growth potential and developing social skills.

In accordance with the principles of self-organization, constant pressure from within encourages us to enter new life stages. This presupposes a systematic search for information that can be stored in memory systems, either unconsciously or only partly available to the ego. At certain crucial points in life, when windows of opportunity are created in the environment, this information becomes available to be reshaped in new forms. In these processes, dreams are at the forefront of development, expressing this through symbols, characters and patterns of behavior. (Vedfelt 2004).

Daniel Stern has described this in relation to child development: "Development occurs in leaps and bounds; qualitative shifts may be one of its most obvious features." He writes: "Parents, pediatricians, psychologists, psychiatrists, and neuroscientists all agree that new integrations arrive in quantum leaps." In the first two years of life, Stern finds documentation for four "quantum leaps in whatever level of organization one wishes to examine, from electroencephalographic recordings to overt behavior to subjective experience. Between these periods of rapid change are periods of relative quiescence, when the new integrations appear to consolidate." Other researchers have investigated the transition to verbal language, the oedipal conflict, sibling rivalries, cognitive progress, and development in imaginative skills at the ages of 4–7 years. Then come the tweens, puberty, entering adulthood with professional life and creating a family.

Even after all this, development continues. An understanding of transitional phases and development by leaps and bounds at a mature age was already proposed by Jung. He saw these transformations of the whole personality during the great transitions of life as core qualities of being human. Jung attempted to map out, so to speak, development from within by examining universal, archetypal symbols for the transitions between the various developmental phases. He expressed this first in his groundbreaking work, *Symbols of Transformation* (Jung 1911–12), and continued doing so throughout his working life. A significant portion of his work in this consisted of comparing the symbolisms in myths, fairytales, rites of initiation and religious beliefs, with the symbols of modern human beings expressed through creativity, fantasies and – not least – dreams. Among Jung's successors, Erich Neumann is especially noteworthy with his descriptions of the inner symbolism in the early phases of development (Neumann 1963, 1973, 1973a).

Robert Hoss (2012) has summarized the results of brain research supporting Jung's understanding of the roles dreams play in ongoing processes of individuation. He highlights particularly the dream-active network in the midline forebrain (anterior cingulate cortex and the medial prefrontal cortex) as responsible for goal-oriented problem solving based on past experience and imagined outcomes. In Edelmanns theory of neuronal selection in the brain during development (chapter 4) there is an adaptive build-up of networks of nerve cells and an epigenetic build-up from within. The adaptive influence on the network is a parallel to the environments influence on inner relationship patterns, the epigenetic changes in the networks corresponds largely to my concept of self-organization.

Age-Related and Prospective Dream Interpretations

Fritz's dream where he was pursued by an adult (Core Quality 3) was interpreted as referring to being burdened with the responsibility of an adult role too early in life. In the dream recounted below, a small boy is about to face a new phase in his development but struggles with stepping into the transition.

Big Decision for a Three-Year-Old Boy

Sam is standing at the edge of a forest. A large man wearing a blue cap comes out of the forest. He cleaves Sam from behind with a sword.

Sam was crying when he awoke. The man was unknown. The blue cap looked like a police cap. The forest was dark and eerie.

In many fairytales the forest is the home of magical and dangerous beings, such as the witch in *Hansel and Gretel* and the wolf in *Little Red Riding Hood*. According to Sam, a policeman was the one who decided what he could or could not do.

In their dreams, as recent systematic research shows, children are much more likely to be victims of aggression than adults – aggression most often committed by men or monsters (Nielsen 2012). Dreams of this intensity must have backstories.

Sam slept well and did not have bad dreams for a long period of time. He lived in safe and secure surroundings. He was an only child with caring parents and he was healthy, smart and well-liked at preschool.

However, one event stood out from Sam's routines: the day before his dream, he agreed to say a final goodbye to his pacifier that he had still used to comfort himself in certain situations. Sam's parents had conducted a small ceremony, serving his favorite cake and presenting him with a gift he had wanted a long time.

The psychological function of pacifiers as mothering substitutes is well-known. British child psychiatrist Donald Winnicott calls them transitional objects. They function as internal objects, substituting for mother's breast and even her whole being, thus aiding children's development toward greater independence, yet only as a small step down that road (Winnicott 1971).

Calvin Hall and Van de Castle classified "cutting, stabbing of the dreamer's body" as castration anxiety (Hall and Van de Castle 1965). In psychoanalytical theory, this is especially seen in boys of Sam's age in connection with the Oedipus Complex. In Erich Neumann's psychology, an adult man represents a transition from matriarchate to patriarchate – from motherly to a fatherly inner world. In these traditions, transitions are connected to willpower and self-discipline processes within the child, which fits the developmental stage Sam was experiencing.

Stated more simply, Sam agreed to go through a 'rite of passage' into a new phase in his life. The effects of this were more 'violent' than expected and we can postulate that he felt split by his big decision (Vedfelt 2003).

Understanding the meaning of Sam's dream came as a great relief to his parents because it did not refer to anything pathological, but rather a normal phenomenon in a child's development. At the same time, Sam's dream suggested that a very strong, inner, masculine force was at work. Sam was allowed to hang on to his pacifier a little while longer and gradually surrendered it at his own volition during the subsequent six months.

Long-Term Predictions in Dreams

Based on a mechanical, will-controlled method, if you try to align seemingly negative or eccentric behavior to behavior you find more appropriate for the individual's age or your own ideas of normality, you may interfere with a high level of Self-organization that needs more time to unfold some unconventional individual skills or special talents.

In some strange way, the process level is proportional over time, and therapy can be experienced as a kind of time machine – the higher the process level we enter into, the more we are able to view into the future. Stated somewhat less mystifyingly, higher process levels contain potentialities that take more time to realize. Here is an example.

A caring parent couple was concerned about their 14-year-old daughter Ida's precocious and experimenting relationship to life.

Ida told me that, in her dreams, *she often had Walt Disney's wacky inventor Gyro Gearloose's Little Helper with his blinking light bulb head as her faithful companion.* Moreover, she related a dream in which *she traveled through many strange cities and always found her way by following a red thread.* She associated these cities with artistic activity and she was intensely interested in this type of activity from a very early age.

In therapy she was creative, had a quick mind and an ability to view issues from surprisingly interesting angles. When I talked with her about things that she was truly interested in, Ida demonstrated wisdom beyond her years.

I regarded her clear and uncomplicated dreams as expressions of a higher level process referring to particular talents that could foster a future career as an artist. The red thread leading through unfamiliar territory was an expression of continuity in her somewhat unorthodox life. I was able to reassure Ida's parents.

Several years later, after receiving education in foreign metropolises, Ida actually became successful and was recognized as an artist. Since then, I had the opportunity to follow her 25-year career from a distance and I am able to confirm that she creates original art valuable to society. Also, I have valid information from other sources that she has a sensible, down-to-earth family life.

Age and Symbol Meaning

The meaning of symbols may be dependent on the dreamer's age. Fertility symbols, for instance, may appear in the dreams of young women and also in those of women who have gone through menopause. Yet the significance of these symbols is completely different. For young women they may refer to a preparation of their minds for biological fertility and, for older women, they may be a symbol of spiritual fertility. Age and life-phase also play crucial roles in interpretation in many other ways. For example, as a rule, your ability to relate to your dreams on an inner level improves as you mature in life.

Forty-five-year-old Anne dreamed that *she was standing in front of a fruit tree on which five big, juicy pears were hanging. She picked them and put the four she wanted to take to the town square to sell in a basket. The fifth one she kept for herself.*

Anne interpreted her dream herself: "The pears represent the fruits of my life. I have four children who are now grown and can take care of themselves. That was the four pears I took to the square so they could be circulated into society. The fifth pear was the fruit of my own personal and professional development, which I am now tasting."

Anne's dream and her interpretation obviously had a 'goodness-of-fit' with a different type of life-phase than Sarah, who is younger and very pregnant (Core Quality 3).

Better Future Energy Distribution

Jack, a 40-year-old father, started therapy after a breakdown where he was suffering from anxiety attacks and often in tears. In the course of his therapy, Jack started a small business parallel to his job. He talked with me a long time of his concerns about whether or not he would succeed. He doubted he is good enough, even though many outer signs and recognition from his surroundings suggested that he would indeed succeed.

Jack dreams: *My stepfather is dead and about to be buried. Afterwards, I'm standing with my wife in our house. She points out that it would be better if we had a more economic distribution of energy in the house. I assign a worker this task. He completes it.*

As a person, Jack's stepfather is a little anxious and neurotic. He is not dead in reality and Jack has no outstanding issues with him currently. We see his death as a transformational symbol – something neurotic and anxious within the dreamer himself has to die to make room for new development.

The scene then moves to Jack's house, which is a symbol of a familiar framework for his self and the life he shares with his wife. His wife plays an important role as the one who creates awareness of the benefits of changing their home's energy distribution, which is psychologically understood as a metaphor for the distribution of the energy in various parts of Jack's mind.

Jack says that his wife is his soulmate. She is a rather calm, down-to-earth and confident person. These are the very qualities within himself that he can potentially integrate. She is also a good role model for creating a small business, and for doing what needs to be done.

Jack's dream is telling him about an opportunity to integrate some of the character traits he attributes to his wife, and also that he has an inner, masculine helper of which he needs to be aware.

No matter if we choose to focus on the present, past or future, we are looking for a 'goodness-of-fit', i.e. the best overlap between dream patterns and our present lives. No ultimate answers are to be found, but rather a likelihood to discover meaning in dreams relevant to the dreamer.

Dreams make us aware of meaningful internal patterns that guide our life at levels beyond conscious understanding.

Dream patterns should be matched with contexts that include dreamers' life histories, current life situations, as well as future developmental opportunities.

References

Bulkeley, K. *et al.* (2005) 'Earliest Remembered Dreams'. *Dreaming*, Vol. 15(3), s. 205–222

Campbell, J. (1989) *The Improbable Machine.* (New York: Simon and Schuster)

Fischer, C. (1960) 'Introduction to Pötzl'. *Psychological Issues*, Vol. II(3), s. 1–40

Fosse, M. J., Fosse, R., Hobson, J. A. and Stickgold, R. J. (2003) 'Dreaming and episodic memory: a functional dissociation?' *Journal of Cognitive Neuroscience*, Jan. 1, 15(1), 1–9

Freud, S. (1900) *The Interpretation of Dreams.* (Sunderland, UK: Dead Dodo Vintage), Kindle edition

Gupta, S. and Hill, C. E. (2013) *Earliest Remembered Dreams versus Recent Remembered Dreams*, Thesis. (Washington, DC: The University of Maryland Libraries)

Hall, C. and Van de Castle, R. (1965) 'An empirical investigation of the castration complex in dreams'. *Journal of Personality*, Vol. 33, s. 20–29

Horton, C. and Malinowski, J. E. (2015) 'Autobiographical memory and hyperassociativity in the dreaming brain: implications for memory consolidation in sleep'. *Frontiers in Psychology*, 6, 874

Hoss, R. J. (2012) 'Jung's transcendent function: neurological support' in D. Barrett and P. McNamara (Eds), *Encyclopedia of Sleep and Dreams.* (Westport, CT: Greenwood Publishing), Kindle edition, location 9832–78

Jung, C. G. (1938–9) *Kinderträume I og II.* (Zürich: Eidgenossische Hochschule)

Jung, C. G. (1911–12/1981) 'Symbols of transformation' in G. Adler, M. Fordham and Sir H. Read (Eds), *The Collected Works of C. G. Jung: Symbols of Transformation*, Vol. 5. (Abingdon, UK: Routledge and Kegan Paul)

Kluger, H. Y. (1955) 'Archetypal dreams and "everyday" dreams'. *Israel's Annals of Psychiatry and Related Disciplines*, Vol. 13, s. 6–47

McClelland, J. L., Rumelhart, D. and Hinton, G. E. (1986) 'The appeal of parallel distributed processing' in D. Rumelhart and J. L. McClelland, *Parallel Distributed Processing, Vol. 1: Explorations in the Microstructure of Cognition Volume Foundations.* (Cambridge, MA: The MIT Press), pp. 3–44

McNamara, P. (2016) 'Are dreams required for memory?' *Psychology Today*, 18 February

Neumann, E. (1963) *The Great Mother.* (Princeton, NJ: Princeton University Press)

Neumann, E. (1973) *The Origins and History of Consciousness.* (Princeton, NJ: Princeton University Press)

Neumann, E. (1973a) *The Child.* (New York: G. P. Putnam's Sons)

Nielsen, T. A. and Zadra, A. *et al.* (2003) 'The typical dreams of Canadian university students'. *Dreaming*, Vol. 13(4), p. 220

Nielsen, T. (2012) 'Characters in dreams' in Barrett, D. and McNamara, P. *Encyclopedia of Sleep and Dreams.* (Westport, CT: Greenwood Publishing), Kindle edition, location 3202–94

Pötzl, O. (1917/1960) 'The relationship between experimentally induced dream images and indirect vision'. *Psychological Issues*, Vol. II(3), No. 3, pp. 41–120

Schredl, M. (2012) 'Continuity hypothesis of dreaming' in D. Barrett and P. McNamara (Eds), *Encyclopedia of Sleep and Dreams* (Westport, CT: Greenwood Publishing), Kindle edition, location 4614–61

Shevrin, H. *et al.* (1958) 'The Measurement of Preconscious Perception: An Investigation of the Poetzl Phenomenon'. *Journal of Abnormal Psychology*, 56, 285–294

Smolensky, P. (1986) 'Information processing in dynamical systems: Foundations of Harmony Theory' in D. Rumelhart and J. L. McClelland, *Parallel Distributed Processing Vol. 2: Explorations in the Microstructure of Cognition Volume Foundations.* (Cambridge, MA: The MIT Press), pp. 194–281

Van Rijn, E. and Eichenlaub, J. B. (2015) 'The dream-lag effect: selective processing of personally significant events during rapid eye movement sleep, but not during slow wave sleep'. *Neurobiology of Learning and Memory*, July, Vol. 122, pp. 98–109

Vedfelt, O. (2003) *The Man and His Inner Women.* (Copenhagen: Gyldendal)

Vedfelt, O. (2004) *Dreams as Unconscious Intelligence: A Cybernetic Theory.* Conference paper, Keynote Presentation for the Annual Conference of International Association for the Study of Dreams, Copenhagen

Winnicott, D. W. (1971) *Playing and Reality.* (London: Tavistock)

Chapter 10

Core Quality 7

Dreams are High-Level Communication

Unconscious intelligence has systems that actively seek dialogue with consciousness through dreams. Since dreams have self-organizing functions and because they deal with matters important to us, they will provide feedback if dreamers relate to their lives in ways that fit with the level of advanced self-regulation.

For instance, the attitude of the waking self can be a goal-oriented and conscious effort to change inappropriate structures of experience and thought that interfere with an individual's life. This is not just a matter of willpower, it is a form of conscious practice where dreamers spend time and energy on being attentive to disturbing thoughts, fantasies and behaviors whenever they might appear.

Ella, a 70-year-old woman, worried about growing old and was haunted by thoughts about her ten-year-older husband's illness. For some time she was almost obsessed with the idea of death and had trouble feeling happy about anything – nothing lasted forever. I suggested she sharpen her awareness of her internal thought patterns. Each time she discovered thoughts about death preoccupying her consciousness, she was to actively stop them and turn her thoughts to the positive matters that were also a part of her life.

Greatly motivated, Ella followed my advice. After some nights she dreamed:

> *I visited my brother-in-law. An apple that he had once given me, but which I lost at the time, was rediscovered lying in a dark corner (I had actually gotten an apple from my brother-in-law a year earlier and, at that time, forgotten it in my jacket pocket where I rediscovered it dried out, shriveled and brown six months later). In the dream, the apple was not shriveled: quite the contrary, it had remained in the dark corner absorbing moisture. I picked the apple up. It had grown, was fresh and beautifully red.*

She had mentally managed to find the level of the dream. Ella's dream seemed to be patting her on the back saying, "You're on the right path." The dream motivated her to continue the practice and overcome the obsessive thoughts.

Feedback from dreams on important decisions depends on whether the decisions are taken seriously. As an example I can mention an author who had finished a book and put the manuscript in an envelope to post to the publisher the following day. That night he dreamed: "I was playing in a soccer match and scored seven goals. But the last one was in my own goal." He suspected that this referred to his latest book, which had seven chapters. He quickly sent the book to some competent friends before sending it to the publisher. It turned out that the seventh chapter was superfluous and did more harm than good. The feedback from the dream was not just negative – it gave a constructive idea of how the book could be improved.

If you want to receive such answers through dreams you have to be so deeply involved in a project that enough energy can be accumulated to fuel your dreams. Anecdotal knowledge exists about famous scientists and artists who have been inspired by dreams to write literature and music. These were all deeply devoted individuals who had struggled with creative themes for the longest possible time (Barrett 2001).

In the case of the author above, he had been busy with this project for a long time and still had an uneasy gut feeling that he could not put into words despite all his efforts. Therefore, a large quantity of goal-oriented, mental energy had been accumulated that was strong enough to provoke an answer from his unconscious intelligence.

Other important situations in life where dreams may provide feedback are when you are choosing education or work, entering into a couple's relationship, having children, etc. What is crucial is that you – with an honest heart – put all your energy into the decision. If you dare not take the first steps and wait for dreams to make the decision for you, then you will simply dream about indecision in some symbolic form.

Decisions about using consciousness in new ways and new spiritual values can also be commented on by dreams. Mie had started going to a dream and mediation group as part of a decision to become more conscious of what she wanted for her life. During the course she dreamed: *I am standing in an unknown house. Some people come flying down and throw money in the windows. I touch the money. It has different shapes and colors – some are triangular and others spherical, etc.* She commented on her dream by saying that her meditations were like "gifts from above." Mie's meditative awareness of inner states had been so colorful and sensual that – like the money in her dream – she felt she "really could pick up and touch them." She admitted she had been skeptical at first because meditation seemed to her to be so abstract – something she could never learn. She had feared she was "throwing money out the window." Her dream told her the opposite was true; material money could be exchanged for spiritual experiences and values.

It is my experience that dreams cannot be manipulated by ego. As previously described, ego represents only a small part of the personality. The lion's share of the information that the entire organism is digesting is done so unconsciously. Dreams have a connection with a more comprehensive personality than does the waking consciousness. They are links in the efforts to create more overriding balance in the personality. They cannot be controlled by superficial wishes and needs. Quite the contrary, if you try to manipulate them, they will reveal that manipulation to you.

This is apparent in the following example with Ingelise, a woman who had just started therapy with me. During our initial conversation, Ingelise recounted this dream she had the previous night: *She had been to the doctor's, but when he asked her for her insurance card, she had given him a fake one.* "You came to me as a kind of doctor of the soul," I said. "What do you think about going to the doctor with a false identity?" My question surprised her. She blushed and sat in silence a long time. Then she said, "It seems that dreams don't lie." She then told me that her intention had been to get me to interpret her dreams so that she could publish them as her own ideas.

Since dreams are a part of the overriding self-regulation of the personality, they open up deeper explanations of why we are trying to cheat ourselves. In Ingelise's case, her false identity went deeper than that particular situation with me. Her continued work with her dreams revolved around why she felt, on a more fundamental level, that she had to present a fake identity to get help.

Ongoing Communication between Dreams and the Waking Self

If you observe the dreams of one person for a longer period of time, it will become easier to see that their dreams are communicating on a level higher than everyday hectic consciousness. They underscore general patterns of behavior and experience found behind current daily events.

Anders is a 30-year-old physician. He is a friendly person and competent professional, yet he is dissatisfied that he has not been recognized at a level that matches his abilities. He feels periodically listless and depressive. One night he dreams that he is *talking to his boss. While they are talking, a threatening biker guy enters the room. Anders hurries out.* The day before the dream Anders actually had a meeting with his boss who then appeared in his dream. Anders said that the meeting was "no trouble." Still, he shakes his head.

During role-playing, Anders played some of other people in his dream. He portrayed his boss as well-spoken and rather grandiose. When he portrayed the biker he felt like "punching his boss in the face," yet, when he returned to his role as Anders, he thought the issue had been blown out of proportion and wanted to stop role-playing.

Afterwards, Anders could see that his desire to stop role-playing corresponded with when he hurried out of the door in his dream. In many ways his boss was a "nice guy," but it was exactly that niceness that made it possible to manipulate Anders into taking on some rather boring routine work that did not provide the professional development to which he was entitled. When he began to consciously stand up for himself in relationship to his boss, it turned out his boss was more cooperative than expected.

A few weeks later he dreamed *that a male head doctor criticizes him. He becomes irritated, but bites his tongue.* It turned out that the day before this dream Anders had felt I had been negative about something he had said. He felt it was too petty to mention. We had a dialogue about it and I found he was actually right in his judgment. This was a relief to him. In a third dream *a captain is scolding an aggressive sailor while Anders passively looks on.* In a fourth *there was an angry caretaker chasing some boys who are running away.* In a fifth *his father tries to persuade him to take a job he does not want. Anders is passive, but a friend insults his father.* In a sixth *a wise old man refuses to give him a diamond.*

In most of these dreams we found corresponding situations where Anders felt he was being dominated, manipulated or went unrecognized, and where he felt his reaction to this had not been optimal.

His dreams reflected variations in relation to the individual situations, yet they also showed a continual and overriding pattern of how Anders perceives the world. The overriding pattern behind all these conflicts was a three-way drama between a manipulating male authority, an aggressive and anarchistic impulse which was personified, and his dream self as a passive, conflict-avoiding main character. At times, the authority figure in the dream was the same person Anders was in conflict with in his waking life. But mostly the dream-authorities were other people.

As his dreamwork progressed Anders became better able to identify these typical situations and then get the recognition to which he was entitled. His depressive state eased simultaneously. His dreams revealed a general pattern that Anders used as the basis for interpreting situations in the outer world. At the very moment someone appeared who looked like an authority, Anders' pattern peaked somewhat sharply in his psychological landscape. This peak attracted all the associations and therefore shut down the ability to see other possibilities.

The task at hand for Anders consisted of reflecting on his reaction patterns to relevant situations and testing his interpretation of the external world. Then the head doctor in his dreams stopped criticizing him. Characters such as angry captains and aggressive sailors appeared less often. Caretaker-like figures became kinder and wise old men in various symbolic forms helped him find what he sought.

Proactive Dreams and High-Level Transitions in Young People

In modern societies the age of transitioning from childhood into adult life is considerably delayed when compared with that of indigenous peoples. However, young men – and also young women – are under pressure to deal with these high-level changes and this is expressed in their dreams. I will demonstrate this with a dream series from a young man named Peter and with other examples from women.

The Initial Dream of a Young Man – Peter

As a rule, in connection with important life transitions, one or more dreams will present themselves that provide particularly representative images of the dreamer's most pressing problems. Dreams that arrive later in the process often point out more particular aspects and issues. Introductory or initial dreams can be crystal-clear and symbolic in their make-up, yet often dreamers only derive a few superficial associations from them. Still, the forms in which their symbols appear provide very central information about the states dreamers experience and about their future opportunities for development. Initial dreams brought into psychotherapy often have these qualities. Freud, Jung and a number of other pioneers of dream analysis have been unified in their observations about initial dreams (Schultz 1969; Vedfelt 2000). We can understand them as proactive, high-level communication from our dreams to our waking selves.

Peter was a young man in his late-twenties. In his first therapy session he said he was engaged to marry a young woman whom he really did not feel was the right one, yet he could not end the relationship. His fiancée was a little older than Peter and ready to start a family. In a way, he was of an age and in a phase in life where men usually enter love relationships that lead to partnership and eventually to creating a family.

Peter had had several lovers, especially during the latter part of his engagement, but even though these relationships had been discovered, his fiancée still did not initiate a break with him. After he had made his first therapy appointment with me he broke up with his fiancée – he hoped that therapy would somehow help him to work through the guilt feelings that his choice left him with, and also because he had strung her along for such a long time.

Peter's initial dream in therapy was that

> *a fat, elderly female physiotherapist makes intimate advances. He finds her physically repulsive, but lets her lick and masturbate him while he remains passive. The dream scenario shifts and he has sexual intercourse in his car with a beautiful and slim, young woman. The young woman has bought tickets to a kind of honeymoon journey. It annoys him because now it will become public knowledge and that makes him feel tied down.*

Analysis of Peter's Initial Dream

I will concentrate on the function of Peter's dream as an initial dream and, therefore, make a systematic analysis for a didactic purpose, which is not the same as the empathetic meeting required for dreamwork.

The Narrative Structure

The narrative structure unfolds in three parts. In the first part, the dream self is subjected to inappropriate advances from an older woman. His feeling is one of repulsion, yet he does not refuse the woman. In the second part, Peter is an active participant in the events. It is his own car. The feelings are pleasure, excitement and satisfaction. In the third part, the figure of the dreamer is passive once again while the woman is active. The feelings are annoyance and a more complex mix of emotions which, in this case, consists of sorrow, anger and revulsion. Apart from this, however, he is still attracted to the young woman.

The Dream Characters

Besides the figure of the dreamer, the characters are unknown. There are no objectively important people from his waking life represented.

The First Associations

The elderly female physiotherapist makes Peter think of an older female therapist who had talked a great deal about herself instead of listening to what Peter had sought treatment for. Repulsion is something he may actually feel in relationship to this elderly woman who talked and talked about herself without listening to him. He characterized the woman he had intercourse with as a slim classic beauty who was the type he has erotic fantasies about in waking life.

Content Analysis

From a formal perspective, this dream is special because men's dreams usually have two men other than the dream self but, in Peter's dream, he was alone with two women (Hall and Domhoff 1963). The car is a central symbol. It often turns up in his dream. Using an interpretation from Calvin Hall suggests that the car, as a metaphor, provides the ego with the ability to move from one place in life to another (Hall 1953).

The older woman is in a caregiver role and at an age that could make her his mother. She can thus be categorized as a mother figure, which naturally raises questions about Peter's relationship to his own mother. Peter explains that he has a close and loving relationship to a good and caring mother. Nothing about the older woman in his dream reminds Peter of his mother. Besides, he had a good, secure childhood and he cannot understand how he had ended up in the situation he was in. The young woman in the dream is clearly different from the mother figure. She is not quite as far along in age and maturity as his fiancée.

Amplification of the Female Figures

At first glance, Peter's dream appears fairly banal, but amplification reveals some other layers. Erich Neumann describes in his book, *The Great Mother*, how the feminine as a phenomenon has usually been described and depicted in art and culture. He makes a distinction between two fundamental forms of the feminine in both old and new civilizations around the world. One is a maternal aspect (the elementary character) that is symbolized by voluptuous, motherly, female forms. This symbolically represents the static, secure, material aspect of the feminine. The therapist in Peter's dream matches this.

The other aspect is the "transformative character" representing the dynamic, soulful, imaginative and inspiring aspect of the feminine (Neumann 1963 24–38). She is symbolized by slim, beautiful, young women and matches well with the young woman Peter has intercourse with in his dream.

Consummated intercourse in dreams not only symbolizes physical sex. It is described by Jung as a symbol of the union of inner opposing forces in the psyche and the creation of wholeness of personality. Jung called this "Coniunctio" (Jung 1955–6). In this sense, intercourse is a symbol of transformation pointing out an opportunity for development that is tugging one forward toward a new phase in life.

On an inner level, the female physiotherapist symbolizes the elemental character, i.e. a static, material personality part that seduces and pacifies Peter, rendering him a passive object.

Literature from Freud, Jung and their successors describe men with "mother complexes" and "oedipal complexes." Attachment theories explain how flaws in an early, sensitive and responsive caregiver causes old patterns to play out in relationships with new partners. A theme that tied the first part of Peter's dream together with the last was that both the motherly woman and the young woman tried to satisfy their own needs without considering whether the young man was prepared.

In session, I mostly remained in a listening and emotionally balanced mode and allowed Peter to tell about his tribulations and moral qualms. I concentrated on highlighting positive and motivating aspects: it was a good, illuminating dream containing a central theme about feeling controlled by the expectations of women and taking a passive role in relationship to this. On the other hand, he was also able to experience erotic attraction and the joy of a beautiful woman. The car in which it took place could, perhaps, symbolize an opportunity to move forward in life. If he wished to continue with the inner process, of which his dream was the first sign, I would recommend that he give himself enough space to explore his inner world without the need to live up to solutions coming from the very consciousness he wanted to change.

Emerging Possibilities in Peter's Dream Series

When it comes to serious difficulties, if our surroundings do not have what is required to meet people in an optimal way – especially early in life – then dreams may contain relevant information hidden in unconscious memory systems. This often happens in a symbolic coded language that is too difficult to decipher, both for our surroundings and for the consciousness our surroundings have helped shape. Dreams can be both regulators of emotion and warnings. The symbolic codes can be perceived as forms of protection against new misunderstandings from the world at large. Also they function as backups when a situation or relationship becomes ripe for new processing.

If an individual is met in a new and understanding way, enfolded potential begins to unfold in new ways. This is obvious in dreams. While Peter's first *dream portrayed him as being caught in a feminine universe, his dreams quickly began to focus on conflicts and fights between him and male figures of the same age.* In connection with these, we worked on feelings of anger within Peter and his inner conflict that made him suppress a portion of his masculinity.

After some time, Peter dreamed that *he is with some friends from a band who want to play some modern music for his father. His father turns on the radio and forces some old-fashioned pop music on them, drowning out Peter and his friends. This leads to Peter changing gender and becoming a woman.*

Recollections of situations where Peter had submitted to his father in a feminine way in order to get acceptance from him began to appear both in a waking state and while dreaming. Several dreams were about that: *supported by some of his friends, he keeps away from his father's dominance.* Other dreams support his attempts to reclaim the masculinity that had no place in his childhood.

Even the female figures became more positive. At one point he met *an especially glowing and fascinating beauty* in his dreams. This was accompanied by a state of euphoria, and then he fell in love with a woman in his waking life in a completely new, happy and whole-hearted way. I have often met this symbolism in men who are on the brink of a breakthrough to an important transitional phase. (For women, their male dream figures are particularly fascinating and radiant.) This very often leads to falling in love. On an inner level, such female figures usually personify men's intuition, feelings, capacity for personal love and their connection to the unconscious, as Jungian Marie-Louise von Franz expresses it (Franz 1964).

Some time later, Peter dreamed that, "together with a girlfriend (from actual life), he finds some dead bodies on his biological family's property. They put them in a coffin and carry them out of his childhood home."

The symbolism in this dream started Peter on an exploration of the 'skeletons in the closet' he had in his childhood. This led to a new dream *in the neighborhood he lived in from birth to age 12. This dream took place in a shop he frequented with his mother. His mother is weak and helpless, frozen in a block of ice. He starts to help her get out with a cutting torch.*

The image this dream presented of his childhood opened hitherto forgotten memories of being mother's small helper and her confidante when she felt misunderstood by his father. Intellectually, he understood he had tied his Eros to her in an unhealthy way, yet this was no easy matter to admit to himself emotionally because he has also been very happy with his mother. After working with these feelings for some time, Peter dreamed that *his mother dies and he feels great sorrow.*

This hurled him into feelings of insecurity and being abandoned, which was reflected in his dreams about *desert landscapes and bombed-out areas.* When faced with such downturns, it is important to offer a form of guidance that can help graduate the process when it comes to the ego's robustness and ability to integrate, and to communicate that this is all a part of a process.

Eventually, *deserts turned to lush landscapes and wastelands became recognizable cityscapes. The female figures in Peter's dreams grew more multifaceted* and could be seen to reflect his own inner emotional life and his ability to enter into relationships.

Male Initiation

One of Peter's dreams he described thus:

> *I was put into a kind of trance by a witch, and had to go through a frighten-*
> *ing, painful ritual where, among other things, my erect penis was measured.*
> *After the ritual had been carried out, I was allowed to rest. A man about*
> *35–40 years of age put his arms around me. He was handsome and mascu-*
> *line, and was dressed in a short, Greek, sun-colored coat. But I felt wonder-*
> *fully secure resting my head against his masculine chest.*

This dream can be compared with the initiation rituals of indigenous peoples where young men leave the women's group and are initiated into the world of the adult men. The young men are brought into altered states of consciousness and submitted to painful rituals. Their masculinity is measured (symbolized in Peter's dream by his erect penis) after which they are included in the male society (Van Gennep 1960).

After this, Peter's dream characters began to communicate in new, positive ways and his dream self's ability of self-reflection increased. The inner conflicts became more nuanced and his mother and father again appeared in his dreams, even as positive characters at times.

Through this process, significant, positive changes entered Peter's emotional life, his relationships and his work life. A few years later, he married that woman he fell in love with and started a family of his own.

His initial dream had placed the focus on the central issue: Peter was caught in a universe of ideas about women's expectations of him and he had a shortage of masculine support.

At first glance, the archetypal symbolism of the union of male and female appeared to be as banal as a one-time-bang in the back of a car. Peter was not emotionally bound to this symbolism until he dreamed of the glowing woman that preceded his falling in love with his future wife.

In later dreams, other women became personifications of emotional competencies and inner helpers in his liberation from the bonds of the past.

What Peter's initial dream oracled was the necessity of moving from one level of development in his life to the next. Such a transition opened new areas of responsibility and brought challenges that his dreams commented on with continued fastidiousness and foresight. I have described Peter's case in more detail in my book, *The Man and His Inner Women* (Vedfelt 2003).

Female Initiation

The menstrual cycle, pregnancy and delivery are very closely tied to female identity. As biological events, they influence dreams while, as dream symbols, they depict female ways of being and areas of experience.

The onset of menstruation, the resulting need for guidance, and possibly even the joy of stepping into the realm of womanhood, can be revealed through dreaming. In dreams, this transition may have the quality of being initiated into a mystery where mature women support and teach girls. A lack of support in waking reality can be reflected in dreams through confusion, lack of self-esteem and symbols representing incomprehensible bodily processes.

During normal menstruation cycles there are clear connections between the possibility of conception and the dream self's relationship to men and women. In the phase leading up to ovulation where the most female sex hormones are produced, there are more positive meetings with men in dreams than at any other point in time. There is also an increase of good sex and greater courage to be in unfamiliar places. At the same time, there are fewer friendly interactions with women than usual. When conception is no longer possible, the dream self is, again, friendlier and more positive towards other women, while men slip into the background. And there is less successful sex (Van de Castle 1994 382ff.).

In the premenstrual phase there is a tendency towards more dreams with negative emotions like aggression, fear, depression and confusion, plus dreams about unlucky or unhappy events (Wiebe, *et al*. 2007).

This is when dreams can help to bring to consciousness deep instinctive forces that control women's relationships to their own and the opposite sex. Throughout life the female cycle symbolizes connectedness with the rhythms of the mind and of life.

Psychological and physical resolve to have children can be detected by the arrival of symbols of motherliness and lushness. Some women have described dreams that predict conception, such as: 'putting unbaked bread into the oven', and 'planting a magic seed', and 'being a fertile field, being plowed'. Conception dreams may also have a quality of almost a 'mystical union with nature' (Van de Castle 1994 393ff.).

Vegetation symbols frequently appear in both fertility myths as well as dreams. The child is a plant growing in mother's womb and a tree growing in a garden. Even small, cute animals are perfect metaphors for an arriving child. Tubs, jars and large fruit, etc. may symbolize the womb and – possibly to an even greater extent – the inner growth potential of women (Neumann 1963).

Dreams about female initiation may anticipate a young woman's urges to have a baby and symbolize a spiritual longing at the same time. Birgit, a young woman whose girlfriends had already started having children, dreamed that *she went into a church. The usual male priest was not standing before the altar, but instead a voluptuous, mature woman with her breasts exposed was there. The woman opened a big, juicy fruit filled with seeds.*

This dream has parallels to sacred mystery initiations for the Great Mother goddess of antiquity. The Great Mother is often depicted with a fruit filled with seeds, which is a symbol of fertility, and her breasts are typically emphasized. The mysteries were both about women's fertility and birth as symbols of the rebirth of the soul and immortality (Neumann 1963 55–63). In this woman's dream, this spiritual aspect was integrated into her own religion and church.

Pregnancy

During pregnancy female identity is challenged once again. An expectant mother's dreams often reflect her changing body-image and her concern for the well-being of her arriving child. A mother's dreams often also reflect her worries and expectations for her own future, and the future of her child and her marriage, plus the expectations she has for the father of her child (Stukane 1985).

During pregnancy – especially for first-timers – there are an unusual number of anxiety-filled dreams and nightmares. These dreams deal with the many potential complications and difficulties, both physically and socially, that may occur, and also reflect the woman's own abilities as a mother. The dreams of pregnant women seem to function as pressure release valves for all the feelings and imaginings that are being held back in waking life. Therefore, the dreams are an excellent point of departure for processing underlying anxiety and preventing post-natal psychological and social complications.

In the second and third trimester of a pregnancy, many more dreams than usual feature the mother of the pregnant woman, encouraging examination of to what extent the dreamer's mother can be utilized as a role model.

References to the baby appear in approximately one third of all dreams after the fifth month of pregnancy. The birth itself is not referred to that often, yet, if it does appear, it frequently has a magical quality, as if the child potentially possesses unusual talents such as being able to walk or talk from birth (Van de Castle 1994). These dreams may reflect the mother's grand expectations of what the child will bring to her life. But this may also be about a new attitude to the life quickly growing inside her.

Unconscious intelligence seeks active dialogue with consciousness through dreaming.

If waking consciousness relates to important themes in life, it can meet dreams on the levels on which they are being played out.

References

Barrett, D. (2001) *The Committee of Sleep*. (New York: Crown Publishers)

Franz, M.-L. von (1964) 'The anima: the woman within' in C. G. Jung, *Man and His Symbols*. (London: Aldu, Books) pp. 177–195

Hall, C. (1953) *The Meaning of Dreams*. (New York: McGraw Hill)

Hall, C. and Domhoff, B. (1963) 'A ubiquitous sex difference in dreams. *The Journal of Abnormal Psychology*, 62, s. 278–280

Jung, C. G. (Author) (1955–6/1981) Adler, G., Fordham, M. and Read, Sir H. (Eds) *The Collected Works of C.G. Jung: Mysterium Coniunctionis* Vol. 14. (Abingdon, UK: Routledge and Kegan Paul)

Neumann, E. (1963) *The Great Mother*. (Princeton, NJ: Princeton University Press)

Schultz, H. (1969) *Zur diagnostischen und prognostischen Bedeutung des Initialtraumes in der Psychotherapie.* Dissertation zur Universität Ulm

Stukane, E. (1985) *The Dream Worlds of Pregnancy.* (New York: W. Morrow)

Van de Castle, R. (1994) *Our Dreaming Mind.* (New York: Ballantine Books)

Van Gennep, A. (1960) *The Rites of Passage.* (Abingdon, UK: Routledge and Kegan Paul)

Vedfelt, O. (2000) *The Dimensions of Dreams.* (London: Jessica Kingsley Publishers)

Vedfelt, O. (2003) *The Man and his Inner Women.* (Copenhagen: Gyldendal Publishers)

Wiebe, S., *et al.* (2007) 'The dreams of women with and without severe emotional behavioral premenstrual symptoms'. *Dreaming,* Vol. 17(4), 199–207

Chapter 11

Core Quality 8

Dreams are Condensed Information

When dreams are viewed by the rational thinking forms of waking consciousness they can appear to be random alloys of elements and relationships that make no immediate sense. Strange jumps in plot, foreign details popping up in well-known surroundings, complex dream figures, and references to many different phases and events in the dreamer's life can, and do, appear in dreams.

In his analysis of dreams Freud found that individual dream elements could be the junctions of many dream-thoughts. He used the term "condensation" for this phenomenon. He remarked that, "The dream, when written down, fills half a page; the analysis, which contains the dream-thoughts, requires six, eight, twelve times as much space..." (Freud 1900, loc. 3925). Jung observed a similar phenomenon, which he called "contamination." He defined it as a central point that links together matters and objects that are not connected in waking life (Jung 1933–5, p. 203). Calvin Hall described it as a stenographic language that provides several bits of information at a time (Hall 1953).

Bisociation – A Creative Understanding of Condensation

My understanding sees this condensed information as a product of the surplus information capacity of dreams. Internal conditions, which to the limited capacity of the analytical waking consciousness look like chaos, turn out to have a more poetic dream language reflecting an order of greater complexity. Due to information density, dreams are akin to the intuitive forms of creativity we know from art, invention and other creative activity (Vedfelt 1999).

This is extensively described by author Arthur Koestler in his great work on creative processes. For instance, Johann Gutenberg, inventor of the printing arts, combined a method of fixing wax seals with a technique for pressing grapes into wine, thereby inventing the letter press. Galileo Galilei made astronomical discoveries using only a telescopic toy to observe the stars. In inventions like these, the decisive jump to innovation was a juxtaposition of planes and levels normally kept separate by the routine conditions of everyday life. Koestler called it "bisociation" to distinguish it from association. If more ideas were brought together he called it "trisociation" or even "multisociation" (Koestler 1964).

As an example of condensing information in a dream, I can mention a woman in my practice who is a good linguist. She dreamed: Ole asks, *How's it going with abeloid and pentatex?* Her associations went to a folder for filing dreams I had given her. *Ab Elo id* is Latin for 'that which comes from Elo' (= Ole). 'Id' she recognized as Freud's term for our unconscious drives. 'Pentatex' made her think of *penta*, which is Greek for the number five, 'tex' gave her the German word *text*: she had given me a folder with five stars in which to keep copies of her dreams. In this, she had played monkey ('abe' in Danish) see, monkey do with me ('abelo').

If you follow dream associations and understand them in context, they turn out to make creative syntheses of ideas that we, in waking consciousness, are inclined to keep separated.

For instance, a woman dreams that *a parrot pecked a hole in her head.* "Parrots are always called Jakob," was her first association, and then, "They repeat themselves, over and over." Then she suddenly thought about Jakob, a handsome guy she could not get close to, even though he had inspired her to say no to one suitor after another for years. In a flash she understood what the "hole in her head" was. A series of feelings and thoughts that had lived a relatively separated existence in her waking state were then synthesized into a new, comprehensive and meaningful entity.

From a neuroscientific point of view, dreams connect memory systems that are separated from each other when we are awake. They are 'hubs' with a high density of connections between the 'spokes'. In dynamic systems theory, these condensations can be understood as 'attractors'. Attractors are a set of values toward which a system tends to evolve (Milnor 2006).

In Chapter 9 on dreams as patter recognition I have shown that dreams can refer to significant aspects of the past, present and future; in principle, they can – as a result of the condensation – refer to all three aspects at the same time.

A dream about '*my childhood home is on fire*' corresponds to the experience of a destructively inflamed atmosphere in the home of one's parents. The memory of this can be triggered by a present-day event where the dreamer is inflamed with emotion or is exposed to this from the surroundings. Fire is also an old symbol of transformation. Therefore, a dream about fire can suggest a potential future transformation, since the dreamer's identity can no longer live in a destructive house. All three patterns of experience are possible – each one individually or all at the same time – as a result of this condensing.

This is how dreams follow the same principles as a dramatist when writing a theater piece or screenplay. A simple, apparently banal sentence often performs many functions at the same time: it illuminates the speaker and the person spoken to; it carries the plot forward; and it may function ironically by sending a message to the audience that means something different from what the characters understand (Styan 1963). The professional term for this is 'subtext'.

For some people it may be more familiar to imagine their associations to these condensed elements as drop-down menus that can be clicked open. Between the various themes in the sub-menus for the individual dream elements you may find interesting links. Your associations need not simply run linearly down the sub-menus. This phenomenon was also recognized by Freud, who phrased it differently (Laplanche and Pontalis 1973, p. 82). To the untrained eye these associations may appear to be random, yet, if you are able to follow the more significant chains, they form patterns that match the dream story on various levels and that tend to move a self-organizing process forward (Vedfelt 2004).

These patterns cannot be pinned down to one specific meaning but must be unfolded in creative processes, which will be described further in connection to the remaining core qualities.

An Example of Dream Condensation – Karen

In the following example I focus on condensation in the present, the past and the future, plus on the objective and subjective levels. This dreamwork took place in a personal development group of 14 people who recounted dreams. My wife and led the group. We met for four entire weekends, 20 hours each weekend, during the course of one year.

Karen, a woman in her late 30s, brought this dream to the group. *She picks up her son and daughter at school. On the way home she discovers, to her great fright, that she has forgotten her daughter. After a series of complications, she makes it back to school. When she is looking for her daughter's classroom, she enters the wrong room. She wants to continue looking, but her shoes are missing. She is about to panic. She wakes up without resolving the issue.*

Karen's daughter had just begun school and felt anxiety about it. Karen's relationship to her daughter is very close and intimate. She is concerned and enters into dialogue with the school, which wants to support the mother and daughter. Her dream self is anxious about doing something wrong and has difficulty orienting herself in this situation. The missing shoes are associated with being unprotected and vulnerable – not dressed for the occasion. This appears to be related to her concern for her daughter in waking reality (the continuity hypothesis). We discuss the issue on the level of cognitive behavior.

Afterwards we look at her daughter as a personification of something in Karen herself (the subjective level). What was her life like when she was her daughter's age? What comes most clearly to her mind is that she remembers having a great deal of difficulty starting school and had no adults to console and support her. She experienced a powerlessness and disorientation just like in her dream. By staying with these feelings of powerlessness and staying in contact with me, Karen is able to notice some sadness she had not been in contact with while we were talking about the issue objectively. I mirror some consoling words she wanted to hear from the adults. She feels relieved.

It is a well-known issue that anxious, protective mothers can create anxiety in their children and a closed cycle of emotions that shuts out helpful surroundings. As sociologist Margaret Nelson puts it, "a great deal of what so many of today's most assiduously devoted mothers do is designed, consciously or not, to assuage their anxiety" (Nelson 2012). It may hurt parents, as well as children, and can be an overreaction to the deeply insensitive parenting methods of earlier generations (Warner 2012).

After her emotional state cleared somewhat, Karen found more energy to work with how she can be more aware of her emotions in situations where mother and daughter experience separation.

One prospective aspect is that the relation to her child is a developmental opportunity for Karen herself to gain maturity and a more integrated personality. On a more social level, she has gone back to school to further her education. Though she manages her life fairly well, she often feels vulnerable and lacking the required life skills. Several times she has been on the verge of giving up, and one reason for this is that her daughter's problems have been so demanding.

We managed to make our way from the present back to the past and then on to the future, and we also looked at the objective and subjective levels, without any of them taking precedence.

The Neuroscientific Perspective of Karen's Dream

From the point of view of neuroscience, the first thing that comes to mind is an activation of the so-called separation distress or panic system. According to Jaak Panksepp, "[It] provides mammals with a sensitive emotional barometer to monitor the level of social support they are receiving. If social contact is lost, organisms experience a painful feeling of separation, and the young protest (cry) vigorously in an attempt to reestablish contact and care." In humans, it is involved in "... everyday loneliness, as well as ... childhood depression and the emergence of panic attacks" (Panksepp 1998, loc. 8234ff).

The separation distress system seems to be intimately connected to social bonding and the process of parenting. At the core of this system is the anterior cingulate gyrus with its extensive connections to several thalamic, hypothalamic and other nuclei such as, for example, the PAG in the brainstem (Solms and Turnbull 2002, p. 129). As earlier described, all these networks can be highly active in dreaming.

The first turning point in Karen's dream is a wake-up call presumably related to the amygdala's "lexicon of fears." Her associations to her dream suggests an intrusion of early unconscious memory into Karen's adult consciousness, which is usually stored in circuits within the amygdala and the right hemisphere (Cozolino 2010).

Her dream is placed in a setting connected to higher levels of the social brain, i.e. contemporary human parenting duties such as picking up at school and driving a car, etc. The maternal care is supported by oxytocin and prolactin – opiates from the separation distress system (Solms and Turnbull 2002 p. 129).

From that point in her dream, the seeking system of her brain must be very active. This will, however, be intruded upon by various symbolic incidents, including the one I mentioned – the missing shoes. This incident may again be an intrusion by an early unconscious memory, this time of shame (not being properly dressed) which, according to Louis Cozolino, is also usually stored by the amygdala and the right brain. Unconscious social memory systems also activate the creation of a relationship to a therapist, technically called transference (Cozolino 2010). On the positive side, this makes it easier for Karen to use me in a consoling role when she emotionally moves herself back to her memories of starting school.

Cozolino states in his description of the social brain that people who are "shame based can find criticism, rejection, and abandonment in nearly every interaction." This can underpin the hypothesis that, perhaps, Karen has a role in her daughter's separation distress and experiences of being abandoned. In that case, emotions can circulate via the unconscious "quick and dirty route," as LeDoux calls it (LeDoux 1998, p. 202), between the amygdala systems of both parties and amplify the feelings of anxiety and being abandoned.

On the positive side, we have the activation of the seeking system and motherly feelings, both of which can be utilized in relationship to her daughter and to Karen's own inner system, because it has an inhibiting effect on separation distress, even from a neuropsychological point of view.

To summarize, we can say that condensation is found in the separation distress system, but the construction of the dream as a whole and the creation of contexts and connections to casual relations and future developmental opportunities must be ascribed to the entire brain, not least with the participation of the vmPFC and the mPFC in the frontal lobe.

Rounding off Karen's Case

In the dreamwork with Karen, I did not go into these technical details. I empathized with her motivation and will to seek solutions to her problem and encouraged the involvement of her motherliness, which could be turned inward toward her own hurting inner child. In connection to the prospective aspect, I mentioned the Greek myth about the mother goddess Demeter's daughter who was kidnapped but then returned transformed and more mature. This theme is described by female Jungian writers as an example of feminine individuation (Skogemann 1984). Myths speak more to the experiential level of dreams than a pathogenic explanation does, thus stimulating the hope of breaking old patterns.

By the next meeting of Karen's group, her daughter's separation distress in connection with being dropped off at school had all but ceased. Karen also appeared more capable of concentrating on furthering her education.

Naturally, these changes can be caused by many factors, yet Karen had another dream to share. "She is together with her husband and two children. After several complications, they go with her – as the one in charge of organization – on a train that is heading in the direction it is supposed to."

This is the high-level communication of dream world. When I later mentioned Karen's last dream to her, she could not immediately remember it but was very happy to be reminded. This is not an uncommon occurrence. If I get the opportunity to observe the dreams between two intense event processes with some amount of time between them, I often see that the level can dip until – shortly before the next meeting – unconscious intelligence takes the lead and picks up the red thread from the previous event.

Condensation in dreams is the creative synthesis of areas and levels of the personality that are separated from each other during the routine thinking of everyday life.

The relevant meanings of dreams condensation must be unfolded through creative processes.

References

Cozolino, L. (2010) *The Neuroscience of Psychotherapy: Healing the Social Brain* (2nd Ed.). (New York: W. W. Norton & Company), Kindle edition, location 1601–20

Freud, S. (1900/2013) *The Interpretation of Dreams*. (Sunderland, UK: Dead Dodo Vintage), Kindle edition, location 145–6

Hall, C. (1953) 'A cognitive theory of dream symbolism'. *Journal of General Psychology*, Vol. 48, 169–186

Jung, C. G. (1933–5) *Modern Psychology I-II*. (Zürich: Eidgenossische Technische Hochschule)

Koestler, A. (1964) *The Act of Creation*. (London: Hutchinson & Co.)

Laplanche, J. and Pontalis, J. B. (1973/2006) *The Language of Psychoanalysis*. (London: Karnac Books)

LeDoux, J. (1998) *The Emotional Brain*. (London: Phoenix Paperback)

Milnor, J. (2006) 'Attractor'. *Scholarpedia*, 1(11), 1815

Nelson, M. K. (2012) *Parenting Out of Control: Anxious Parents in Uncertain Times*. (New York: NYU Press)

Panksepp, J. (1998) *Affective Neuroscience: The Foundations of Human and Animal Emotions* (series in Affective Science). (Oxford, UK: Oxford University Press)

Skogemann, P. (1984) *Femininity in Growth [Kvindelighed i vækst]*. (Copenhagen: Borgen)

Solms, M. and Turnbull, O. (2002) *The Brain and the Inner World*. (New York: Other Press)

Styan, J. L. (1963/1985) *The Elements of Drama*. (Cambridge: Cambridge University Press)

Vedfelt, O. (1999) *The Dreams Many Faces*. Conference paper for The International Association for the Study of Dreams. (Santa Cruz, CA: University of California)

Vedfelt, O. (2004) *Dreams as Unconscious Intelligence – A Cybernetic Theory*. Conference paper, keynote presentation for the Annual Conference of International Association for the Study of Dreams, Copenhagen

Warner, J. (2012) 'Smother mother. Why intensive child-rearing hurts parents and kids'. *Time Magazine: Life and Style*, 13 July

Chapter 12

Core Quality 9

Dreams are Experiences of Wholeness

A common perception in Western philosophy and the world of ideas is that consciousness is equivalent with verbal thought activity. Other "modalities" of experience such as emotions, imagery, bodily sensations and movement impulses have been held in less regard. We deem them of lesser importance and pay less attention to them than we do our thoughts.

Nonetheless, each personal experience is a 'wholeness', and each living experience is stored in our memories – this applies to all the aforementioned experience-modalities. Modern infant research has shown that we, from the moment of birth, have an innate ability to transfer impressions from one modality to another. For instance, one experiment has shown that a two- to three-week old infant is capable of mimicking adults who stick out their tongues or open their mouths. In this case, visual impression is transferred into movement. When this experiment was broadened, the infant first had a pacifier put in its mouth so the child could not stick out its tongue. When the pacifier was removed 150 seconds later, the infant could still remember the movement (Meltzoff and Moore 1977). When they are only weeks old, infants can determine that facial movements on a video are out of sync with the audio track. They prefer faces that are synchronized with speech and speaking the same language as the infant's mother (Chamberlain 1988). They are actually capable of matching the intensity of sound and visual impressions.

Apparently, we have from birth an internal 'supramodal' experience space that contains the wholeness of experience. Our culture has very little awareness of the importance of this supramodal ability to the formation of consciousness. Learning is communicated through language that is then seen as true consciousness. Normal waking consciousness keeps quite busy performing the tasks it has been trained to do. There is rarely any energy left over to feel, sense and notice wholeness.

Yet this supramodal ability is always active in everyday life. We simply do not think about it. An experience of a scent can be associated with a visual memory, and the sight of a flower may awaken a certain feeling. A thought may be accompanied by a bodily sensation. Our language is also filled with supramodal expressions. A person is described as hard or soft, cold or warm. Thinking can be sharp and prices inflated. Tenderness is disarming. We are weighed down by sorrow and winded after exertion. We go through ups and downs, and get stoned or high.

If we lacked a supramodal language we would not be able to describe the many complex relations to the world that give our lives meaning and a sense of fullness. We experience this in poetry and novels, film and theater, art and music, and even more intensely in our own dreaming lives.

In dreams our supramodal ability manages to unfold fully. There, feelings, life-like images, thoughts, actions, movements and bodily expressions are gathered into an entirety.

Dream Theories and Experiential Modalities

The various traditions of dream research and dreamwork put primary focus on differing experiential modalities.

In classic psychoanalysis, consciousness was defined as verbalized thought (Fenichel 1977) and even early cognitive therapy focused primarily on verbal thought (Beck 1971). In Jung's writings, words *and* images play central roles so, for instance, in painting and active imagination dream characters are central. Art therapy for dreams and "symbol therapy" are also methods that place particular emphasis on painting and drawing images when exploring dreams.

As described in Chapter 2, many dream theories based in neuroscience consider emotion regulation as one of the primary functions of dreams. For instance, Ernest Hartmann (2011, p. 12), proposes the theory that "emotion guides the dream," and that "the central image of the dream pictures and measures the emotion." Even Perls' dreamwork attached the greatest import to the liberation and transformation of emotions and also underscored the significance of body language.

Methods that include the body in dreamwork in more specific ways are rarer. Eugene Gendlin introduced body sensing – "the felt sense" – to dreamwork (Gendlin 1986), while Jungian Arnold Mindell particularly emphasizes the relationship between body sensations and dream images (Mindell 1984).

A Supramodal Method of Dreamwork

I have developed methods that provide equal attention to all the various experiential modalities – imagery, thinking, feeling, body sensing, and kinesthetic (Vedfelt 2001). When habitual thinking begins to control the flow of associations, I do not assume that unconscious content is being repressed. Rather, emotional intensity expresses itself in an experiential modality that is not controlled by consciousness, such as movements, facial expressions, sensations in the body or images. Paying attention to an energy-charged modality may reveal new emotions. If these emotions are explored, the intensity may move to an inner sensation, a visual image, a memory, a relational experience, and so on. When you pay attention to the 'supramodal' flow, you are not being lured away; you are engaging in a creative process that circumscribes the dream's entire experiential spectrum.

Vera, a young woman, brought the following dream to therapy: *I was visiting some or other man, and he had many German Shepherds, which growled and barked. I was afraid of them. They were locked in a wooden cage, but it seemed like they could get out at any moment.*

This dream gave Vera a "basic mood" (background emotion) of unpleasantness. Afterwards, she closed her eyes and saw the situation before her (visual modality). She noticed her anxiety (primary emotion). This awakened memories about a conflict with her partner. Her stomach muscles tightened (inner bodily sensation). She noticed the anxiety again (primary emotion). She tried to role-play one of the German Shepherds (movement and imagination abilities). She then noticed that she was angry (primary emotion).

Vera concluded that she was anxious about the consequences of getting angry (verbal cognitive modality). This could be in her relationship to a partner if her partner shut her out or left her. This could also be at work. Together with me, she devised a strategy for how to say no without becoming like a German Shepherd that has just broken out of a cage.

She moved back and forth between the thought modality and her feelings, strengthening connections. The dreamwork gave her a global supramodal experience of power and aliveness.

The Brain and Levels of Feeling

Comparing how different researchers use the words 'emotion' and 'feeling' is not an easy task. Yet, to many authors, feeling seems to implicitly indicate a more differentiated product than emotion or affect, and the word connotes a 'sensing' or 'being aware of'.

Neuroscientist Antonio Damasio distinguishes between background emotions – primary emotions – and secondary or social emotions. Background emotions are the most fundamental. They refer to internal global states exemplified by words such as "calm, tense, edgy, discouraged, enthusiastic, down, cheerful" and so on (Damasio 2000, pp. 51–3). These global states are induced by a network of nuclei in the brainstem that further activates all the other emotional systems, and they are related to the somatic marker system described in Chapter 2.

The brainstem network contains 'maps' of the visceral functions and body images, and represents changes in the body's internal situation, plus the most basic embodiment and feeling of your "self" (Solms and Turnbull 2002, p. 90). So-called primary emotions, such as happiness, sadness, fear, anger, surprise, disgust, etc., relate to more specific systems in the emotional brain. As Damasio explains: "The induction and experience of sadness, anger, fear and happiness lead to activation of several sites [in the brain]... but the pattern for each emotion is distinctive."

According to Damasio, experiencing, knowing you feel, and reflecting on emotions represent three different levels in the mind and the brain. Emotion presupposes first order neural maps representing changes in body states. Feeling an emotion is mediated by second-order structures, a proto-self (primitive ego) that senses changes in the body. "Reflection on feeling is yet another step up" from having a feeling. Feedback loops connect the different levels, but common to these three phenomena is their body relatedness (Damasio 2000).

An Example of Cultivating Feelings through Dreamwork – Paul

According to Solms and Turnbull, "The core of the emotion generating systems of the brain is identical to those that generate the background state of consciousness," (2002, p. 107). As I understand it, tuning into this background state and awakening hidden emotions in a process of supramodal association is a possibility. The focus of this second example is on shared background emotions and the acknowledgement of feelings in relationships (Vedfelt 2009).

In a group sharing on the second day of a two-and-a-half-day personal development course, Paul recounted the night's dream: *a woman gives him a thermos jug. Looking into the jug, he sees it is broken inside.*

Paul had no immediate idea of what the dream is telling him and he mentioned no particular feelings or emotions. When asked for details, he said that in waking life the dream woman was actually married to a good friend. The jug was red and had a spherical shape, just like the ones we used for tea during the course. I recalled that the foregoing evening I had mentioned that a figure he had drawn from another dream seemed to have a motherly function. Immediately after having made the comment, I had a slightly uneasy feeling that I could not specify. Soon my attention was drawn to other group members and the uneasiness disappeared, yet it was evoked again when I heard Paul's dream about the jug.

Because Paul was new to the group, I also wondered aloud if the dream might reflect some feelings about being on the course. He answered that he did feel uneasy about my comment the day before; he was gay and tired of stereotyped psychoanalytic explanations about homosexual men being dominated by controlling mothers. I told him that was not what I had in mind. I was actually thinking of the nurturing and caring aspects of the feminine.

He loosened up and, in a following one-to-one session with me, he drew the red jug in oil pastel on a big sheet of paper. He visualized the woman giving him the jug and described a global feeling of pleasure. Expressed in a drawing, the feeling became a present wrapped in gift-paper. When contemplating the drawing, he affectionately remembered Christmases in waking life spent with the woman, her husband, and their children. They have been a kind of "new family" for him for years. In acknowledging this, he sensed an expansion in his chest and a feeling of quiet joy.

A separate drawing of the broken insides of the jug evoked a background emotion of disappointment. This emotion was not related to his "new family" but conjured up emotion-laden memories from the age of eight. His primary family had split up and he was sent to a boarding school. Before that he recalled feelings of joy, contentment, and closeness in his family. Reflecting on this he recognized that, since then, a hidden fear of loss or rejection has made him apprehensive about really owning his feelings of togetherness with the new family. He found it uplifting and joyful to allow feelings of love and friendship to be present.

With the supramodal method, analytic understanding can be used in conjunction with the whole of the experiential spectrum. Emotions can be consciously regulated instead of separated from consciousness through isolated cathartic reactions or acting out. This method is one of 'cultivating', in the sense that the dreamer is implicitly trained to be aware of emotions and feelings, and then sense them in the body. A therapist's understanding of the bodily expression of emotions, his or her awareness of any resonating background emotion coupled with an ability to respond empathically and non-intrusively facilitate this process.

Bodily Associations to Dreams – Alice

Bodily associations with dreams are often overlooked even though they may provide very important perspectives. In the following example, it turned out that body language led to revealing what was perhaps the most important point of the dream.

Alice, nine months pregnant, dreamed: *My father and mother had kidnapped my child. They had conspired, so I wasn't able to get in touch with the child!*

Immediately afterwards Alice could not make the theme of the dream fit with anything in her waking reality. She said she had invited her mother to help look after both her baby and herself just after delivery. It seemed completely absurd to her that this would cause any trouble. To the context belongs the child (a boy) shortly before had turned away from the normal birth position.

As she talked about her dream, Alice sat with eyes wide open and one hand in front of her face in a gesture of dismay. I suggested she return to this position and go deeper into her experience. She then started thinking that, when her mother was pregnant with her, her maternal grandmother had never accepted it. This put her in touch with an experience of being unwanted and a feeling of inadequacy. This sense of inadequacy even applied to her ability to be the mother of her arriving child.

Alice then realized that her true motive for her arrangement with her mother after delivery was to allow her to take over the mother role, instead of taking it upon herself. She also noticed that she felt an anxiety behind this – her mother might "hijack" her baby. Seen in this perspective, her dream made sense. She had a conspiracy taking place within herself trying to separate her from her child. After this, Alice decided to take care of her baby by herself and involve her partner more than she had originally intended.

The key to understanding this dream was Alice's gesture of dismay, which she was quite unconscious of at the time. Even though we use our supramodal ability all the time, we almost always do so unconsciously. Therefore, it demands both courage and practice to give modalities other than our thinking activity a chance.

An important part of this story is that, the night after this dreamwork, Alice's unborn child moved back to a normal position. That very night she dreamed that *she got in touch with the boy while he was in her belly. She encouraged him and asked if he didn't feel like "coming down," (i.e. being born). He said "yes" to this.* Soon after a healthy baby was born without complication and she and the husband succeeded with the planned parental care.

In Core Quality 5 I discussed the issue of limiting dreamwork. Including all experiential modalities does not make dreamwork more unmanageable – on the contrary, it gives the work greater precision.

Dreams combine all modalities of experience – emotions, feelings and thoughts, imagery, bodily sensations and movement impulses – into a wholeness.

Inclusion of all experiential modalities provides dreamwork with greater precision.

References

Beck, A. (1971/2004) 'Cognitive patterns in dreams and daydreams' in R. Rosner, W. Lyddon, *et al.*, *Cognitive Therapy and Dreams.* (New York: Springer Publishing), pp. 27–32

Chamberlain, D. (1988) *Babies Remember Birth.* (New York: Jeremy P. Tarcher Inc.)

Damasio, A. (2000) *The Feeling of What Happens.* (London: Vintage)

Fenichel, O. (1977) *The Psychoanalytical Theory of Neurosis.* (Abingdon, UK: Routledge and Kegan Paul)

Gendlin, E. T. (1986) *Let Your Body Interpret Your Dreams.* (Asheville, NC: Chiron Publications)

Hartmann, E. (2011) *The Nature and Functions of Dreaming.* (Oxford: Oxford University Press)

Meltzoff A. N. and Moore, K. (1977) 'Imitation of facial and manual gestures by human neonates'. *Science*, 198, 75–78

Mindell, A. (1984) *Dreambody.* (Abingdon, UK: Routledge)

Solms, M. and Turnbull, O. (2002) *The Brain and the Inner World.* (New York: Other Press)

Vedfelt, O. (2001) *The Supramodal Space: A Missing Link between Body, Soul and Spirit.* Conference paper, conference on Body-psychotherapy. (Zürich: Institute for Biosynthesis)

Vedfelt, O. (2009) 'Cultivating feelings through working with dreams'. *Jung Journal: Culture & Psyche*, Vol. 3(4), 88–102

Chapter 13

Core Quality 10

Dreams are Psychological Energy Landscapes

In every individual's life there are many areas of interest that are important. A competition between the most meaningful themes of our lives takes place in our internal network. What motivates us most at any given moment is not only dependent on rational considerations, but equally so on the intensity of unconscious patterns of experience and behavior.

In a network model, the balance between the patterns that regulate personality can be depicted as 'energy landscapes' with sharp peaks and low hills. Dominating patterns are sharp peaks in the landscape, while flexible patterns are lower hills and valleys (Rumelhart *et al*. 1986).

In dominating patterns, information is packed tightly together. If such a pattern is activated, it has a tendency to siphon energy from all other patterns. In flexible patterns, the bonds between the individual parts are weaker so associations can flow more freely within the network.

When a waking situation demands a decision, a particular pattern must take control and attract energy from other patterns so unified action can be initiated. For instance, if you seek a pattern that fits a situation, the pattern having the most associations will rise up like a sharp peak and take control (Rumelhart *et al*. 1986). This can be compared with searching the internet where the website with the most hits appears at the top of the search results.

In the dreaming state where we are liberated from the limitations of waking life and not forced to make decisions, we move into unconscious energy landscapes. Here we can see deeper motives for our actions and how these motives compete and are balanced in relationship to each other.

This is demonstrated by how some elements in our dreams are more emotionally charged and contain more energy than others. The most energy-charged dream elements immediately attract special interest. Thoughts may linger around them and the images are especially clear. If we draw or paint them, a great deal of extra paint may be applied, or the brush pressed especially hard, or they may be accompanied by certain bodily sensations and powerful memories.

Network function is explained on the basis of a 'harmony theory', so called because the interpreting schemas activated seek out that which is most 'harmonious', i.e. the most likely states in the surroundings with which to harmonize. In dreams, the self-organizing system properties search for optimal harmony within high-level personality dynamics under the given circumstances. The system starts up at 'high temperatures', performs a search process, which starts by combing local solutions, but then cools and ends with a global solution to which it 'freezes', latching on. Thus, the system moves from a fluid state to one that is increasingly solid. During this process many exchanges occur between units that mutually adjust each other until a pattern is found that has the maximum harmony (Bernsen and Ulbæk 1993, Smolensky 1986).

The Sharp Peaks and Low Hills of Energy Landscapes

In the following example, Linda, a woman in her forties, dreamed:

> *I'm in a waiting room. Ahead of me is a family. The mother is complaining to a little girl all the time. A boy, who is slightly bigger, sits expectantly looking around with curiosity. He seems to be full of life. The father is a strikingly handsome younger man. He comforts the mother and leads her out of the waiting room. I can now see the mother's back. Her back has some scar-like stripes.*

"Whiner," Linda called the mother in her dream. This statement immediately attracted the most interest. "I complain way too much at home instead of finding joy in my husband and children," Linda said. "It bothers me that, as recently as yesterday, I was irritated and created a bad mood at home. In reality I got mad about a trifle. I really don't understand why I do that."

The way our waking consciousness functions gives us a tendency to lock on to the first intuitive interpretation. Yet, that interpretation is probably closest to what we already know. At that point, if we start determining the rational consequences of our behavior and practical lives, we can miss out on broader information about what really motivates us. If we unravel the dream in a creative way instead, space will be created for the emotionally charged aspects that have the most psychological energy available.

I suggested that Linda draw her dream with crayons on a large sheet of paper. This in itself is an associative process where the unconscious is allowed to make itself heard. In her drawing, the mother sat at the center in a black dress. This central placement probably symbolized her strong position in the energy landscape. "She's a true matron," Linda said. In front of her sat a 'tween' girl, drawn more vaguely.

The father was seen on the right of the drawing leading the mother out. "I can't draw it clearly," Linda said, "but he was younger and a very handsome man in my dream." The woman being led out looked different from the matron in the center of her drawing.

"She looks younger, more like me," Linda said. Her back was bare, and the scars were drawn clearly in red. Particular energy had been applied to drawing the scars. This made Linda think of "psychological scars." She said, "My mother and father got divorced when I was 12. It was a terrible time and still affects me. This is probably where my scars come from."

It suddenly hit her that the "whiner" in the middle of the drawing looked like her maternal grandmother who was constantly complaining about everyone. About the little girl, Linda said, "That's me, of course, sitting and listening to my grandmother. I lived with her mostly for a period after their divorce. I had to sit and listen to her whining all of the time. She always knew best. Look at her sitting there on her throne. She always puts everyone down. Especially my father."

"I liked my father a lot. He actually reminds me of my dream. He was a very handsome man." Linda's eyes glistened a moment and sorrow tugged at her mouth, "I miss him terribly. Ah, ha! It's just a sad waiting room. I sat there hoping my father would come and take me away."

"Like the father in your dream did?" I asked. She nodded. After a while, her associations continued: "My father once gave me a nativity scene with Joseph, Mary and the holy family. My grandmother thought it was ugly and distasteful. I sat in my room and looked at it for hours. I longed for the togetherness of that family."

Linda became more and more emotionally moved by her dream. She cried, but after a while calmed down again and then felt relieved. I pointed out that we still needed to look at the curious boy in her dream. That made her think of her big brother. When her father took her away from her grandmother's "waiting room", they went to his summerhouse. Her big brother was there and she remembered they could always relax and have fun together.

"It's like that sometimes with my husband and children, too," she said. "But part of me is sitting in that waiting room – a heavy person dressed in black. That's when I haven't managed to do what's important to me. That's how I end up blaming myself and getting irritable."

She felt relieved and was ready to meet herself – and her family – in a new way.

In Linda's case, we allowed her unconscious intelligence to express through her drawing how her psychic energy was distributed.

Using this method – which took both intellectual understanding and energetic aspects into consideration – her awareness shifted. She no longer focused on finding an ultimate and true interpretation, but stimulated whatever worked instead.

On the subjective level the whiner, the younger woman with scars, the tween girl, the curious boy and the father were understood as representations of personified parts of Linda. They seemed to reflect subsystems of distributed energy that the dream and the creative dreamwork tried to reorganize from a stagnated and conflictual state to a more dynamic and harmonious state. On the objective level this transformation had the potential to energize and harmonize her current family system. In a more collective perspective it was a search to align with a general human ideation of a harmonious holy family.

Peak Experience Dreams

The frequency of sharp peaks and low hills varies for different types of dreams. Dreams are the leading edge of important life transitions and anticipate the most important scenarios of the future. In especially meaningful "peak experience" dreams, the energy seems to activate higher levels of self-organization while the experienced self simultaneously feels recharged with energy and finds the gusto to jump into new life projects. Such dreams have always attracted a great deal of attention and stick in our memories with particular strength. People lacking any special knowledge of dreams often intuitively understand that a dream like this is extremely important and may, in retrospect, see it linked to drastic changes in their lives.

At the age of 20, Marc Chagall, the famous Russian painter, lived illegally in abject poverty in St Petersburg. He had flunked out of art school and the police were after him. When everything looked hopeless, he had this dream:

I find myself in a large room. In the corner is a single bed and I'm in it. It gets dark. Suddenly the ceiling cracks open and a winged creature floats noisily down, radiating and filling the room with movement and clouds. I hear the rustle of wings being dragged. I think: 'An angel.' I cannot open my eyes. It's too bright, too radiant. Once the angel has poked around everywhere, it rises up and leaves the room through the ceiling crack taking everything luminous and divine with it. It gets dark again, and I wake.

(Dieckmann, 1984.)

This dream gave Chagall renewed faith in his calling as a painter.

Close ties exist between this kind of dream and certain types of intensely experienced states of consciousness in waking life. The first to psychologically describe these experiences was William James who, under the heading "religious experiences," described a broad spectrum of individual breakthroughs in consciousness (James 1902). Jung called them "numinous" experiences, referring to religious historian Rudolf Otto's mystical, awe-inspiring and fascinating aspects of the experience of "the sacred" (Otto 1917/1958). Humanistic psychologist Abraham Maslow coined the term "peak experiences" and described their phenomenology in human life (Maslow 1976). Similar states of consciousness are known from eastern philosophers and schools of meditation, and also from transpersonal psychology where they are systematically induced. I call them 'information-dense states' (Vedfelt 1996). They have been described in connection to near-death experiences and creative breakthroughs.

Common to the descriptions of these experiences is a surrender of ego and consciousness to something sensed as greater and more intense than the reality known up to that point. Greater clarity, freedom, presence, harmony, union of oppositions, and altruistic love for humankind and the world is experienced. These experiences convey a fascinating and energy-recharging force. They can move a person to euphoria and lead to drastic changes in personality.

I call these experiences information-dense states because of their special ability to condense valuable high-level information. Dream series provide excellent opportunities to follow how peak experiences are built up, and how high-order personality changes can subsequently be integrated into an individual's life in a harmonious way.

Theories of Particularly Important Dreams

Carl O'Nell, in his book *Dreams, Culture and the Individual*, has described how most tribal peoples and ancient cultures distinguish between important dreams and those of lesser importance (O'Nell 1976, pp. 77–80). Another fine source for this theme is an anthology by Kelly Bulkeley (2001) on the religious, cultural, and psychological dimensions of dreaming.

Important dreams mediate contact to the gods and the spirits of the ancestors, and provide societies with omens of impending catastrophes or new opportunities. Significant dreams were most often recounted by shamans, prophets and very creative people. If ordinary members of a society had such dreams, they would be interpreted by one of the above-mentioned specialists (O'Nell 1976, pp. 77–80). In some cultures dreams were seen as more real than waking reality. In other words, these dreams represented a higher and truer reality (O'Nell 1976, p. 26ff).

Even in psychological dream research, a distinction between more and less important dreams has gained ground and prompted further systematic research. In his most central essay on the nature of dreams, Jung distinguishes between "little" or "insignificant" dreams that, he finds, "are restricted to the day-to-day fluctuations of the psychic balance," and "big" or "significant" dreams that "are often remembered for a lifetime." Big dreams "not infrequently, prove to be the richest jewels in the treasure-house of psychic experience." Little dreams, according to Jung, have less meaning and less prospective potential; they come from what he calls the personal unconscious. Big dreams come from the collective unconscious, which he considers to be a more universal and archetypal level of the psyche. They are so full of meaning it can take many years to understand them. Such dreams occur mostly during critical phases of life – puberty, early youth and the onset of middle age (Jung 1945/48, par. 554–5). As we can see from his memoirs, earliest remembered childhood dreams can have that significance (Jung 1961). Jung also described "synchronicity" as a phenomenon related to big dreams. He understood synchronicity to be the coincidence of a psychologically significant inner occurrence and an external event with no reasonable, external causal relation (Jung 1952).

As Jung understands it, archetypes – the foundations of big dreams – have dynamic qualities. This has been systematically studied by Israeli Jungian analyst Yehezkiel Kluger. He examined the dreams of 218 individuals, the majority of whom had not been in analysis, and compared them with people who were in deep-reaching Jungian analysis. In accordance with Jung's theory, Kluger found the following criteria for a dream's archetypality:

1   mythological parallel;
2   heightened affect;
3   non-rational imagery or behavior;
4   remoteness from "everydayness."

All four criteria could be measured as strong, moderate or distant.

Kluger found that childhood dreams were 56 percent archetypal. Old dreams, which were still vividly recalled, were 65 percent archetypal. But dreams that were included solely because they were the most recent were only 20 percent archetypal. In contrast, 38 percent of the most recent dreams of Jungian analysands were archetypal (Kluger 1955).

Using Kluger's method, P. A. Faber, another Jungian analyst, found that archetypal dreams were more frequent in persons who experienced "altered states of consciousness" in the form of active imagination, relaxed fantasy journeys or through meditation, for example (Faber *et al.* 1978, 1983).

Another tool that has been used in the study of Jung's concept of "big dreams" has been developed by Kelly Bulkeley based on Calvin Hall and Robert Van de Castle's statistical methods of analysis. It is called the "Good Fortune Scale" of dreams and can, according to Bulkeley, be helpful in identifying big dreams (Bulkeley 2006):

1   wishes come true;
2   flying;
3   helpful forces in the environment;
4   magical objects;
5   extraordinary powers;
6   characters return from the dead.

Ernest Hartmann's theory of a Central Image (CI) can, as I mentioned in Core Quality 9, be seen as an attempt to measure the importance of an image and the intensity of the emotions contained in it – the Central Image Intensity (CII). A Central Image is defined as "a striking, arresting, or compelling image – not simply a story – but an image, which stands out by virtue of being especially powerful, vivid, bizarre, or detailed." The CII was measured by using questionnaires rated by independent observers with meticulously elaborated methods (Hartmann 2011). The CI does not include the narrative that is central to Kluger's way of measuring the importance of a dream.

Hartmann made a list of related emotions. I have divided the list in two, which is of practical value for dreamwork.

The first part of the list contains strong negative emotions: fear, terror, helplessness, vulnerability, being trapped, being immobilized, anxiety, vigilance, despair, hopelessness (giving up), anger, frustration, disturbing cognitive dissonance, disorientation, weirdness, guilt, grief, loss, sadness, abandonment, disappointment, shame, inadequacy, disgust and repulsion.

The second part of the list contains experiences with strong and positive emotional charges: power, mastery, supremacy, awe, wonder, mystery, happiness, joy, excitement, hope, peace, restfulness, longing, relief, safety and (relationship) love.

One may discuss if all should be called emotions. To me some of the experiences mentioned are feeling states of consciousness or emotionally charged situations. What is relevant in the present context is their strong charges of psychic energy.

This first part of the list are experiences likely to appear in traumatic dreams, while the second part of the list contains experiences that I think would belong to the category of peak experience dreams.

The Synthesis of the Observations

The more universal the dream narratives and images are, the stronger the energy charges, meaningfulness and prospective power a dream is assumed to contain. The less a dream has elements from everyday reality, the more important these elements may be. Peak experience dreams especially occur during critical phases in life. The value, meaningfulness and intensity of a dream can be graduated employing various tools, both in research and in practical dreamwork.

The more dreamers are involved in self-development and therapeutic work, plus consciously involving themselves in imagination activities and meditation, the more of the above-mentioned qualities are likely to appear in dreams.

Yet, as Jung and his followers have often pointed out, an emphasis on "big dreams" may be overwhelming for the ego and normal waking self. It can lead to "inflation" of the ego (Jung 1928, par. 250), loss of grounding and even cause psychosis (Dieckmann 1984). Thus, there must be a reasonable balance between the peak experience dreams and the various levels of everydayness, no matter how spiritually 'developed' the dreamer may be.

Certain cautionary rules should be employed in connection with strongly charged negative emotions. This is a theme I will look at more closely below in connection with traumatic dreams.

Whether dreams have individual or collective meanings, I believe, depends on which aspects one chooses to focus on and the context in general. All dreams can be utilized in groups to shed light on themes that are of common interest to the group members. They can be used to investigate general social and cultural similarities and differences, and they can be found meaningful to an individual's attitude toward work or social group.

Peak experience dreams occur during important life transitions, creative breakthroughs and as initial dreams. They may also be reactions to traumatic events that mobilize extraordinary and, in children, often precocious qualities.

Children and Peak Experience Dreams

Peak experiences often take place in children from the ages of 5–7, give or take a year or two. Children often have difficulty formulating what they experience because it can be so foreign to them and therefore so rarely understood by the adults close to them. Not until later in life are experiences and dreams tied to an event recalled, and this usually happens only if the individual receives cues from the surroundings. I have systematically researched this theme and written extensively about it in other contexts (Vedfelt 2013).

One criterion for a peak experience is that it makes a very deep, long-lasting impression. The earliest remembered childhood dreams can be seen as significant dreams for that very reason alone. Yet there can be certain traits that enhance the impression.

At the age of five, Rikke dreamed that *her friend Inga says that God is in the hallway and that Rikke should come out and look. Rikke is frightened that God will be judgmental toward her, in contrast to Inga who is so kind. But God is standing there great and luminous, looking with love and acceptance at both girls, who are standing hand in hand.*

The dream involved a supernatural being and had the same luminous quality as Chagall's dream. It can be categorized as archetypal. It also contained a magical quality and the feelings of awe, wonder, mystery, happiness, hope, peace and love, as mentioned by Hartmann. The dream also seemed to have consequences in her life and close relationships. Rikke had a very strict father. After this dream she was less anxious in her relationship with him.

In the section in Core Quality 6 on earliest remembered childhood dreams, I referred to Jack, a male musician who, when starting school, "fell off the edge of the rainbow leading to the home of the gods." This dream, which has a strong mythological parallel in Norse mythology, was related to a crucial event and may even be related to the expulsion from Eden.

All the earliest remembered childhood dreams mentioned were subjectively experienced as meaningful patterns in the dreamers' personalities and as themes they had to deal with throughout life. They all had abstract, non-rational and non-everydayness qualities.

Peak Experience Dreams in Puberty

Fourteen-year-old Ida's dreams (Core Quality 6) about Gyro Gearloose's Little Helper that always followed her, symbolized an inner genius and inventiveness that, much later, proved to be of great help in her life and career. Her dream of a red thread that led through many strange cities has an archetypal parallel in the thread of Ariadne that guided Greek hero Theseus through a dangerous labyrinth. There was no everydayness in the two dreams that Ida mentioned. Her dreams had helpful forces in the environment, magical objects, extraordinary power and mastery from the Good Fortune Scale. They were encouraging for her and had long-term consequences.

The Peak Experience Dream of a Young Man – Peter

The dream Peter – the man in his late twenties who had trouble making serious commitments to women (Core Quality 7) – dreamed did not appear at first to be a peak experience dream even though it was an initial dream. Retrospectively, Peter's dream was especially significant and contained important archetypal symbolism: the intercourse with the young woman – "coniunctio" – as Jung called it (Jung 1955–6). However, this sequence was framed by other dream sequences about repulsion and a lack of situation mastery in his relations with women. Peter's conscious experience of the (dream) intercourse with a young woman lacked the 'soul' quality that lies at the heart of Jung's definition of the feminine as an archetype in the male personality. Later in his process, it turned out that Peter needed to liberate a masculinity tied up in old patterns before he could integrate the energy that was contained in the coniunctio symbol. Not until after an internal revolt with the father did Peter have a peak experience dream of "meeting and melting together with a beautiful, fascinating woman," accompanied by the ability to fall in love. His dream also required extensive inner post-processing.

Peak Experiences and Vulnerability

Another facet of peak experience dreams is the vulnerability of the mental states that peak experience dreams are reflecting. We see this in pregnant Sarah's dreams described in Core Quality 3. In a dream after having been rejected by the mother, she experienced life-threatening persecution. A few days later she dreamed of being together with her motherhood group and her husband with her child. The second dream was understood as a rallying and harmonizing of forces in her psyche into a new wholeness around her own inner child. Just as Peter's dream did, it required some post-processing to build up and secure her new position in life.

A 40-Year-Old Woman's Peak Experience Dream – Emma

People who work intensively with meditation, self-development and their dreams can have dreams where the archetypal nature stands out very clearly in crucial transitional life phases. A friend of mine told of a dream she had when she was 40 years old and which she had remembered 25 years later as one of the most important dreams of her life.

> She is flying over a landscape. It feels very light and happy. The colors are supernaturally intense and radiant. She flies over the edge of a beach and can see something lying on the sand glittering in the sun. She lands and sees that it is jewelry. She especially notices a blue gemstone and a royal scepter. She picks up the scepter and holds it out toward the sea. The seas part and she

can walk on the floor of the sea. She is aware she is dreaming at times. The dreamer does not remember if she picked up the blue gemstone, but after her dream she experienced many synchronistic coincidences with the color blue.

This woman had been in Jungian analysis for a few years where sand-play and dreams had significant roles. In addition to this, she was in an intensive meditation group with which she was very pleased. She had broken out of a marriage several years before and was in love with a man she was starting a family with. She and her new man were in business together, which she was also happy about, yet she felt it was difficult to live up to him because he had more professional experience. At the time of her dream she had been encouraged to lead her own groups in meditation and personal development – completely after her own heart.

Archetypality

A strong mythological parallel is the tale in the Old Testament about the parting of the Red Sea by Moses with his staff, who then leads his oppressed people away from the persecution of the Egyptians. The flying in her dream has a weaker parallel in the myth about Icarus who fled together with his father and was told not to fly too high or too low. Jung describes the finding of jewelry and gemstones as a motive from alchemy, "the treasure hard to attain," is a symbol of achieving inner wisdom (Jung 1944 fig. 172). In addition, her dream had heightened affect, non-rational imagery and remoteness from "everydayness."

The Good Fortune Scale

Her dream has four of the six qualities on the Good Fortune Scale: flying, helpful forces in the environment, magical objects and extraordinary powers. From the positive end of Hartmann's list of intense emotional experiences, we find power, mastery, supremacy, awe, wonder, mystery, happiness, joy and excitement.

This dream made an indelible impression on the dreamer and became the beginning of many years work with her own groups, parallel to her work with her new partner.

She says that her dream became an enormous driving force in her life. She suffered great anxiety when she began to work alone as the leader of self-development courses. Yet it was as if a hitherto unknown force carried her through.

The Peak Experience Dream of Antonio –
80 Years Old

Antonio, an 80-year-old engineer, told me of a dream that had left a big impression on him.

His daughter-in-law shows him 'his new house,' with a view out to a beautiful nature area. She leads him up a twisting staircase to a big platform on the roof. He is met there by an old (now deceased) high school teacher who had supported him in his youth. 'UFOs can land here,' the teacher says and then explains that the crafts will bring friendly-minded beings of superior wisdom. That fills Antonio with happy expectation.

The day before his dream, Antonio had put his summerhouse up for sale because he could no longer manage the upkeep. This would also put an end to a debilitating feud with his neighbor. His decision brought him a great sense of relief.

His daughter-in-law was a woman he liked to whom he could talk in terms of a philosophy of life.

The teacher in Antonio's dream was a warm and open person from his high school years who had awakened his interest in religion, phenomena of consciousness and esoteric matters.

After Antonio had this dream, he was very surprised to find he had been liberated from a fear of dying that had plagued him since retiring. His daughter-in-law later said that she thought he had changed, becoming milder and more well-rounded.

Antonio's dream is packed with archetypal symbolism and matches remarkably well Jung's theory of individuation in mature life (see Chapter 1). The new house in the dream may symbolize a new overall frame for Antonio's personality. The ending of a feud with the neighbor opens for a letting go of hostile and aggressive projections i.e. the work with "the shadow". The philosophical woman in the dream is the "anima", a feminine personification in the male that must be integrated after the work with the shadow. She is a spiritual guide of souls, "a psychopomp that leads the way to god and assures immortality (Hillman 1985 p. 52)." This corresponds to Antonio's liberation from the fear of dying. The spiritual teacher symbolizes, in Jung's developmental sequence, a continuation of the animas guidance. He represents the "wise old man", the innermost self of Antonio. "Flying saucers", Jung found typically in dreams that referred to the individuation process of the dreamer. He understood the flying saucer as a symbol of a higher transcendent reality and a compensation for the spiritual and crisis of modern man (Jung 1958).

Lucid Dreaming

A particular type of dream that may appear as a high peak in the psychological energy landscape is a lucid dream. A lucid dream is defined as a dream where you are conscious that you are dreaming (LaBerge 2007).

Lucid dreams are spontaneous phenomena in general. For the most part, they are experienced as especially vivid and intense, and they belong to the kind of dreams we typically remember a long time. Between one fourth and one half of us have lucid dreams from time to time. They most frequently appear in connection with intense situations and important transitional phases in life.

Some people seem to have a special disposition for lucid dreaming and experience it relatively often. It can also be connected to states of anxiety where consciousness seems to leave the body and observe itself from outside (out-of-body experiences) (Vedfelt 2000).

If the lucid state is maintained, it is possible to gain a certain amount of control of the dream, for instance, flying to the place one wishes.

Being conscious that you are dreaming is often noticed shortly after the dream begins when you discover something improbable such as, for instance: flying, or an unknown piece of furniture is in your office, or a lion with zebra-stripes.

There are several levels of lucidity, depending on how long you can remain conscious that you are dreaming. It might be difficult to stay in that state of consciousness without slipping into a normal dream. On the other hand, the discovery of being in a lucid dream may be so exciting that you are awakened by the excitement in your mind.

One way to maintain the lucid state is by keeping your mind completely calm. The ability to remain lucid is reminiscent of the ability to stay in intensive states of meditation. Lucid dreaming therefore has been of interest to practices that employ meditative training, such as Buddhism (Tse-fu Kuan 2008).

Meditation, visualization and disconnecting from everyday stress, on vacation for instance, increase the probability of having lucid dreams. Practicing to remember dreaming increases your chances of lucid dreams. Analyzing your dreams and paying particular attention to any overlooked elements of lucidity sharpens your awareness when dreaming (Garfield 1974).

While dreaming, you focus on a body part – your hands, for instance. The effect is probably due to the fact that the dreamer's body belongs to the most stable elements in a dream. In case of anxiety, it is suggested that you remind yourself that it is only a dream and nothing can happen. Thus, the emotional tension that might lead to awakening is reduced (Barrett 1992).

Lucid dreams are phenomena that fascinate many people, partly because they are very intense and contain adventurous activities that provide dreamers a certain degree of control of the events. Yet this wish for control may be influenced by narcissistic needs from the ego – in exact opposition to the self-regulating function of dreams. Therefore, almost everyone who seriously works with lucid dreaming acknowledges that there has to be an ethical base and purpose for the activity that goes beyond the individual dreamer's ego and narcissistic needs (Sparrow 1982). Through this, interest in controlling the dream-plots wanes. The benefit in this is that you allow yourself to be carried towards something bigger than the ego, something that illuminates consciousness.

From a neuroscientific point of view, it seems that recognition is dependent on activity in the dorsolateral prefrontal cortex, which is normally deactivated during REM-sleep. Intense activity in visual areas of the cortex and the pons continues, and it is likely that the areas in the emotional brain, particularly the amygdala, are not active enough to awaken the dreamer (Muzur *et al.* 2002).

Parapsychological Dreams

Another type of dream, which is likely to be experienced as very lively and intense, are dreams related to parapsychological experiences. They are remembered long after and may be tied to especially fateful or exalted moods.

Parapsychological dreams are experiences that seem to transgress the limits of our culture's adopted notions of time, space and energy. They fascinate people in general (Dwyer 2004), they have been studied in the therapeutic setting and experiments have been conducted in the sleep laboratories. These experiences can be divided into four types that overlap each other to a certain extent (Vedfelt 2000).

Precognitive Dreams

Precognitive dreams tell about things that later come to pass in actual, outer reality. Louisa Rhine, a pioneer in the study of paranormal dreams collected more than seven thousand anecdotal reports from popular dream books of paranormal experiences. The majority of the accounts involved dreams. Robert Van de Castle studied 413 precognitive dreams from her files that seemed to predict future events. Death was the most prominent, accidents and injuries was next on the list. Close blood ties were involved in about half of the dreams. Spouses and friends were frequently involved. Women were twice as often receivers as men (Van de Castle 1994 p. 409).

Also dreams of great collective importance were recounted. Only days before his actual assassination, President Abraham Lincoln described, a dream to his wife and secretary about his own funeral after an assassination (Krippner 1975). British psychiatrist John Barker found in a systematic research examples of seemingly precognitive dreams prior to a coalmine disaster. Before the disaster a little girl told her mother a dream: "we go to school but there is no school there; something black has come down all over it". Few days later she and 118 children were crushed or buried alive under a huge slag deposit. (Barker1967).

More positively, I have in my practice and in my own life, experienced dreams that seem to predict conception and pregnancy, moving into new homes, and budding love affairs, etc.

Telepathic Dreams

The dreamer receives thoughts or images from another person. Dream researcher Montague Ullman has described transference of visualized paintings from a psychic medium to a dreamer in a sleep laboratory (Ullman 1969). The experiment was criticized by David Foulkes, who was unable to replicate the result in his sleep laboratory (Foulkes 1972). However, Foulkes later admitted a case of telepathy from his own laboratory, as recounted by Robert van de Castle (1994) Another researcher, Alan Rechtschaffen found that persons who dreamt at the same time in his sleep laboratory experienced corresponding themes. Further certain states of consciousness for instance hypnosis seemed to improve the telepathic communication (Rechtschaffen 1970).

Synchronicity

Synchronicity is described by Jung as a meaningful coincidence of two events without any probable outer causality. For instance, one of Jung's patients dreamed that someone had given her a very valuable piece of jewelry: a golden scarab. Scarabs are a species of beetle that had a great symbolic value to the ancient Egyptians. Just as this woman was telling Jung about her dream, a very rare Swiss golden beetle was tapping gently on the window-pane (Jung 1952). Jung found that parapsychological experiences are mediated through the collective unconsious. Therefore they typically occur in archetypal (universally human) situations, dvs. de vigtigste overgange i livet, som fødsel, pubertet, situationer omkring partnerskab, midtvejskrise og død. phenomena (Main 1997, Franz 1975). Also creative processes and important of cultural and societal events can activate synchronistic and precognitive dreams. In his memoirs, Jungs gives interesting examples of his own dreams with alledged collective meanings (Jung 1961).

Out-of-body Experiences

Dreamers experience being outside of their own bodies and perhaps watching themselves sleeping, or have the experience of being able to move to other times and places, without physical limitations. They may in occur in peak experience dreams, lucid dreams, precognitive dreams, and telepathic dreams. They are also frequent features in traumatized, and even psychotic persons dreams as an automatic cope with intolerable pain, fear or abandonment (see Chapter 14).

Parapsychological dreams, according to many clinicians my experience, may appear when important emotional communication has become difficult on other levels, like between parents and children, between lovers or within therapeutic relationships with strong, unconscious transferences. (Servadio 1970, Eisenbud 1952, Ullman 1969, Franz 1964, Van de castle 1994 and Vedfelt 2000)

Dreams may be warnings or encouragements to prepare for the future. Certain contextual conditions, or a particularly intense and undeniable mood, may support solid interpretation. Yet most dreams may benefit from being interpreted psychologically and as symbolic inner-happenings, which Freud, Jung and their successors recommended. For instance, if a parent dies in a dream, this may symbolize a psychological liberation process from the influence that the parents have exacted. Other dreams about a fear of death may also be about unprocessed sorrow deriving from earlier in life, and may not be telepathic in a literal sense.

If parapsychological dreams appear to an individual frequently this may indicate both great sensitivity and/or a lack of grounding. If parapsychological experiences actually take place, they probably do so more frequently than we are aware of, because our attention is tied to tangible life tasks, and our sensitivity and mindset are trained to register other categories of phenomena.

Conclusion

There is no sharp division between peak experience dreams and the dreams of everyday life. A complexity of qualities determines how sharp the peaks are in the psychological energy landscape, and how valuable a dream will be in the context of a person's life.

If we consciously begin to relate to these dreams and work through their most urgent themes, the energy landscapes will spread out and become lower hills. The important themes in the dreamer's life become more nuanced. Dreams can point out several important interests simultaneously and provide an image of their mutual strength levels at any given moment.

References

Barker, J. C. (1967): 'Premonitions of the Aberfan Disaster.' *J. the Society for Psychical Research* 44, s. 169–181. London.

Barrett, D. (1992) *The Effectiveness of Dreams for Problem Solving*, paper presented at the 1992 Annual Convention of the Association for the Study of Dreams.

Belvedere, E., Foulkes, D. (1972): Long distance, Sensory Bombardment. ESP in Dreams: a failure to replicate. *Percept Mot. Skills*. 35(3), s. 731–34, US.

Bernsen, N. and Ulbæk, I. (1993) *Natural and Artificial Intelligence*. (Copenhagen: New Nordic Publishers)

Bulkeley, K. (2006) 'Revision of the Good Fortune Scale: a new tool for the study of "Big Dreams".' *Dreaming*, Vol 16(1), pp. 11–21

Bulkeley, K. (Ed.) (2001) *Dreams: A Reader on Religious, Cultural, and Psychological Dimensions of Dreaming*. (London: Palgrave Macmillan)

Dieckmann, H. (1984) *Träume als Sprache der Seele*. (Stuttgart, Germany: Bonz)

Dwyer, R. (2004): Panel discussion on dreams. Annual conference for the IASD.

Eisenbud, J. (1952): 'The use of the telepathy hypothesis' in *Specialized Techniques in Psychotherapy* (US) pp. 41–63

Faber, P. A. *et al.* (1978) 'Meditation and archetypal content of nocturnal dreams'. *Journal of Analytical Psychology*, Vol. 23, pp.1–22

Faber, P. A. *et al.* (1983) 'Induced waking fantasy: its effects upon the archetypal content of nocturnal dreams'. *Journal of Analytical Psychology*, 28(2), pp.141–64

Foulkes, D. (1972): Long distance, Sensory Bombardment. ESP in Dreams: a failure to replicate. *Percept Mot. Skills*. 35(3) s. 731–34, USA

Freud, S. (1922) "Dreams and Telepathy" in *The Standard Edition of the Complete Psychological Works of Sigmund Freud* Vol. 18. (New York: Hogarth Press), pp. 200–220

Freud, S. (1933A [1932]): *Dreams and Occultism* s.7-30 In New Introductory Lectures on Psychoanalysis, S.E. Vol. XXII

Garfield, P. (1974) *Creative Dreaming*. (New York: Ballantine Books)

Hartmann, E. (2011) *The Nature and Functions of Dreaming*. (Oxford, UK: Oxford University Press), Kindle edition

Hillman, J. (1985) *Anima. An Anatomy of a Personified Notion*. (Spring Publications, Inc. Woodstock. Connecticut)

James, W. (1902) *The Varieties of Religious Experience*. (London: Longmans, Green and Co.)

Jung, C. G. (1928/1981) 'The relation between the ego and the unconscious' in G. Adler and R. F. C. Hull (Eds), *The Collected Works of C.G. Jung: Two Essays on Analytical Psychology*, Vol. 7. (Abingdon, UK: Routledge and Kegan Paul)

Jung C. G. (1944/1981) 'Psychology and alchemy' in G. Adler and R. F. C. Hull (Eds), *The Collected Works of C.G. Jung: Psychology and Alchemy*, Vol. 12. (Abingdon, UK: Routledge and Kegan Paul)

Jung, C. G. (1945/48/1981) *On the Nature of Dreams* in G. Adler, M. Fordham and Sir H. Read (Eds), *The Collected Works of C.G. Jung: The Structure and Dynamics of the Psyche*, Vol. 8. (Abingdon, UK: Routledge and Kegan Paul), par. 530–69

Jung, C. G. (1952/1981) 'Synchronicity. An acausal connecting principle' in G. Adler, M. Fordham and Sir H. Read (Eds), *The Collected Works of C.G. Jung: The Structure and Dynamics of the Psyche*, Vol. 8. (Abingdon, UK: Routledge and Kegan Paul), par. 816–997

Jung, C. G. (Author), G. Adler and R. F. C. Hull (Eds) (1955–6/1981) *The Collected Works of C.G. Jung: Mysterium Coniunctionis*, Vol. 14. (Abingdon, UK: Routledge and Kegan Paul)

Jung, C. G. (1958/1981) 'Flying Saucers: a modern myth of things seen in the skies' in G. Adler and R. F. C. Hull (Eds), *The Collected Works of C.G. Jung: Civilization in Transition*, Vol. 10. (Abingdon, UK: Routledge and Kegan Paul)

Jung, C. G. (1961) *Memories, Dreams, Reflections*. (New York: Random House)

Kluger, H. Y. (1955) 'Archetypal dreams and "everyday" dreams'. *Israel's Annals of Psychiatry and Related Disciplines*, Vol. 13, pp. 6–47

Krippner, S. (1975) 'Dreams and other altered conscious states'. *Journal of Communication*, Vol. 25(1), pp. 173–82

LaBerge, S. (2007) 'Lucid dreaming' in D. Barrett and P. McNamara (Eds), *The New Science of Dreaming: Content, Recall, and Personality Correlates* (Vol. 2). (Westport, CT: Praeger), pp. 307–328

Main, R. (1997) *Jung on synchronicity and the paranormal. Keyreadings selected and introduced by Roderick Main*. (Routledge, London)

Maslow, A. (1976) *Religions, Values and Peak-experiences*. (London: Penguin Books)

McClelland, J.L. Rumelhart, D. and Hinton, G. E. (1986) 'The appeal of parallel distributed processing' in D. Rumelhart and J. L. McClelland (Eds), *Parallel Distributed Processing Vol. 1: Explorations in the Microstructure of Cognition Volume Foundations*. (Cambridge, MA: The MIT Press), pp. 3–44

Muzur, A., Pace-Schott, E. F. and Hobson, A. (2002) 'The prefrontal cortex in sleep'. *Trends in Cognitive Sciences*, 1, 2(11), 475–81

O'Nell, C. (1976) *Dreams, Culture and the Individual*. (San Francisco, CA: Chandler and Sharp)

Otto, R. (1917/1958) *The Idea of the Holy*. (Oxford, UK: Oxford University Press)

Rechtschaffen, A. (1970). "Sleep and dream states: An experimental design." In R. Cavanna, (Ed.), *Psi favorable states of consciousness* pp. 87–120. (New York: Parapsychological Foundation)

Rumelhart, D. *et al.* (1986) 'Schemata and sequential thought' in J. L. McClelland and D. Rumelhart (Eds), *Parallel Distributed Processing Vol 2: Explorations in the Microstructure of Cognition: Psychological and Biological Models.* (Cambridge, MA: The MIT Press), pp.7–57

Servadio, E. (1970): *Psychoanalysis and telepathy* in Devereux, G. Ed. *Int. Univ. Press* pp. 210–220

Smolensky, P. (1986) 'Information processing in dynamical systems' in D. Rumelhart and J. L. McClelland (Eds), *Parallel Distributed Processing Vol 1: Explorations in the Microstructure of Cognition Volume Foundations.* (Cambridge, MA: The MIT Press), pp. 194–281

Sparrow, G. S. (1982) *Lucid Dreaming.* (Virginia Beach, VA: A.R.E. Press)

Tse-fu Kuan (2008) *Mindfulness in Early Buddhism: New Approaches through Psychology and Textual Analysis of Pali, Chinese and Sanskrit Sources* (Abingdon, UK: Routledge)

Ullman, M. (1969) 'Telepathy and dreams'. *Experimental Medicine and Surgery*, 27, s. 9–38

Vedfelt, O. (2000) *The Dimensions of Dreams.* (London: Jessica Kingsley Publishers)

Vedfelt, O. (2013) 'The phenomenology of the spirit in childhood memories. Early numinous experiences in a desacralized world' in E. Kiehl (Ed.), *Copenhagen 2013, 100 Years On: Origins, Innovations and Controversies: Proceedings of the 19th Congress of the International Association for Analytical Psychology.* (Einsiedeln, Switzerland: Daimon Verlag)

Chapter 14

Dreams and Trauma

Severe traumatic experiences of war and violence, accidental fires and natural disasters, rape and sexual abuse, disease and painful treatment may produce echoes in dreams long after the events, perhaps even throughout an entire lifetime.

If the trauma is not psychologically processed, reminiscences may appear as highly charged energy peaks in the overall dream landscapes. In single, isolated dreams, memory traces may also be present as redundant information where many elements, themes or characters recurrently refer to traumatic events with strongly charged associative links.

Seemingly insignificant cues from the previous day or from generally stressing life situations may arouse energy charged trauma patterns and initiate inappropriate and seemingly irrational actions, the causes of which are unconscious to the actors.

Severe trauma always interferes with personal development as a whole. Trauma may halt or slow normal developmental processes in various respects. Due to highly charged energy, they may activate information-dense states and peak experiences, as well as social, imaginative and creative skills in precocious ways. Traumatic memories may live hidden in the unconscious memory systems for years before being awakened, and also add complications to important phases in life. This often leads to the severe fragmenting of various areas of the personality.

Traumas may be divided into two categories, 'characterological traumas' and 'shock traumas', the latter causing Post Traumatic Stress Disorder – PTSD (Joergensen 1992). However, these two types of trauma have many overlapping properties. Characterological traumas are representative of a long series of dysfunctional, character-forming occurrences with shared content. I have exemplified such traumas in Linda's dream about the waiting room (Core Quality 10), in Henrik's dream with the broken key from the unreliable father (Core Quality 6), and in the sexualizing, incestuous mother figure in Peter's dream (Core Quality 6). The psychologically recurring experiences that these dreams portray are not powerful enough to produce PTSD, but may have a persistent and inadequate influence on character.

These dreams may offer important contributions when dealing with the phenomenon in all its complexity. When dreams refer to traumatic events, the cluster of associations they attract are meaningful on many levels, if the opportunity to unfold them in a larger context presents itself.

The PTSD Diagnosis

The criteria for the PTSD diagnosis, as described by the American Psychiatric Association's diagnostic manual (DSM-IV), is:

1. An individual felt his life threatened, suffered possibly severe physical harm, or was witness to another person's death, serious injury or menace to life.
2. a) An individual's reaction was intense anxiety, helplessness or terror. In children, this can also be manifested by disorganized or nervously agitated behavior.
    b) The traumatic event is persistently relived in one or more of the following ways: disturbing recollections of the incident in dreams, acting or feeling as if the incident has returned, or psychic disturbances and reactions toward inner or outer experiences which symbolize or resemble parts of the traumatic event. In children, aspects of the trauma might be played out in games or behavior.
    c) Persistent attempts to avoid influences that are associated with the trauma, and a blunting or numbing of the general receptivity. This leads to a reduction of conduct of the individual's life and emotional life, and also includes an inability to recall important aspects of the trauma.
    d) An increased arousal referring to an overalertness and overwariness that makes relaxing difficult. This can manifest itself as difficulty sleeping, a lowered fright-threshold, irritability, unrestrainable anger and concentration difficulties.

Unlike an 'adjustment disorder' (for example caused by characterological traumas) the influence has to be extreme, i.e. the situation must be experienced as life-threatening. Direct threats do not necessarily have to be made towards the individual or another. This may also be in connection with the unexpected or violent death of a relative or loved one. If this state persists for less than three months it is termed acute. If it continues beyond that, it is chronic (American Psychiatric Association 1994).

How Traumatic Events Appear in Dreams

Both Freud and Jung were aware that extreme traumatic events, such as shell shock and other mental injuries, exposed the victims to persistent, repetitive dreams. These dreams were similar to exact replays of the traumatic events.

Freud suggested that because the repression mechanism relaxes during sleep, traumatic memories will be active and thus awaken the sleeping person. He saw it as a failure in dreamwork – the compulsion to repeat overrides the wish fulfillment function (Nagera 1981). Jung found that traumatic dreams could hardly have the compensatory function he generally ascribed to dreams (Jung 1916/1948). They both had difficulty seeing constructive aspects in these dreams, in general.

Yet later research by Ernest Hartmann suggests that recurrent nightmares with exact replay of traumatic events are not dreams at all, but memory intrusions of traumatic waking experiences that can disturb any stage of sleep. Ordinary nightmares, usually defined as frightening dreams, show the same great variation in content as other dreams (Hartmann 1996). This also applies to war veterans whose difficulties are the primary impetus for the interest in recurring nightmares. Thus, useful approaches for dealing with nightmares of Iraq combat veterans has been described (Paulson and Krippner 2007).

Today, therapists and researchers generally assume that there is a continuum from normal dreams to traumatic nightmares. They also assume, as highlighted by Kelley Bulkeley, that, as healing takes place, nightmares about traumatizing events progress into more 'normal' dreams in which the events are woven into other life concerns (Bulkeley 2003).

According to Hartmann, dreams as well as therapy can create connections between trauma and the other parts of a patient's life. Emotions become less powerful and overwhelming as the trauma is gradually integrated into the rest of life (Hartmann 1998, p. 7).

As stated, these dreams are never exact replays of waking events. Memory fragments from trauma are woven into dream structure. They are also creatively associated with narratives and symbols that shed light on the dreamer's personality and provide background for individual ways of reacting.

Kathleen Nader, who is an international adviser concerned with traumatized children, writes in a comprehensive study of childhood trauma:

> Preschool children exposed to a hurricane, dreamed of being chased by an eye (they had heard of the eye of the hurricane) and of a variety of monsters. Headstart children exposed to the Los Angeles riots in 1992 dreamed of monsters, witches, fires and guns. Preschool children undergoing bone marrow transplants and medical procedures dreamed of ghosts coming to take them away, dragons threatening them, or being chased by mutilators. School age children may replace these ghosts with nondescript monsters sometimes taken from the movie screen. Monster dreams may occur at any age, although less frequent in adults.
>
> (Nader 1996.)

A study by Alan Siegel of adults who had escaped firestorms demonstrated that fire frequently appeared in the initial dreams after the event. Later, however, the participants recounted dreams about other types of frightening events, such as tidal waves or being chased by groups of criminals (Siegel 1996).

Ernest Hartmann describes the dreams of a young woman who was raped. The rapist, who was approximately 18 years old, climbed in her window, through the curtains and then threatened to strangle her with the curtains. In her dreams shortly after this trauma: *a gang of male adolescents started attacking a child. I tried to free the child, but I realized that my clothing was being torn off.* In other dreams: "some curtains began to choke me … a train is coming right at me … a whirlwind comes and envelops me …" and *"… snakes choke me."* She awoke from all these dreams very frightened. The rape as such was not directly portrayed in the dreams. As the process of healing progresses, there will be fewer allusions to the traumas in dreams according to Hartmann (1998).

The more intense and persistent traumatic events are, the more they will be associated to in the dreams. Swedish doctor of psychology Binnie Kristal-Andersson has described dreamwork with torture victims and their associations to each other's dreams. For instance, a seemingly harmless boat rope was associated to a friend who was hanged in prison. A train whistle became a signal that torture would start. Dancing could awaken reminiscences of squirming or wriggling during torture and not being able to run away. Looking at separate dreams, these types of associations would not be likely to come from individuals who had not experienced such terrible situations (Kristal-Andersson 2001).

However, the process of healing is complex. During recovery, there may be a reduction of the numbing that is typical in trauma victims, and an exacerbation of symptoms may occur. Kathleen Nader writes in her study of children's nightmares: "Each child establishes its own rhythm of trauma review." The dreams may also, "…incorporate psychodynamic issues, for example issues of protection, betrayal, loss, or accountability" (Nader 1996), and there may be guilt and shame for being the person who survived, while closely related persons died (Hartmann 1998, p. 8).

Frederick Stoddard, who leads a psychiatric ward at a clinical research hospital in Boston and who is a specialist in treating burns, describes night terrors where children talk about fear or seeing fire in the early phases after being burned. Yet these could appear much later, for instance, if a child returns to the hospital for follow-up surgery. If trauma is not treated psychotherapeutically, the effects of the trauma will typically last well into adult life and also be reflected in dreams, according to Stoddard et al. (1996, p. 32).

Precautions When Working with Post-Traumatic Dreams

Since traumas are highly charged events and since memories of traumatic events are high peaks in an individual's memory and dream landscapes, they attract many associations. The more they are evoked, the more dominating the pattern becomes.

According to cybernetic understanding, this may cause a relearning of a traumatic experience that increases its power. Therefore, traumatic dreams must be treated with great care and the energetic charge should be reorganized into more constructive experiential patterns.

As Siegel describes it, a trauma can make a person hypersensitive to subsequent life crises and stress, and these might retrigger the experience. Even in the absence of PTSD symptoms, it may be important to look for adaptation problems for many years to come (Siegel 1996, p. 176).

I have observed this understanding in many experienced clinicians of various observations. Body-psychotherapists Peter Levine and Ann Frederick

> visualize (the trauma) as an external force rupturing the protective container (banks) of our experience (...) With the rupture, an explosive rushing out of life-energy creates a trauma vortex. (...) It is common for traumatized individuals either to get sucked into the trauma vortex or to avoid the breach entirely by staying distanced from the region where the breach (trauma) occurred. We re-enact and relive our traumas when we get sucked into the trauma vortex, thus opening the possibility for emotional flooding and re-traumatization.
>
> (Levine and Frederick 1997, pp. 196–198.)

The trauma vortex can be seen as another metaphor for a high peak in the psychic energy landscape.

Barry Krakow, who is a specialist in sleep disturbances and nightmares, describes how people suffering from severe nightmares can be caught up in a "victim paradigm" because they have a tendency to overdo exercises and interpretations of nightmares, despite therapists' warnings (Krakow 2004).

Creative Imagination and Post-Traumatic Dreams

In an overview of the literature, clinical psychologist Johanna King finds that, although nightmares and bad dreams almost always accompany severe trauma, mainstream psychology and psychiatry has not made much use of dreams. "Sometimes suggestions are offered about drugs that might be administered to reduce nightmares," she writes, "but rarely is the dream or nightmare considered an important psychological experience in and of itself, full of meaning and potential for the trauma victim and the clinician" (King 2012).

As we can see, a good deal of psychological knowledge exists about post-traumatic dreams. Mostly, they are viewed in a pathological perspective. This is valuable in itself since caution is needed when working with traumatic dreams. Yet it is important to understand the healing and even prospective aspects of post-traumatic dreams.

Peter Levine suggests that organisms have evolved exquisite processes to heal the effects of trauma in much the same way as I have described self-organizing processes in connection with Core Quality 1. He describes the therapist function supporting the organism's "own intelligent healing processes" (Levine and Frederick 1997, p. 199).

The same kind of processes may play out in dreams, according to Ernest Hartmann who found many similarities between dreams and psychotherapy (Hartmann 1995). Kelley Bulkeley (2003, p.15) gives examples of how post-traumatic nightmares reflect the continued healthy functioning of a person's creative imagination.

Special attention to the value of creative imagination in trauma can be found within Jungian psychology with its notion of a "creative unconscious" (Neumann 1959). In his book, The Inner World of Trauma, post-Jungian analyst Donald Kalsched describes a severely traumatized boy's fantasies of being an African boy-king with heavenly parents while living under terrible conditions in Germany during the Second World War. These fantasies brought him hope, well-being and even sexual pleasure. Kalsched assumes that the psyche's capacity to invent such a fantasy "keeps the ego-germ alive physically and psychically" as a result of self-organization (Kalsched 1996).

Another Jungian analyst, Jean Knox, emphasizes the explorative functions of fantasy in traumatized persons, and also finds support for this from attachment theorist Peter Fonagy, who is particularly known for his work on mentalizing processes (Knox 2003). For my own part, I have described in various papers how self-organizing fantasies are activated with special intensity in traumatized children and adults (Vedfelt 1996, 2014).

Trauma and Individuation – Hell and Heaven

Traumatic events are always a challenge to personal development. They are best known for their destructive impact but they may also mobilize hitherto unknown creative forces that push development forward.

Kelly Bulkeley suggests, "Dreams following a crisis do not aim simply at making the person 'normal' again, with no other goal than restoring the state of affairs that existed previously – rather they aim at the development of a whole new understanding of self and world that is slowly created out of the broken ruins of the dreamer's pretrauma self" (Bulkeley 2003, p. 200).

Time and again, I have witnessed that highly charged traumatic experiences arouse and overlap information-dense experiences with transformative high peaks in personal development (Vedfelt 1996, 2014). However, it is more compli-cated than in normal development. As a result of trauma, an individual may swing between grandiose fantasies, feelings of depression and low self-esteem (Kohut 1983). However, as Jung described "inflation" and "deflation", it is also common in connection with the breakthrough of individuation (Jung 1928). From the perspective of body-psychotherapy, Peter Levine imagines it as expansion and contraction where a person, "... wobbles between heavenly rapture and hellish nightmare in an ever-constricting vortex of energy. This buffeting between the extreme polarities of heaven and hell generates the rhythm essential for the transformation of trauma."

An Example of Character Trauma and Mature Individuation – Torsten

From my own therapeutic experience, I will exemplify this with the experiences and dreams of Torsten, a 50-year-old leading psychologist. Outwardly, he had a fine career. Yet he had always suffered from nervousness and mood swings, sometimes launching into great altruistic projects and even coming close to collapsing under pressure at times.

Torsten had been in therapy for two years as part of a mature individuation process. He often talked about his father – an aggression-inhibited man who felt that he should have been something greater in life than what he had become. Torsten's father was plagued by financial difficulties. He could become extremely irritable and explode in unpredictable outbursts of rage for which he reproached himself afterwards.

Several times, Torsten had mentioned an episode from when he was three years of age: he approached his father in an attempt at contact, but the latter unexpectedly went into a tantrum and threw Torsten against a closet door.

Torsten worked through this traumatic event in group therapy and followed up with individual sessions. The group session started with drawing the incident. It included role-play and bodywork, and was accompanied by strong emotional and bodily discharge. Deeply immersed in role-play, Torsten found rest and consolation at his grandmother's house which was his safest place as a child.

In meditation the next day, Torsten experienced a powerful light descend over his head. He felt it was a connection to his grandmother and described the light as divine. He had a dream in which he was in therapy with me and passed through: *a blissful heavenly sequence*. In other dreams: *he could walk in the air*. This was a type of dream he had never had before. For some time after this, he was in a high, almost euphoric mood.

Since his youth, Torsten had been bothered by difficulty in sleeping and frequently took sleeping pills but, after this work in therapy, he ostensibly slept, "…incredibly well and soundly." He experienced that his breathing had become calm and often felt intense tranquility and bodily warmth. In work situations where he was usually nervous, he would often recall the feeling he had experienced in relation to his grandmother. Then Torsten became calm and relaxed. His wife said that he was more loving and open than she had ever experienced him.

This happy state lasted for nearly a month. Then bad dreams appeared. *One of them dealt with a bomb threat*. After this, Torsten suddenly went into a panic over his personal finances because he had slightly overdrawn his bank account. He felt his chest constrict, his stomach tense, general anxiety and distaste for everything. When he immersed himself in the anxiety with therapeutic support, he found it was associated with memories of the father going bankrupt when Torsten was in puberty. His family had been scattered to the four winds. After this therapy work, he could clearly see that his finances were not threatened. Torsten had a secure and well-paid position and his overdraft could easily be covered.

Rather than seeing new trauma memories as accidental, I suggested that the work with his very early trauma had activated memories of the later trauma. The repercussions of this work were, as I saw it, a replaying of the trauma with this typical splitting: a positive transpersonal experience, and the reactivation of memories with a related emotional experience of catastrophy.

Torsten's dreams of flying had been followed by dreams of the fear of falling. In one dream *he hovered up under the ceiling and looked down at the other dream-characters*. This type of elevating oneself above the physical level could be a reminiscence of an out-of-body experience during a trauma, where it is common that victims feel they are hovering above the situations and looking down on what is happening (Herman 1992).

All of the emotions that, as a prelude, had come up in connection with the work with his father's assault – the grief, the rage, the abandonment on one hand, and the love and trust on the other – had to be lived through with much greater depth. Or, as it was expressed in one dream: "A little child runs about freely. I must watch out that it doesn't get run over."

Healing PTSD Nightmares in a Young Woman – Lisa

In the following case, I will show how post-traumatic dreams contain all the core qualities that I describe in this book, and how they are valuable to practical dreamwork.

Lisa, a young woman in her early 20s, sought out my help with terrifying recurrent nightmares. In an email request for therapy she wrote that she suffered from a severe cancer illness at the age of 11. She underwent treatment for a couple of years, including surgeries and lengthy chemotherapy, which had severe side-effects for her. Everything was painful and uncomfortable. She stayed in the hospital for long periods of time. Lisa had difficulty sleeping and acted out on her surroundings very aggressively. When awake, she had her father read stories to her, trying to escape into other worlds. Her nightmares began in this period and have stayed with her ever since.

Now she has fully recovered without any lasting physical effects. Lisa wrote that, even though she was ailing at the time, she primarily remembers the love and support given to her by the people she met in this difficult period. Unfortunately, the horrific nightmares still plague her every single night. She hopes therapy will give her back the good dreams she had before her illness.

At the hospital, a psychologist evaluated that, emotionally, Lisa was a well and healthy girl who reacted with natural aggressiveness of the treatment.

In her first hour with me, an image develops of an intelligent, articulate young woman with an altruistic value base. Lisa has musical talents and is studying the humanities. She loves reading, drawing, dancing and creativity. For the most part, she keeps to herself. During the session, she is intense, dedicated, very attentive and she talks about her life in broad terms.

I ask her about her nightmares. Lisa tells me that they are usually about her getting lost, being banished or abandoned to a desolate place, like after a nuclear war perhaps, and no one is there to help her.

I asked her to write down recent dreams. Lisa felt her dreams were banal and therefore did not record them. When I ask her to tell me about a recent, tangible dream anyway, she mentions that: she is somewhere where the ground is being flooded and a lot of alligators are approaching. It all seems so very hopeless.

In another dream she arrives at a place that looks like the old Mayan culture. Some gorillas are the rulers and they have contact with the gods. There is one particularly aggressive male gorilla that wants to wipe out the world because humankind has destroyed it with their technology.

I ask whether experiencing the end of the world, feeling abandoned and being threatened by something might somehow reflect her experiences during her illness. Lisa has not thought of it that way and I can see she is moved.

I ask if she can describe these two dreams in greater detail. She then realizes that, in the second dream, she manages to make some contact and communicate with a gorilla. This makes her think about there being a baby alligator in her first dream that she can communicate with, even though it all still seems so hopeless.

I tell her that being able to communicate with a baby alligator and an angry male gorilla are fantastic abilities. My comments make her visibly moved and happy.

In the second session, Lisa tells about a new dream that she calls "The (Almost) Great Escape."

> *I'm on vacation in an exotic place with my mother and father. I have a big fight with my mother. I end up getting grounded. I manage to sneak out. The escape makes me feel excitement. The Great Escape. Great adventure. Am I finally free? Great sense of freedom without fear or nervousness. Torn free of my mother's control – finally free in a world of opportunities. During the escape, I fall in love with my helper. We kiss each other ...*

Yet the dream ends with: *I'm returned to my mother. I still have a great sense of satisfaction at having made it so far alone. Rebellion.*

This is an initial dream. It is not post-traumatic, but instead appears to open up a universal theme of the development of a young woman – breaking free of her parents and especially from her dependence on her mother, and the devotion to a partner and the freedom connected with that. The conclusion reflects an externalized rebellion that does not suceed. Yet, she has preserved the enthusiastic feeling of freedom and motivation to succeed later.

Despite this dream, Lisa says that it is hard to think about separating from her mother. She still lives at home and has a close relationship with her. Her mother is her best friend.

Lisa recounts more dreams in her following sessions. They are long and rich with imagery, so I summarize them here for brevity.

Lisa dreams that *she tries to help some people who want to commit suicide but they really don't. This repeats itself several times in her dream. In the end, she finds them an emergency exit.*

Lisa's first thoughts are about her present, working life. She talks about some young women who are sexually harassed at a job and who she tries to help. I acknowledge her helpfulness. I ask if anything in her own life could have been so difficult that she had wanted to kill herself. "I guess so," she says, "but it was a long time ago ... the chemo and all that." Then she changes the subject.

In a dream at a following session *she has to move but is having trouble finding a suitable place. First, there are some cardboard boxes that people can just steal from her. And then a tent that she could not lock.*

Lisa tells me that she plans to move away from home. She is having a hard time finding somewhere acceptable to live. This is the actual life situation part of the context. When she visualizes and associates to the dream, she remembers that she liked to make a little fort out of random material with her father. They sat in it and he read stories. However, sometimes it was removed by the staff or she was moved to another hospital or department.

Six weeks into her therapy, she dreams:

> *I find myself in a well-known harbor town that is safe and idyllic, but some-thing tells me that danger is lurking. Someone says I have a baby. My father is there and he offers to look after my baby for me. I am surprised – my father is not known for being energetic. I look him over an extra time – he looks perfect with my baby. I become extremely secure with the situation – he is radiating enormous vitality and happiness. Then the mood suddenly changes: I remember he is dead. It hurts. This man had such a passion and vitality. I am really sad that I will never meet this man again (in reality).*

Lisa's father was loving but he was very busy with his work. At one point, he had a problem with alcohol that made their contact insecure. He died six months before her therapy started.

I see this dream as a 'transference dream' testing me as 'the good father'. It conjures up 'extreme security' in this situation that did not exist in real life. I do not wish to disturb Lisa's image-making so I only mention that the baby can be a symbol of something new in her which has been born out of her dreamwork. I ask her to dwell on her feeling of extreme security.

A Post-Traumatic Dream

Two months into the process, Lisa spoke of a very emotional family event. She was shaken and felt deep indignation that her father, who had recently died, was never again mentioned by his closest relatives. It was as if he had been "nonexistent."

Lisa had two long, frightening dreams that were thematically related. We will look at the last one first. She recounts it in full and we then examine it step-by-step: *I'm in a place where creatures are tortured, perhaps a concentration camp or some place very dangerous, maybe with radioactivity or acid. I flee on my horse which can transform into a small cat animal with magic powers. But he has gone through terrible things. His flesh has melted away so only the skeleton remains.*

This dream leaves a deep emotional impression on Lisa, but she has difficulty making sense of it.

Her dream continues: *People become frightened when they see us. Maybe they will kill us. They believe we are evil, and death incarnated.*

This part of the dream makes Lisa think about the father again. His relatives somehow had "killed him in their minds," and had made him "nonexistent." This leads her thoughts to her stays in the hospital as a child where she shuddered to think that, if she had died, she would have become nonexistent and forgotten by everyone.

The grim details of the first part of her dream suddenly makes sense to her. These details reflect the pain Lisa endured battling cancer with repeated chemotherapy, as well as hair and weight loss. It was like being in a concentration camp. She could then see the remainder of her dream as a reflection of events during her illness.

She continued, "In my dream, I was very lonely." She had been ferried by orderlies to countless tests and then left waiting for the results. Unknown adults talked over her head about matters she did not comprehend.

Her dream continued: *I'm flooded with sorrow because I know I will never be loved by anyone. No one will ever be with me again.*

This is the most terrible part of Lisa's dream, she feels. It reminds her of experiences in childhood where she believed that no one could ever love her in that condition. In the present waking reality, Lisa is a beautiful, lively and loving woman. Yet she can still be overwhelmed by the sorrow reflected in her dream. She sobbed when she woke after the dream and remembered that part.

Her dream continues: *We ride through the woods and come out of it. Children were there. My horse suddenly has another form with flesh and all. He tells me that he can change me, too. He does so and I become human again. But this is an illusion and I'm afraid the illusion will break if I touch the horse. Yet I still keep leaning up against him.*

This sequence reminds Lisa of the ebb and flow of her hope for recovery and her anxiety that all the various treatments would not help her. She also remembers her father reading stories to her when she was in the hospital. She was especially interested in stories about power animals that were magical helpers. They filled her world with fantasy and brought her joy.

Lisa's dream continues: *I try to entertain the children – play with them so they don't go away again. I do so throughout the night and when the children do go home it's like a knife to my heart. They leave one-by-one. It's almost like they are oxygen to me – my lungs deflate. I've moved away from my horse and become terrified, but then find out that the magic spell still works even without physical contact.*

While in the hospital, Lisa was deprived of any normal companionship with other children. She sat in a wheelchair most of the time. She suffered numerous bodily discomforts, pain and was generally in poor condition.

The dream continues: *In the morning, the parents arrive to check on their children. They get mad because they see me and the horse as a threat to their children. They become terrified. They can't understand we mean the children no harm. We simply want to spend time with them. The mother of one of the children threatens to summon a fairy. I'm not frightened by her threat. A fairy is probably not that afraid of something that looks scary.*

Lisa explains that she felt different back then. She experienced that parents of both the ill children and visiting children treated her with exaggerated concern, trying to convince her that everything would be all right. They seemed so afraid of doing something wrong that they did not dare to really relate to her. Perhaps some of them were terrified when she looked the most ill, just like in her dream. This may have made them think of the fate of their own children.

Lisa continues: *The fairy is standing at the gates of the realm of the elves. The horse and I jump into the elven realm. We find many delightful fruits and plants there. We are very hungry and nibble here and there, but the elves get angry. It turns out that a great famine has fallen on their realm and that almost all the food must be saved until winter.*

We understand the gates of the elven realm as an entry into the realm of the imagination. We talk about the delightful fruits and plants. I mention that her inner life will surely bring her nourishment and the finest taste sensations.

Lisa's Case Dreams and the 10 Core Qualities

Now I will explore Lisa's dream from the perspective of the Ten Core Qualities.

Core Quality 1: Dreams Deal with Matters Important to Us

Lisa sought therapy because of nightmares caused by trauma. Overlooked resources in her dreams were recognized and qualified. Her dreams suggested the need to integrate trauma work with an overall development of personality and organization of self.

Core Quality 2: Dreams Symbolize

Clarification and Elaboration

Elaboration and clarification of the actual content of Lisa's dreams revealed that she omitted important problem-solving details when recounting her first dreams. For instance, she spoke about a threatening, aggressive male gorilla in a very general way, but she left out that she could communicate with the animal. This is a general problem for dreamers. If we are not trained, we often view dreams with the very consciousness that the dream is attempting to affect, thus overlooking important details. This is especially true of traumatic dreams where imminent threat often weighs most heavily.

Amplification

In her post-traumatic dream, the horse is an important symbol. Jung has presented examples of dreams where he found horses symbolize the body (Mattoon 1978). Freud compared horses with drives and instincts that carry an individual. The horse is also known in the history of symbols to have magical abilities (Ronnberg and Martin 2010). For Lisa, the horse has a special meaning because she created fantasies, power animals and magical abilities. We talked about her use of this as a resource to overcome imagination.

The plants and delightful fruits could possibly be interpreted by using Erich Neumann's descriptions of the good mother archetype. He describes the "Lady of the Plants" as a universally significant symbol of the Great Mother Goddess that is connected to psychological and emotional nourishment in the earliest life phases (Neumann 1963). In Melanie Klein's object relations theory, fruits will typically be interpreted as "The Good Breast," which refers to a good early relationship to the mother. In the history of symbols, fruits are also tied to spiritual abundance and fertility (Cirlot 1967), which would correspond to Lisa's abundant imagination and creativity. I also often find vegetation in dreams when people disconnect very fundamentally from stress and create contact between body and soul. I was not very explicit about this but used it in my assessment of her resources and my emotional attunement to her.

Core Quality 3: Dreams Personify

For Lisa, her dream self was examining and tenacious. This suggested enough strength and vitality to integrate her new experiences and insights about herself. In her post-traumatic dream, we concentrated on the outer aspects of the traumatic situation and the adult's need to distance themselves from her. On an inner level, this distancing could refer to her own anxiety and her own adult idealization in the beginning of therapy of how she was being met by her surroundings when she was sick.

As mentioned earlier, the children in her dreams may represent creative developmental sides as well as childish, non-socialized aspects of the personality. Both spectrums could be explored in therapy.

On the subjective level, being deprived of contact with the inner child and confronted with angry and terrified parents has dire consequences. This, I think, is when she feels weak and dependent, when she in the beginning of therapy idealized the grownups behavior during her illness, and when in her actual life the moving away from the childhood home stopped.

On the other hand the inner parent systems reluctance to deal with the deeper feelings might be a survival strategy in herself, a protection against being sucked in to the "trauma vortex", "victim paradigm," or, as I call it the traumatic sharp peak in the psychological energy landscape. The therapist's job will then be to facilitate the gentle unfolding of her real feelings at a pace where she learn to cope with and integrate them in a more harmonious way.

Core Quality 4: Dreams are Trial Runs in a Safe Place

The dramatic structure of Lisa's post-traumatic dream inspired great ingenuity in the dream self. The structure winds its way through many turning points toward an increasingly more human and recognizable condition. An important turning point is the revelation about the adults' rejections of – and anxiety for – suffering.

The dream self relates to reality on multiple levels of consciousness. Lisa knows it is an illusion that she will get flesh to return to a body, yet still feels that this illusion is vital to her life. This is a recognition of her imaginative ability. The dream's solution – an imaginary mother (elf) – allows Lisa and the horse to pass through because they are the guards of the gates to the realm of elves.

Core Quality 5: Dreams are Online to Unconscious Intelligence

Lisa's very vivid and rich dream imagery was stimulated simply by being recounted. Just like her dream self, Lisa demonstrated good instinctive and nonverbal communication skills. She had developed a sensitivity toward the nonverbal communications of others and her own inner resources. She was responsive to emotional attunement with body language, tone of voice, and choice of words from my side and her imaginative ability made it possible to plug into her own unconscious intelligence.

Core Quality 6: Dreams are Pattern Recognition

The 'goodness-of-fit landscapes' of her dreams matched several contexts.

Continuity with Actual Waking Life

The awareness the dreamwork brought to the interaction between Lisa's dreams and events in her daily life strengthened her self and increased her awareness of her own vulnerabilities in relation to inner and outer influences.

Past Important Life Events

One important issue was finding out what contributed to building up Lisa's personality before the trauma, and how her relatively robust and imaginative self had been formed. The literature about what makes children vulnerable or resilient when faced with stress demonstrates with great clarity that secure attachments to understanding and empathetic caregivers early in life are the best protections against outer strain. Long-term, the sense of self and the ability to regulate inner emotional states are strengthened (Luthar and Ziegler 1991).

British child psychiatrist Donald Winnicott coined the term a "good-enough mother" for a mother who "starts off with an almost complete adaptation to her infant's needs and, as time proceeds, this adaption gradually becomes less and less complete, in accordance with her infant's growing ability to deal with her failure" (Winnicott 1953). Based on what Lisa herself told about her childhood before the trauma, and based on her way of being in therapy, I assessed that she had received good-enough mothering.

Also well-studied when a child has been exposed to traumatic events is whether the surroundings' abilities to respond sensitively and consolingly are crucial to the child's possibilities to reestablish balance and develop emotional self-regulation (Luthar and Ziegler 1991). From training staff at hospices and in many other contexts, it is my experience that people, in general, often have difficulty dealing with life-threatening illness, and that Lisa's experience of the adult's understandable yet critical lack of competence in facing her illness was not unrealistic. It was Lisa's sense that the surroundings vigorously overcompensated – resorting to cognitive explanations and forward-thinking solutions – the cost of which was no empathy or consoling. It reassured and consoled her that I shared my general knowledge about flaws in communication abilities in some children's wards.

Core Quality 7: Dreams are High-Level Communication

The fact that dreams are proactive and at the leading edge of development was most easily observed when we got further into the process and were able to view Lisa's dreams as a series, and saw how they unfolded in therapy after her long, post-traumatic dream.

"The end of the world" was the most violent of post-traumatic themes. After working with Lisa's post-traumatic dream, this theme continued to appear, though it was increasingly sporadic and decreasingly dominant. For the first 7–8 months, it appeared as: *a new world-wide ice age* … and … *a relapse to the hospital*. A … *dystophic, post-apocalyptic world* … and … *a widespread epidemic*. In the meantime, more and more *helpful people* began to appear in these dreams. Her other dreams were populated with a mix of close family members, friends, lovers and unknown figures, which are all typical of young people (Hall and Van de Castle 1966), and their themes were typical of young women in general. As were themes such as liberation from parental ties, love, choice of partner, work, study, friends and non-professional interests. In one dream, Lisa trial-ran her own wedding while critically watching the reactions of her father and mother to the events. In a later dream she experienced what it was like to be pregnant.

We employed post-traumatic dream elements as omens for a mismatch between Lisa's inner and outer realities. Situations could arise that provoked her fear of being abandoned (for instance, after minor disagreements with her boyfriend), or rejected (for instance, after an employment application), or belonging to the wrong category of people, if she behaved outside the norms.

Lisa's positive dreams were like perfect test scores confirming sound choices.

Core Quality 8: Dreams are Condensed Information

Lisa's dreams synthesized her post-traumatic reminiscences with future development themes, as well as her present situation in life. At the outset, the dreams also synthesized her father's security-creating qualities with the trust-evoking qualities of the therapist. Later, *she was critical of her father* in her dreams, while endowing me with magical healing abilities. When I was on a long holiday, however, she dreamed she *had been selected for space exploration to places no one had ever been before. Desolate, uncivilized places. Exciting but difficult. Some of the sponsors backed out. And when I came back: a helpful doctor assisted her.*

The associations to the densely packed, post-traumatic dream continued to unfold a long time after our first session with the dream. The dangerous radioactivity in the beginning of this dream was associated with the x-ray room she had had to enter. She panicked. The adults consoled her, but then went out and waved at her through a window. Thus with their actual behaviour they communicated that x-rays were dangerous anyway. The acid that melted flesh away was re-experienced as the chemotherapy. A brochure entitled "Chemo Casper Helps You" was supposed to get her to accept chemotherapy more readily. Lisa hated Chemo Casper. In reality, he marked the beginning of long-lasting suffering.

Core Quality 9: Dreams are Experiences of Wholeness

Lisa's thoughts and verbal communications were quick and unproblematic, both in relation to cognitive understanding and metaphorical thinking.

Her visual modality was keenly represented by her lively dream imagery. Lisa found it easy to visualize with her eyes closed and this gave access to a rich, emotionally-charged network of associations.

Emotions

Before therapy, anxiety was the dominant feeling of Lisa's dream self. In her initial dream, she felt a great sense of relief and freedom, and interest was the primary driving force.

Many emotions were present in the post-traumatic dream, yet they were placed outside the dream self. Anger was experienced as the murderous intentions of the surroundings toward the dream self and the horse. Disgust and shame corresponded to the dream self and horse being viewed as evil by the others. Sorrow and hopelessness were personified by the non-self figures' retreat from the world of real relations.

As the dreamwork progressed, her dreams demonstrated a wide register of emotions expressed by her dream self. Anger and rage, disgust, calm, joy, happiness, gratitude, love, compassion and exhilaration. As the process developed, sadness, sorrow, and later, guilt and shame arose, and again happiness, gratitude, love, compassion.

Through this work, emotions were gradually transformed into consciously experienced feelings in the sphere of the self, moving from having an emotion, to knowing you feel an emotion and reflecting on it, to integrating it in practical life.

The Body

Lisa's body language was spontaneously very expressive, and she did tremendous work in reflecting on the dreams and her states of mind. Methodically, we employed some body sensing, and emotional attunement was a ubiquitous tool.

Core Quality 10: Dreams are Psychological Energy Landscapes

Lisa's traumatic experiences created a sharp peak in her psychological energy landscape. She vented the emotional charge in her nightly nightmares and she had adapted to a limited life during the day. Aided by her dreams in therapy, we took our point of departure in the low hills of her energy landscape, stimulated her inner self-organization and strengthened her self, so a more harmonious integration of the various areas in Lisa's mind became possible.

On the outer level, Lisa moved away from home but maintained good contact with her mother. She finished her studies and performed her part-time job satisfactorily, and managed to maneuver nicely into the joys and challenges of a love-life in a timely fashion.

Trauma had thrown Lisa into a reality where certain abilities and developmental opportunities where repressed while others were developed in a precocious way. The sensitive and creative ways of experiencing she had been forced into during her traumatic period were acknowledged and turned into strengths. Her guardedness was transformed into healthy skepticism. Her willingness to fight helped Lisa find her own identity and her own set of values independent of the pressure from her surroundings.

The ability to use her own powers of imagination to transform negative states into positive ones appeared in a dream shortly before she had an exam with a woman whom she experienced as cold, strict and authoritarian (a personification of the terrible mother). Lisa dreamed that *she communicates with a growling bear. It turns into a young man with pearls in his hair. They dance and have fun. She discovers she can fly. The dream ends with a sense of relief she has not experienced before.* Lisa was completely calm during her exam. She felt fine and did well. We interpreted the bear as a hefty rage awakened by her notions about the cold, unempathetic instructor, and that Lisa's meditative, self-observing attitude led to an emotional transformation.

In another dream Lisa (dream self as an adult) *meets a girl who is being haunted by ghosts at night. She consoles the girl. Morning arrives, the light returns and the ghosts disappear.* She visualized and contemplated the meeting with girl. I held her hand while she was crying softly and deeply for a long time. Afterwards she said that it was first now that she could allow herself to fully sense her deepest loneliness and sorrow, knowing that she could come back to ordinary consciousness again. When we discussed this dream, Lisa recognized the girl as a version of herself during the traumatizing period. Yet it was not the dream self exposed to the horrors but rather a part of her personality that Lisa's self can relate to and console in a way that makes the monsters vanish.

With time the terrifying nightmares vanished. 'Bad dreams' and 'good dreams' became guides to navigate through life with all its complexity.

References

American Psychiatric Association (1994) *Diagnostic and Statistical Manual of Mental Disorders* (4th Ed.). (Washington, DC: APA), pp. 424–29

Bulkeley, K. (2003) *Dreams of Healing: Transforming Nightmares into Visions of Hope.* (New York: Paulist Press)

Cirlot, J. E. (1967) *A Dictionary of Symbols.* (Abingdon, UK: Routledge and Kegan Paul)

Hall, C. and Van de Castle, R. (1965) 'An empirical investigation of the castration complex in dreams'. *Journal of Personality*, Vol. 33, pp. 20–9

Hall, C. and Van de Castle, R. (1966) *The Content Analysis of Dreams.* (New York: Appleton-Century-Crofts)

Hartmann, E. (1995) 'Making connections in a safe place: is dreaming psychotherapy?' *Dreaming*, Vol. 5, pp. 213–28

Hartmann, E. (1996) 'Who develops PTSD nightmares and who doesn't' D. Barrett (Ed.), *Trauma and Dreams.* (Cambridge, MA: Harvard University Press), pp. 100–14

Hartmann, E. (1998) *Dreams and Nightmare.* (New York: Plenum)

Herman, J. L. (1992) *Trauma and recovery.* (New York: Basic Books)

Joergensen, S. (1992) 'Bodynamic analytic work with shock and post-traumatic stress. Energy and character'. *The Journal of Biosynthesis*. Sept., Vol. 23(2), pp. 30–47

Jung C. G. (1916/1948/1981) 'General aspects of dream psychology' in G. Adler, M. Fordham and Sir H. Read (Eds), *Collected Works of C.G. Jung Vol. 8: The Structure and Dynamics of the Psyche.* (Abingdon, UK: Routledge and Kegan Paul), pp. 237–280

Jung, C. G. (1928/1981) 'The relations between the ego and the unconscious' in G. Adler and R. F. C. Hull (Eds), *Collected Works of C.G. Jung Vol. 7: Two Essays in Analytical Psychology.* (Abingdon, UK: Routledge and Kegan Paul)

Kalsched, D. (1996) *The Inner World of Trauma. Archetypal Defenses of the Personal Spirit.* (Abingdon, UK: Routledge)

King, J. (2012) 'Trauma treatment and dreams' in D. Barrett and P. McNamara (Eds), *Encyclopedia of Sleep and Dreams.* (Santa Barbara, CA: Greenwood Publishing), Kindle edition, location 19903ff

Knox, J. (2003/2012) *Archetypes, Attachment, Analysis: Jungian Psychology and the Emergent Mind.* (Abingdon, UK: Routledge)

Kohut, H. (1983) *The Analysis of the Self.* (Madison, CT: International Universities Press)

Krakow, B. (2004) 'Imagery rehearsal therapy for chronic post-traumatic nightmares' in R. Rosner and W. Lyddon, et al. (Eds), *Cognitive Therapy and Dreams.* (New York: Springer Publishing), pp. 89–109

Kristal-Andersson, B. (2001) 'From wound to scar: easing the pain of trauma and torture experiences through dreamwork'. *Drömdialog* (member issue for the Swedish för dreamgroupe forum), No. 1, pp. 9–17

Levine, P. A. and Frederick, A. (1997) *Waking the Tiger: Healing Trauma.* (Berkeley, CA: North Atlantic Books), Kindle edition. p. 196–8

Luthar, S. S. and Zigler, E. (1991) 'Vulnerability and competence: a review of research on resilience in childhood'. *American Journal of Orthopsychiatry,* pp. 148–149, 61, 6–22

Mattoon, M. A. (1978) *Applied Dream Analysis.* (Chichester, UK: John Wiley & Sons)

Nader, K. (1996) 'Children's traumatic dreams' in D. Barrett (Ed.) *Trauma and Dreams.* (Cambridge, MA: Harvard University Press), pp. 9–24

Nagera, H. (1981) *Basic Psychoanalytic Concepts on the Theory of Dreams.* (London: Karnac, Maresfield Reprints)

Neumann, E. (1959) *Art and The Creative Unconscious.* (Princeton, NJ: Princeton University Press)

Neumann, E. (1963) *The Great Mother.* (Princeton, NJ: Princeton University Press)

Paulson, D. S. and Krippner, S. C. (2007) *Haunted by Combat: Understanding PTSD in War Veterans Including Women, Reservists, and Those Coming Back from Iraq.* (Westport, CT: Praeger), Kindle edition, location 404–23

Ronnberg, A. and Martin, K. (2010) *The Book of Symbols: Reflections on Archetypal Images.* (Cologne, Germany: Taschen)

Siegel, A. (1996) 'Dreams of firestorm survivors' in D. Barrett (Ed.) *Trauma and Dreams.* (Cambridge, MA: Harvard University Press), pp. 159–178

Stoddard, F. et al. (1996) 'Dreams and nightmares of burned children' in D. Barrett (Ed.) *Trauma and Dreams.* (Cambridge, MA: Harvard University Press)

Vedfelt, O. (1996) *Consciousness: The Levels of Consciousness.* (Copenhagen: Bevidsthed)

Vedfelt, O. (2014) 'The phenomenology of the spirit in childhood memories: early numinous experiences in a desacralized world' in E. Kiehl (Ed.), *Copenhagen 2013 100 Years On: Origins, Innovations and Controversies: Proceedings of the 19th Congress of the International Association for Analytical Psychology.* (Einsiedeln, Switzerland: Daimon Verlag)

Winnicott, D. (1953) 'Transitional objects and transitional phenomena'. *International Journal of Psychoanalysis,* 34, 89–97

Wurmser, L. (2000) *The Power of the Inner Judge: Psychodynamic Treatment of the Severe Neuroses.* (Northvale, NJ: Jason Aronson Inc.)

Part III

Principles and Exercises for Practical Dreamwork

Chapter 15

Working with Core Qualities 1–5

GOOD DREAMWORK WITH CORE QUALITY 1: DREAMS DEAL WITH MATTERS IMPORTANT TO US

I have now described ten Core Qualities of dreams based on valid knowledge from the dream schools and also from natural scientific research. The theoretical and methodical background for dreamwork has been accounted for and many examples provided.

In this overview we will revisit these core qualities and focus on how each one can contribute to practical dreamwork in various contexts. Each category of good dreamwork corresponds to one core quality, so you can easily refer to the more detailed explanations and examples presented earlier. The Core Qualities do not, however, stand alone. They are tied to a complex network where characteristics and examples from one core quality can be employed to shed light on characteristics in another. Therefore, when presenting the practical application of each, I will refer more broadly to described examples from other core qualities. Some examples will be utilized in several contexts because they are ideal in highlighting several aspects of dream life. Most references can still be found in the individual chapters about the corresponding core qualities, yet some new references will be added.

A Safe Place for Dreamwork

Key to the Ten Core Qualities theory is the insight that dreams deal with important matters. Dreams contain complex high-level information and they can provide access to energy-charged psychological content.

As soon as you begin committing yourself to working with dreams, a mutual feedback system is created between waking consciousness and unconscious intelligence. This system is dynamic and will eventually take your work to higher and more energy-charged levels of self-organization. If you include a therapist, another helper or confidant, that person will become part of your dreamwork system.

The therapeutic setting – both individually and in groups – is an important laboratory for developing the principles of practical dreamwork. Dreamwork can, however, be included in many other contexts such as self-help and counselling, as well as groups for personal development or even social functions. Within the various contexts, different levels of skills must be developed reflecting the complexity of the work.

The approach to and outcome of dreamwork is dependent on the dreamer's self-knowledge, age, prior knowledge of dreamwork, ego-strength and ability to contain and reflect on the material. When therapists or other helpers are involved, it is also dependent on:

1   the helper's skills concerning verbal and nonverbal communication;
2   the relationship between dreamer and helper as it develops in the process;
3   the helper's skills and knowledge of dreamwork and the limitations of the applied method.

The more complexity a dreamwork system can handle, the more it can facilitate the emerging flow of information in an integrative way. The loading and limiting of unconscious material varies from a relatively open-ended strategy to a more focus-oriented one; from long-term depth psychology to more cognitive approaches; from experiential and cathartic ways of working to more verbal and analytical methods.

In order to secure a safe place for the dreamwork some ethical rules must apply. Any professional dreamworker must provide access to his qualifications and affiliations. The dreamer's right to share or not share material concerning dreams should be respected. Communication about dreams must respect dreamer integrity and dignity at all levels of dreamwork. A mutual agreement on the degree of privacy and confidentiality should be reached (Duesbury 2011).

Dreamworkers must maintain awareness of their role as potential transference objects and as role models for communication. They must take measures to deal with this in constructive ways. An understanding that dream material can be processed on various levels – each of which demands its own approach and due caution - should be communicated.

Professional training in dreamwork usually starts with personally experienced dreamwork. This will then be followed by a kind of apprenticeship adapted to the theory employed and accompanied by theoretical education and supervision of how this functions in practice.

Creating Motivation

When it comes to good dreamwork with Core Quality 1, we will especially focus on the outset of work. As I have described, a seeking system in the brain is activated during dreaming that normally arouses curiosity, interest, and expectancy, and even ensures that something 'good' will happen if we explore the environment or interact with objects. My own findings – through my practice and reaffirmed by the described dreamwork literature – demonstrate that needs can be uncovered in any dreams that have not been sufficiently valued by the dreamers themselves or their surroundings.

A first step in the process is developing motivation to invest any time at all into dreams by providing dreamers with the opportunity to express their expectations, longings and what they are curiously hoping to discover.

Many people experience more or less hidden anxieties that their dreams might reveal something bad about them as human beings. For the sake of motivation, it is important that these anxieties are met and consoled by emphasizing the self-organizing resources in dreams. If dreams are experienced as positive contributions to the formation of new understandings of the individual's situation in life, then this in itself will create motivation.

Focus on Resources in Pleasant Dreams

Important principles behind my resource-oriented dreamwork have been acquired from Rosenthal and Jacobson's studies (1992) of how the positive expectations of teachers enhance student performance. These principles have also benefitted from Aaron Antonovski's (1987) constructive "salutogenic" focus on the causes of healing, rather than focusing on what makes people ill or feel bad.

Choosing to focus on resources is not the same as avoiding conflict. It is a practical method of developing trust in the wisdom of dreams through experience. If a dream is pleasant, you may find qualities in your life that you do not sufficiently utilize during waking states.

As an example, I described pregnant Sarah (Core Quality 3) who dreamed that she was in her motherhood support group where the atmosphere was good and enthusiastic, surrounded by friends and her husband, feeling happy and safe. This dream brought Sarah greater awareness about nourishing herself with positive motherliness during her pregnancy. Another example is 14-year-old Ida, the girl who dreamed of Gyro Gearloose, the little helper who helped me in consoling her parents that her eccentric behavior signified talent rather than some deeper problem within. Further, I can point to the peak experience dreams described in Core Quality 10 – and many other dreams – that seemingly reinforce dreamers' confidence in their own resources.

Resources in Unpleasant Dreams

Many seemingly negative experiences in dreams may turn out to facilitate development and quality of life if they are understood on a higher level than the conflict level in the manifest dream. Examples of this are Henrik's dream of the red sports car with a broken key (Core Quality 6) and Victor's dream of his jealous feelings (Core Quality 6). Both of these dreams led to greater insight into the dreamers' own developmental patterns, which in turn was conducive to promoting emotional balance and personal development. Hidden potentials for healing are revealed with particular clarity in traumatic dreams (Chapter 14).

Apparent in the dream series I have described is that an interplay between pleasant and unpleasant dreams takes place in life that contributes – in its own way – to the balance and self-organization of the psyche. For instance, we can think of Sarah's pleasant dream about her motherwood support group, mentioned above, and compare it with her earlier dream about her family being persecuted by Nazis. We understood the Nazi dream to be a message to Sarah from the dream world about her vulnerability and need to protect herself from 'bad mother' experiences (Core Quality 3). Another example was the negative female figures in Peter's dreams who were in later dreams replaced by more positive ones (Core Quality 7).

Experientially Reorganizing Bad Dreams

If a dreamer cannot find resources in a dream and has no other dreams to recount, the content of the dream can be reorganized in an experiential way.

I have provided many examples of reorganization of unpleasant dreams recounted either in individual sessions or through more long-term work. In reorganization, you investigate dreamers' imaginings of what they would have liked their dreams to be. What does each dreamer need? What would it be like if the dream self behaved in a fashion that was experienced as satisfactory? Can any positive, loving, helpful, protective characters or an otherwise supportive environment be added?

If the dreams contain references to powerful and traumatic memories, or are difficult recurring nightmares, then they require the special methods (see Chapter 14 on traumatic dreams).

First Steps to Unfolding Dreams

When starting an individual therapy I let the client do the talking. If dreamers experience being seen, heard and understood on their own terms, trust will develop that enables more spontaneous expression. This might be created in the first context and through the first associations that a client presents. Thus an interpretation or understanding should – as much as possible – be based on what the individuals themselves spontaneously express. This stimulates a sense of empowerment.

When it comes to group work, after an introduction of the process and ethical rules, I begin with a mindfulness exercise where participants can let go of the tensions created by daily life, thus increasing their opportunities to sense what is taking place within. For a limited period of time after this, the participants are allowed to talk freely about whatever expectations they may have about the process without comment from myself or others.

In a group convening for a day or a weekend, I let the first round of sharing be followed by an experiential session – relaxation and inner journey based on a selected dream or life experience. Afterwards, that dream or experience can, for instance, be drawn with crayons on large sheets of paper. (Or you can let the dreamer choose what colors and format of paper he prefers depending on the method.) So far, no feedback has been offered on the material – simply an opening into dream-world states has been created that facilitates associations and creative thinking.

A dream can also be processed through dialogue with another group participant who has been instructed to maintain an attitude of mirroring, acknowledgement and empathy. Then the pair can look for resources in the dream together, which the dreamer can later visualize or reflect on before sleeping. In this group concept I am discussing here, this process of unfolding can be followed up in subsequent days.

Remembering Dreams

A primary and essential condition for actively working with dreams is remembering them. Most people remember one or two dreams a week. Few of these dreams leave such deep impressions that they remain in the waking memory. Others' dreams slip back into oblivion if they are not written down or discussed with others. If you wish to work more systematically with dreams, there are various rules of thumb that can be helpful.

- Preparation: Before lying down to sleep, you can decide to try to remember dreams and work out how you will register them. You can write them down or dictate them into a smartphone. Speaking into a smartphone will ease the registration of your dreams and they can be transcribed to a computer or your dream book later. These tools should be at hand. If you share a bed with someone you should plan how you will manage a light or speaking out loud.
- Awakening: When you wake of your own accord it is almost invariably from a dream phase. If you use an alarm clock to wake up, it can disrupt a deep dreaming phase and you will be unable to remember your dreams. We have the liveliest dreams latest, so a good time to remember dreams is when we spontaneously wake up in the wee hours of the morning before the alarm clock sounds.
- Body position: Dreams are coded together with the body position in which you dream. When you wake, lie completely still a moment and pay attention to any dream images that appear. But you should not lie there too long, because you can easily slip into a new dream phase and forget your dream. If you have problems remembering a dream, it may be because you turn over in bed just before waking. Carefully try to shift your body back into the dreaming position.
- Relaxation: Meditation, visualization and creativity increase the number of remembered dreams. Holidays, weekends and days off allow the best opportunities for both remembering dreams and working with them.

- Motivation: This is important. It may be there from the start or appear along the way as you discover that your dreams are an important addition to your life. Motivation will often come when you are being challenged in a manner that demands that you think in completely new ways about fundamental life-attitudes and your existential choices. When your life gets back on track, then it would be good to remember just how much help your dreams have been.

GOOD DREAMWORK WITH CORE QUALITY 2: DREAMS SYMBOLIZE

In dreamwork, our point of departure when working with symbols is the complexity theory. Starting with a relatively limited amount of information about a phenomenon to be examined, a model simulation is done that can harvest new information and then another model simulation, etc. until there is a "goodness of fit" within the framework available for the dreamwork. This enables a flexible and pragmatic use of understanding symbols with a continual assessment of the suitability of the method for the purpose of the dreamwork, or adjustment of that purpose based on the harvested information.

Learning Symbolic Thinking

Tools employed when working with symbols might be: experientially unfolding dream symbols, matching everyday metaphors, appreciative dialogue, personal associations, elaboration, amplifications, examining the levels and context of symbols, etc.

The order in which these tools are used can vary from situation to situation and switch from one to another in a hermeneutic circle working from partial understanding, to understanding of the whole, and back again. An overriding principle is to explore subjective experience, then give feedback on it from a more general knowledge-based viewpoint and finally return to the subjective experience.

Using Metaphors from Everyday Life

A quick route to understanding symbols might be that a dreamer has a feeling of knowing the meaning of a symbol as a metaphor that is also used in everyday life. For instance: The dreamer found herself in a parking lot, and then the dreamer made the comment, "I feel my life has been parked."

A Symbol as a Kōan

As an exercise, you could contemplate a metaphor and say, "That's what my life is like right now." Or you can simply keep it in mind in your everyday life and see if it – in moments of illumination – suddenly matches a background mood or situation in life. This is somewhat similar to a Japanese Kōan from the Zen tradition – a story or metaphor that challenges a student's habitual perception of the world and of life.

Experientially Unfolding a Dream Symbol

This could be inner journeys, meditation, drawings, movements, body sensing or personal associations, etc. that come to us in connection with other core qualities.

Finding the Emotional Charge in a Dream Drawing

Drawing dreams may provide an indication of what elements contain the strongest energetic charges. Begin with what dreamers remember themselves about any impressions they had and what seemed significant or odd during the drawing process. Then look for any elements that revel intensity because of their color, shape or placement. There may be areas where there is a deep color saturation, a repeating pattern or a placement central in the drawing. Even areas in a drawing where a dreamer dwelled without being able to make a decision about what to draw might be indicating an investment of psychic energy.

If there is any material that provokes anxiety, focus can be moved to areas drawn more softly (low hills). You can still point out the energy-laden areas (sharp peaks) in the dream landscape without awakening emotional associations, or maybe even reframe them. The primary task is to look for and find resources.

Appreciative Dialogue with a Helper

When an individual's experience is mirrored, acknowledged and received with empathy, it can be integrated into the self and the sphere of consciousness in new ways. Many recurring thoughts and feelings in everyday life do not quite fit our patterns of self-perception. Not necessarily unconscious, they still do not contain enough energy to form a pattern that can compete with and defeat our stagnated habitual conceptions. An appreciative dialogue can enhance a feeling of knowing or feeling of rightness. Dreamers might be struggling to believe in this feeling yet still desire to explore it further and reveal new possibilities.

A verbal method for opening up to dreamers' experiences and subjective meanings is psychologist Harville Hendrix's Imago model of communication (Brown and Reinhold 1999). His model was developed in couples' therapy where communication in conflicted situations could be disrupted by unconscious emotion. This is also relevant in dreamwork that contains a great deal of unconscious material in the form of imagery, feelings and dramatic stories, etc. Hendrix's method can also guard against biased interpretation and premature closure of the process, and it can be employed on many levels. Imago has three steps or elements: mirroring, validation and empathy.

Mirroring

Mirroring can be a verbatim recounting or a summary of content that has been recounted. It mandates that the helper is truly listening. Dreamers are also provided with opportunities to correct or elaborate on the content of their messages and clarify or expand on their own interpretations.

Validation

Validation is the recognition that what dreamers say makes sense within their own frames of reference. Helpers might have different perceptions or interpretations, yet the task at hand is to validate the dreamers' universes of experience.

Empathy

Empathy means that helpers feel what they believe dreamers are feeling and attempt to express this. For example: A drawing done of the dream about the parking lot (mentioned above) made the dreamer aware that there was a similar parking space near her place of work (clarification of the dream).

Mirroring

Helper: "Aha, so the parking space reminds you of one near your job?"
Dreamer: "Yes, it actually does … and I don't go in to work, but I don't go away either."
Helper: "You don't go in, but you don't go away either?"
Dreamer: "No, that's what happens, I go in circles. I don't do anything."
Helper: "So you don't do anything?"
Dreamer: "No, and I've actually been offered another job."
Helper: "Aha?"
Dreamer: "It's even more interesting and better paid. It's a little absurd that I don't say yes."

Validation

Helper: "It makes sense that it seems a little absurd that you don't say yes when offered a job that is more interesting and better paid."
Dreamer: "Yes, but I'm familiar with the job I have, and I can manage on the salary I'm getting."

Empathy

Helper: "I can see it must be hard to choose."
Dreamer: "Yes, just the thought of the new job makes my stomach flutter."

Helper: "Oh, I can almost feel it in my stomach, too."
Dreamer: "You can? Then you understand it's not an easy decision."
Helper: "I really can. You must feel powerless, too."
Dreamer: "Yes, of course."

This dialogue helped the dreamer to get in touch with a deeper sense of power-lessness and to seek out a broader foundation for decision making.

Externally

Would it be possible to make the present job more interesting if the dreamer became more involved? Would her present employer support her doing so? Is there any chance of getting a sense of the potential working conditions and climate at her new workplace? Would her family support her if she took the new, more insecure job?

Internally

Would this demand working on processing the old patterns controlling her feel-ings of powerlessness and anxiety? Was her dream pointing out people or courses of action that contained resources within herself she could work on? Did the dialogue suggest 'false' ambitions created by influences from her surroundings that were in conflict with her overriding inner balance and quality of life?

I do not want to tell which job opportunity this individual chose because the point in this is that we often make decisions based on too little information, and that dreamwork can help provide deeper understanding of the more overriding patterns behind our actions and decisions.

Steps to Interpretation

Personal Associations

Associations can appear in long chains in relaxed states, during validating dialogue or as quick intuitive impulses. As an example of a short chain of asso-ciations, I described the young man who connected coffee to something refined to be imbibed while out, and tea as something less exquisite to be consumed at home. Longer chains of associations employing all experiential modalities are found in Laura's unfolding of the loss of her father through experiential work with symbols in Core Quality 2. Other examples are Paul who dreamed of a broken thermos jug (Core Quality 9) and Linda's dream about a sad waiting room (Core Quality 10).

Elaboration of Symbols

Elaboration of symbols means carefully examining symbols and clarifying their characteristics. For instance, you may explore the characteristics of a bird in a dream. Is it a migratory bird, a seabird or a forest bird? Is it a bird of prey? Domesticated or wild? Does it have a specific color? Is the sex of the bird explicit in the dream? One example of this is Tue's dream about the caged birds in his childhood home (Core Quality 4).

Amplification

Amplification means enlarging the understanding of symbols by drawing parallels to the more general symbol understanding found in Jungian psychology, especially through myths and fairytales. Some amplification is relatively easy to access, for example: a woman dreamed she was cleaning an older woman's house. She saw this as analogous to the Cinderella fairytale and recalled situations in her childhood where she felt exploited.

Other examples are transformation symbols (Core Quality 2), the male and female initiation rituals for Peter and Birgit (Core Quality 7), and the mythological parallels to Emma's and Antonio's peak experience dreams (Core Quality 10).

Other symbols may be less obvious, but can still be enriched through amplification. Dreams of death and burial, for instance, might seem frightening but may turn out to contain positive meaning. Dead people in dreams can refer to loss of loved ones who need to be mourned, as is the case with Laura (Core Quality 2) and Lisa (Chapter 14). Yet dead people may also refer to aspects of the dreamer that are no longer useful in the forms in which they are being implemented.

Death as a symbol of an approaching transformation of the personality is dominant in Jung's interpretation of the symbolism in alchemical processes and dreams (Jung 1944). This was further developed by James Hillman who has explained suicide as a misinterpretation of potential transformation of the soul in his famous book on the subject (Hillman 1964).

I have presented several examples of this in earlier chapters. In a dream, Pernille buried her excessive self-criticism personified by her great aunt (Core Quality 3). Peter described the death of his mother in Core Quality 7 as an important step in his work in liberating himself from his "mother complex," in order to enable maturation in his relations with women. While dreaming, Jack experienced the burial of his neurotic stepfather, followed by a more economic distribution of energy in his own house (Core Quality 6).

Levels and Contexts of Symbols

We usually view symbols in relationship to the rest of a dream. There can be several levels of interpreting the same symbol so, for example, the symbol 'nakedness' can refer to embarrassment and shame if the dream self is exposed in a public place. It can also be a symbol of naturalness connected to intimacy and sexuality. Further, nakedness may be a decisive symbol of transformation as in alchemical symbolism where it, according to Jung, refers to a stage of experiencing "the naked truth" about oneself (Jung 1946).

A symbol such as riding in a car or on a train can refer to everyday situations or to being on one's way in life in a much more extensive manner, such as Karen's dream about being on her way with her family (Core Quality 8).

In initial phases, understanding symbols is similar to translating from one language to another. It takes practice and playfulness, which then opens our eyes to the metaphoric and poetic ways of thinking we constantly use without being very conscious of them.

GOOD DREAMWORK WITH CORE QUALITY 3: DREAMS PERSONIFY

The characters in our dreams may reflect both parts of ourselves and/or our perceptions of people in the world at large.

The Dream Self

The dream self is the central character in almost all dreams. The dream self is the figure in the dream whose behavior and experiences are closest to that of the waking self. You can explore the dream self's level of activity, actions, ability to reflect, positive feelings, positive motives, ability to contact others, and problem solving.

1   Is the dream self active and participatory in the events taking place? This capacity grows during childhood with the development of the ego (see Core Quality 3).
2   What is the tone of the dream self's interactions with the other characters – friendly, hostile or neutral? This may disclose social competences as well as an ability or failure to induce cooperation between various inner, psychic areas. During important phases of development and as age and maturity increase, the dream self creates space for the activities of other positive characters and uses them as training opportunities for future development. This was the case with Pernille whose worried, insecure great aunt was replaced in a dream by a caring, dynamic and judicious masculine character who supported Pernille when she was confronted by some rigid Catholic priests (Core Quality 3). Seemingly negative characters, if confronted and dealt with, may be transformed into constructive initiative or socializing activity: for instance, Anders (Core Quality 7) who dreamed about a tough biker he was trying to avoid. Through systematic dreamwork, Anders was able to integrate the biker's aggressiveness, transforming it into a positive, self-affirming continence.
3   How well does the dream self mentalize and reflect? This may mirror the dreamer's level of maturity and introspective abilities. Damasio's (2000) three levels of emotional consciousness may be a useful tool in this (Core Quality 9):

      a   Having an emotion: Fritz, the boy persecuted by an adult male (Core Quality 3);

      b   Knowing you have an emotion: Linda in the waiting room (Core Quality 10);

      c   Reflecting on the emotion: Kevin (Core Quality 3) mentalizing complex feelings;

      d   A further step is to find a general pattern for this activity in waking life, and explore how it can be used constructively (exemplified in the dream series in Core Quality 7 and Chapter 14).

4   Does the dream self have a theory of mind about other characters? This might suggest the potential for empathy towards others and sympathetic insight into oneself.

Objective (Exterior) and Subjective (Interior) Interpretation

Pernille's dream (Core Quality 3) is a primary example of the complexity of using these two different approaches. Furthermore, in Core Qualities 8–10, detailed examples have been provided of complex feedback processes between the exterior and the interior levels. Some rules of thumb are as follows.

- The exterior level is explored if dream characters are important persons in the dreamer's actual life, and if they appear in the dream in a realistic way. A man dreams: *I'm arguing with my father*. The dreamer's father is alive and recently spent time with the dreamer. When the man examines his dream, he realizes that he and his father disagree about something important to which he has not paid sufficient attention.
- The interior level of understanding is more relevant when it comes to distant relationships, insignificant acquaintances or unknown people or historical and fantasy figures, as well as composite or distorted characters. A similar dream from another dreamer in a different context may be interpreted on the interior level: his father died a long time ago. He usually saw the father as a rather rigid person. His dream mirrored a conflict within himself about rigid aspects of his personality.

Typical Dream Figures

Children in Dreams

Children in dreams may provide useful information about children you relate to in actual life on the objective level. On the interior level, they may refer to leaps in personal development and/or creativity that needs to be developed. The age of the child can reflect a phase in childhood containing untapped potential that has been in hibernation and is now ready to be utilized. Or it might refer to earlier life events that limited the unfolding of your potentials.

1   Entering or preparing a new phase of personal development. Pregnancy in dreams, for instance, can be a first step in the birth of a new personality aspect and is often dreamed by women entering a midlife phase. Likewise, playing with or even nursing a child in a dream can indicate that you are constructively dealing with new developments. This is often dreamed after a breakthrough therapy session that has provided new direction in life. In Jungian terms, this indicates individuation (see Chapter 1).

2   Creative projects that the individual is deeply involved in and needs to complete. Example: Amanda dreams *about a little girl who is sitting by herself on the steps of a university. Amanda approaches her. The girl reaches out her arms. She can't be more than two years old. Amanda started her Master's thesis two years earlier. She is stuck. The child reminds her of the importance of getting her thesis done. She can sense it would feel good to have a more playful attitude toward her thesis.*

3   Childhood stages where particular incidents took place that affected the personality. Chantal dreamed that *a crying infant is lying outside a public building. No one can see the child and the dreamer cannot cross the street because of traffic.* The dreamer was adopted at an early age because of a war incident. She has no idea what happened to her biological mother. Chantal has dreams like these when she is under pressure or depressed. The dream pointed to a need for help to work further on feelings of loss and abandonment.

One complex example is Karen (Core Quality 8) who dreamed she forgot her daughter at school. This dream was interpreted on the outer level as relating to her daughter's school troubles. On the interior level, it was connected to Karen's childhood where she experienced the same problems as her daughter and, finally, on the prospective level, the daughter was seen as a developmental possibility within Karen herself.

Generally, children in dreams indicate development and creativity. However, they may also be pointing out childish and inappropriate behavior. Many children depicted in dreams can refer to potentialities that may not yet have reached a stage where they can be realized. It is important to examine whether the dream self or other dream characters are able to communicate with, support and care for the figures of children. Under any circumstances, you will have to enter into dialogue with these aspects of your personality to reveal why the children are appearing and what they are trying to communicate, rather than suppressing them.

Parental Figures

Parental figures can be characters in dreams with protective, caring, controlling or authoritative functions. Associating to these types of characters may help reveal confining and negative childhood experiential patterns, as well as positive experiences that facilitate connections to valuable areas of the personality. Impersonal parental figures may also be representations of societal norms, tradition or wisdom. For more detailed descriptions of parental figures see Core Quality 3.

Examples of various interpretation levels for father figures are found in Anders's dream series in Core Quality 7 and the figures in Lisa's dream series including her father, the therapist and other male helpers (Chapter 14). A variety of mother images are found in Peter's dream series, the young man in Core Quality 7 and Linda's dream of the mother in the waiting room.

Dream Characters' Professions

Dream characters' professions often have symbolic meanings – for example, a judge may refer to conscientiousness and fairness. A cleaner at work can symbolize internal cleansing. The presence of a communications expert might be referring to the importance of communicating with others or to formulating contact with inner parts of the personality.

Individual Character Traits

The individual character traits of the dream figures – for example, if a person is introverted or extroverted, kind or hostile, emotional or cold, etc. – may also suggest unconscious character traits worthy of consideration.

Gender of Dream Characters

In many dreams the general human qualities of the dream characters are more interesting than their gender. Yet human self-perception and developmental psychology are built on a consolidation of masculine or feminine gender identities, and the opposite gender in dreams often represents a more unconscious gender identity.

During important developmental phases, gender may take on a special meaning as an expression of characteristics that could be developed in order to further the personality. Jung described this especially in connection with the process of individuation around the age of 40. This can, however, be expanded to apply to all transitional phases and ages.

Important questions about dreams where gender plays a special role are:

- What do dreams tell us about:
  - the dreamer's own gender and perceptions of gender identity?
  - the dreamer's understanding of the opposite gender's characteristics?
  - how dreamers differentiate and integrate their own perceptions of gender into their personal development toward greater maturity and flexibility?

Here are some of the many examples of these gender issues described in the Core Qualities:

- Fritz, the boy who was approaching puberty and felt pressured into developing an adult male identity (Core Quality 3).
- Peter was overwhelmed by women in his initial dream, but then created a balance between masculinity and femininity through a therapeutic process (Core Quality 7).
- Birgit dreamed of female initiation with a female priest in a church (Core Quality 7).
- Pernille's dream about the burial of her old aunt testified to the necessity of integrating positive masculine attributes (Core Quality 3).
- Antonio, an 80-year-old engineer, was brought up to a new mental level in a dream by his wise and philosophically inclined daughter-in-law (Core Quality 10).

Working with Children's Dreams

Working with the dreams of children requires special care. All children have lively dreams. Some of these are experienced as exciting and containing positive material. Other dreams are frightening – bad dreams and nightmares. As I have demonstrated through many examples, all these dreams make good sense and can be utilized to improve the quality of life and personal development of children (see Core Quality 3).

A child's ability to recount dreams increases from the age of three years and onward. Children's motivation to talk about their dreams depends on whether they find themselves in a receptive home. A welcoming attitude encourages children to tell their dreams, perhaps, in the morning, after being picked up at school or at weekends when quality time is available. Yet these reminiscences can come out at any time (Baudet 2008).

When working with children's frightening dreams, you should not reduce them, but instead listen and empathize with the children's experiences (Garfield 1984; Siegel and Bulkeley 1998; Mallon 2002). Just speaking with a trusted caregiver is consoling in itself. Their dreams can be unfolded in drawings or even reenacted. A child or grown-up can question a monster, asking it what it wants, for instance. Just as with the dreams of adults, children's dreams can be subjected to experiential reorganization by asking: How would you like your dream to be? Is there anyone you wish had been in your dream? Can we draw it, replay it or enact it through sandplay?

If a child is afraid of a monster under the bed, you can start by asking her or him about the room, the bed and other safer, more realistic qualities in the surroundings. The child will slowly open up and become less afraid. American psychiatrist Robert Moradi (2016), who employs this technique, emphasizes that children's dreams can be seen as messages to society, if the demands of society and school, for instance, are too far out of step with children's needs and individual abilities.

In a setting for children suffering from nightmares after burn injury, Frederick Stoddard and his co-workers used a pencil in a pretend interview as a "dream machine" that pointed toward a sleeping doll and asked, "What is the doll dreaming." This was even more effective in small groups where the children could listen to each other's dreams. If the nightmares are not processed in childhood, they may haunt individuals for the rest of their life (Stoddard *et al.* 1996). Compare this with my description of Lisa's case in Chapter 14.

GOOD DREAMWORK WITH CORE QUALITY 4: DREAMS AS TRIAL RUNS IN A SAFE PLACE

The dream state can be perceived as a safe place where our unconscious intelligence can make trial runs of intended actions without any practical consequences. In this sense, dreams simulate models of future possibilities in life and they may play these out on various levels. It is helpful to look at how this anticipatory function expresses itself in the dramatic or narrative structure of dreams. Dramatic structure can generally be relived and analyzed based on the following model:

1   Time and place. Where does the dream take place? Is the place known or unknown? Childhood home? Present location? Is it a composite of elements from different places?
2   Characters. Who are the characters? What is the role of the dream self? Are the characters known or unknown?
3   Storyline. What initiates the storyline? Is a problem introduced? Are new characters added?
4   Complications. Does anything in the dream get changed? Does something dramatic happen?
5   Turning points. Is there more than one complication/turning point/subplot or is the storyline simply linear?
6   Crucial climax. Found just before the end, it is the point of no return.
7   Dramatic resolution. How does the dream end?

Of all potential interpretations of the dramatic structures of dreams, I will focus on four possibilities recommended for exploration. Each of these four possible interpretations will be summarized with examples from Core Quality 3.

1   Is a seemingly bad dream really a wise warning of the negative consequences of actions a dreamer is considering? For instance, Pia's dream about a knife that transformed into a suction cup before meeting her ex-husband. The interpretation revealed she was not aware of her emotional state, which led to post-processing her emotional state rather than meeting with him – which was doomed to fail.

2   Does the narrative reflect solutions to problems that provide the dreamer with new developmental directions? For instance, Tue's dream (Core Quality 3): Some birds in a cage at his mother's home are set free and turn out to have remarkable abilities of flight. This was interpreted as referring to the context of a liberation of his intuitive and creative abilities.

3   Is the dream self-entangled in processes that simply get worse and worse? Does this mirror experiential patterns in waking life that are counterproductive and self-destructive? In Louise's example (Core Quality 4), *she had a dream where she had to find her way to a certain place. She became increasingly disoriented and, in the end, found herself in a foreign city without identity documents.* This dream was recurring – it revisited her if she was pushing herself too hard in waking life. She would then become drawn into a spiral of increasingly negative thinking and a deepening sense of being abandoned. Yet this type of 'chain reaction' dream may also occur in milder forms in creative people, freelancers and high achievers who challenge themselves to the upper limit of their abilities.

4   Does the dream storyline describe various stances that – each in its own way – are valuable and will benefit from being nuanced and brought into balance? In the example with Denice, positive elements and complications were found at both the beginning and the end of her dream. The dream suggested finding greater balance between her extroverted way of emotional expression and her wish for more introverted, contemplative states and knowledge seeking. In Lisa's post-traumatic dream (Chapter 14), a complex, cyclical structure was unraveled, allowing it to spiral up toward increasingly acceptable solutions to her severe abandonment.

When we work with dreams what often happens is we become captivated by particularly intensive images and emotions. We immediately immerse ourselves in these or attempt to find a concrete answer to problems with which we are preoccupied.

The dramaturgical model I have expounded is a valuable tool to gain an overview of dreams. This can be exercised on all the example dreams I have presented. If you choose to focus on the most intensive and eye-popping elements in your dream, and relate them to particular contexts or psychological theories, you can still keep my model in the back of your mind as an aid to discovering resources that might otherwise be overlooked.

GOOD DREAMWORK WITH CORE QUALITY 5: DREAMS ARE ONLINE TO UNCONSCIOUS INTELLIGENCE

In the dreaming state our consciousness is online to unconscious intelligence. In waking life, we can intensify dreamwork by stimulating altered states of consciousness that have more characteristics in common with dreams than the coping strategies of the ego and our normal, everyday consciousness. The various schools of dream psychology are essentially focused on stimulating altered states in their experiential dreamwork.

In Core Quality 5, I described how the knowledge and experience of the different dream schools can be integrated into a model for dreamwork where immature or conflicted patterns are reorganized cybernetically into more harmonious ones. Cybernetic reorganization means that normal consciousness is rendered unstable, enabling the transformation of habitual patterns of experience into new, higher levels of integration.

Composition of a Complete Dreamwork Session

We can now describe a comprehensive model for creating dreamwork with experiential, relational, analytical and cognitive qualities.

1   Establishing a safe place when approaching dreams in the appreciative ways I described in Good Dreamwork with Core Qualities 1 and 2. When working with ourselves alone, routines can be developed within a mental and physical 'sacred space' where our minds are attuned to a deeper state than that of everyday life.

2   Online to unconscious intelligence. Within that safe place, we can load consciousness with associations, imaginings, inner journeys, creative expression, role-playing, body awareness, meditation or even inspiring and emotionally moving dialogue. Our personalities then connect to other memory systems and may gain access to self-organizing resources.

3   Maintaining balance. Our abilities to relate to complexity are dependent on a balance between the freedom and limitation of choice, between contingency and constraints. Having many possible choices unleashes our creativity; having fewer choices strengthens focused thinking. However, in dreamwork a balance must be maintained between the inflow of information and the ability to integrate the information constructively.

4   Cybernetic reorganization can range from small 'golden moments' of insight and recognition, to extensive transformations heralding turning points in our lives. Working with the dream about the parking place (Good Dreamwork with Core Quality 2) is an example of a dreamwork group that had great 'aha' experiences. The dreamer saw herself as being "parked in life." Her 'golden moment' was experienced together with a peer who had been instructed in appreciative dialogue.

The dreamwork with Laura, Paul and Linda (Core Qualities 2, 9 and 10) included group work and extensive one-to-one therapeutic work in a group. Throughout this dreamwork, a pendulum moved between positive and negative experiences. Every new step brought a release of energy that was transformed into positive experiences, bringing more harmony and progression in life.

In long-term, professional, individual dreamwork, the safe therapeutic alliance evokes positive internal systems in dreamers that can counterbalance destabilized states, creating space for increasingly extensive reorganization of negative, traumatizing experiences, and the integration of positive, mature and creative states (see, for instance, Torsten's and Lisa's cases in Chapter 14 – Dreams and Trauma).

5   Exit ritual. After the experiential part of dreamwork, individuals return to a normal, more pragmatic state of the self and are then 'dressed' to return to the pulse of life. A conflicted and unrested state is replaced by greater depth and harmony. The protagonist is encouraged to sense his or her body and is in touch with the ground. The self is consolidated and the nervous system is calm. Metaphorically, the whole process can be seen as a psychodrama. When the stage play comes to the end, we take down the set and actively step out of our imaginary roles. Some time may be needed to memorize the completed work, in order to create better connections between the creative states and the more focused memory systems of everyday life.

6   Summary and evaluation. When a collected state has been achieved, talk can turn to the work as such and what consequences all this might have on the dreamer's practical life. Is there anything the dreamer can be aware of until the next session that may be beneficial? Examples of this are changes in perception of oneself and others, or influences that disturb emotional equilibrium the individual had not been aware of earlier.

7   Conscious homework. One, two or three issues are chosen for the individual to be aware of for instance – pay attention to changes in relationships. Take note that dreams processed on a higher level are not necessarily understandable to others. Protect your experience against disturbing comments from other levels. Homework could also be meditation, visualizations or other exercises related to the dreamwork.

8   Unconscious post-processing. Unfolding developmental potentials that consciousness has touched on during these rather intense and information-dense states can take place on various levels in various dimensions of time. The effects may be deep and long-term, and the self may not be in touch with them. However, you can sharpen your attention to the changes that take place in your life and your relations. If the level of everyday consciousness falls back into old patterns in the intervals between sessions or modules of dreamwork, this will be commented on in new dreams (Core Quality 7).

Check list for the composition of experiential dreamwork:

1   How is a safe place for the dreamer established?
2   In what ways are you loading and limiting consciousness in dreamwork?
3   How is a cybernetic reorganization ensured?
4   Which exit rituals strengthen the connection between the higher level of experience and everyday consciousness?

5   How does the summary and evaluation take place?
6   Which recommendations can be made for conscious homework?
7   How can you follow unconscious post-processing?

References

Antonovski, A. (1987) *Unravelling the Mystery of Health.* (San Francisco, CA: Jossey-Bass Inc.)

Baudet, D. (2008) *Dream Guider: Open the Door to Your Child's Dreams.* (Charlottesville, VA: Hampton Road Publishing Company Inc.)

Brown, R. and Reinhold, T. (1999) 'Foreword by Harville Hendrix' in *Imago Relationship Therapy. An Introduction to Theory and Practice.* (New York: Wiley and Sons, Inc.)

Bulkeley, K. *et al.* (2005) 'Earliest remembered dreams'. *Dreaming*, Sept., Vol. 15(3), pp. 205–22

Damasio, A. (2000) *The Feeling of What Happens.* (London: Vintage)

Duesbury E. (2011) *The Counselor's Guide for Facilitating the Interpretation of Dreams.* (Abingdon, UK: Routledge)

Foulkes, D. (1978) *A Grammar of Dreams.* (Brighton, UK: The Harvester Press)

Garfield, P. (1984) *Your Child's Dreams.* (New York: Ballantine Books)

Hillman, J. (1964/2016) *Suicide and the Soul.* (Dallas, TX: Spring Publications, Inc.) Kindle edition

Jung, C. G. (Author), Adler, G., Fordham, M. and Read, Sir H. (Eds) (1944) *The Collected Works of C.G. Jung: Psychology and Alchemy*, Vol. 12. (Abingdon, UK: Routledge and Kegan Paul)

Jung, C. (1946/1981) 'The psychology of the transference' in G. Adler, M. Fordham and Sir H. Read (Eds), *The Collected Works of C. G. Jung: Practice of Psychotherapy*, Vol. 16. (Abingdon, UK: Routledge and Kegan Paul)

Jung, C. G. and Kerenyi, C. (1951) 'The psychology of the child archetype' in C. G. Jung and C. Kerenyi, *Introduction to a Science of Mythology: Essays on the Myth of the Divine Child and the Mysteries of Eleusis.* (Abingdon, UK: Routledge and Kegan Paul), pp. 95–118

Mallon, B. (2002) *Dream Time with Children.* (London: Jessica Kingsley Publishers)

Moradi, R. (2016) *Nightmares of Children: An Image of the World's Interconnectedness.* Presentation at the 20th Congress of the International Association for Analytical Psychology, Kyoto

Rosenthal, R. and Jacobson, L. (1992) *Pygmalion in the Classroom* (Expanded ed.). (New York: Irvington)

Siegel, A. B. (2005) 'Children's dreams and nightmares: emerging trends in research'. *Dreaming* (Special Issue), Vol. 15(3), pp. 147–154

Siegel, A. and Bulkeley, K. (1998) *Dreamcatching: Every Parents' Guide to Exploring and Understanding Children's Dreams and Nightmares.* (New York: Three Rivers Press)

Stoddard, F., Chedekel, D. *et al.* (1996) 'Dreams and nightmares of burned children' in D. Barrett (Ed.), *Trauma and Dreams.* (Cambridge, MA: Harvard University Press), pp. 25–45

Von Franz, M. L. (1964) 'The anima: the woman within' in C. G. Jung, *Man and His Symbols.* (London: Aldus Books), pp. 177–195

Chapter 16

Working with Core Qualities 6–10

GOOD DREAMWORK WITH CORE QUALITY 6: DREAMS ARE PATTERN RECOGNITION

When you have made an initial collection of material pertaining to your dream, you may begin to look at it in context with your life. What context provides an especially strong goodness of fit with your dream? Personal associations may come to you before symbol comprehension, or you may discover what your dream's structure is telling you about your waking actions in intuitive glimpses. Usually you have to try matching various contexts and then return to the dream – in a hermeneutic circle – for new associations, symbol understandings or insights into the structure of your dream. For practical reasons, I have divided life contexts into five points. You will find systematic exemplifications of the uses of these contexts in my description in Core Quality 6, and many more examples in the other Core Qualities, as well as in Chapter 14 about traumatic dreams.

Matching Dream Material with Life Contexts

Here are a few questions you can ask yourself or a dreamer with whom you are working:

1   Day-residues and recent events:
    - What did you do the previous day?
    - What was especially important the previous day?

Emotionally significant day-residues are often found relatively far from the self and the sphere of consciousness. These emotionally salient patterns of experience are activated by subliminal cues. As a rule, a good deal of work is required to reveal day-residues.

Keeping a journal and writing down what happened the previous day can be helpful. Mindfulness about your inner life and knowledge of your typical patterns of behavior and sore spots may also be helpful. My experience as a therapist is that people in general need some contemplation, inspiration and aid in order to uncover day-residues because we look at dreams through the eyes of our daily consciousness. Our dreams are trying to change that very consciousness. The day residue perspective is very beneficial because it links the strange world of dreams to our everyday life experiences.

2   Present life situation in a broader sense:

- What has occupied you recently?
- What interests/troubles you? Any acute crises?
- What are your most important, present relationships (partner, children, friends, parents, colleagues, teachers, therapist, etc.)?

Again, this requires immersion. Important clues are often revealed in a general talk before you even start discussing the dream, and people will freely share from their hearts after a group meditation or in a safe place with a psychotherapist, etc. Then, when the dream is presented, you can use these clues in a hermeneutic circle with the dream material.

3   Life history and relational patterns in childhood:

- What strikes you as especially important in your childhood?
- Do you remember important developments in your childhood?
- Who were your resource-people?
- Do you remember people who caused you problems?
- Do you remember crises and traumas that may be relevant?
- What is the earliest dream you can remember?

Dreams do not provide complete scenes from childhood – they contain individual elements which, directly or symbolically, arouse associations to childhood. These associations may be about our personal fathers or mothers, or about figures with fatherly or motherly qualities. Locations, objects and childhood figures often appear. Memories are almost never complete – they are fragmented and reintegrated in the dream narrative.

When we turn our attention to aspects of childhood in dreams, memories are awakened in the waking state that, in turn, arouse new memories in dreams. Thus a process of mutual remembering has been initiated.

4   The age and life-phase of the dreamer:

- What do you perceive as typical accomplishments for your age level?
- What are your reasons for living up to these, or choosing not to?

At all ages dreams speak to us about the maturation of our personalities and the obstacles holding us back. How do our dreams comment on opportunities, commitment to adult relationships, parenthood, career choices, midlife crises, retirement and other inevitable transitional periods in our human lives? In my description of the Core Qualities I have provided many examples that demonstrate that dreams can contribute to answering these questions, irrespective of age.

5   Future life transitions:

- How do you envisage your future?
- Are there any returning fantasies about life changes you have not addressed?
- Is there anything important you would like to manifest in your life?

Prospective dreams usually contain an increased occurrence of universal, impersonal symbols of transformation that may be, for instance, finding new roads, experiencing sexual unification, emerging from a dark tunnel, being bathed in a light of unusual clarity, meeting a particularly wise person or talking animal, valuable objects, fountains of youth, angels, and majestic birds. Squares, circles, cones, crosses and oriental mandala patterns may symbolize new orders arising in the inner cosmos (Jung 1912, 1944).

I mentioned that dreams about death and burial might be signaling the need to leave something behind. Further along in the process, our dreams reveal this by the appearance of unexpected helpers, meeting our personified ideals, births, sprouting fields, having a baby, crossing a river, venturing out across a bridge, getting a new house or participating in its construction.

Themes of transformations are especially obvious in initial dreams (Core Quality 6) and peak experience dreams (Core Quality 10).

GOOD DREAMWORK WITH CORE QUALITY 7: DREAMS ARE HIGH-LEVEL COMMUNICATION

Since dreams reflect self-organizing functions and because they deal with important matters they will provide feedback on any serious considerations of the waking self about important life issues – including working with dreams. The advantage of this is that you do not have to exert yourself trying to find the 'perfect' understanding of a dream. Your dreams will inevitably comment on your serious considerations. In order to evaluate the process, dreamers can ask the following questions about any dream and try to understand the dream in a symbolic fashion.

- Does the dream confirm that the dreamer is on the right track when working with an important issue? An example from Core Quality 7 is 70-year-old Ella who employed a mindfulness practice to overcome her fear of death after dreaming about a dried, shriveled apple that had grown and become fresh and beautifully red.
- Does the dream correspond to a question the dreamer has posed to him or herself? Also from Core Quality 7, Mie speculated about whether meditation was something she would be able to learn. After attempting to meditate, her

dreams responded and put her in an unknown house with people swooping down from the sky throwing valuable objects in through the windows.
- Does the dream suggest any corrections in dealing with an important matter preoccupying the dreamer? Again from Core Quality 7 – my colleague who scored in his own goal in a dream, and Ingelise who came to her first therapy session and recounted a dream where she gave the doctor a false insurance card.

High-level communication is described in more detail in Peter's dream series in Core Quality 7, and in Lisa's case in Chapter 14 about traumatic dreams.

Levels of Communicating about Dreamwork in Groups

The processing of dream material happens on various levels and all communication about this unconscious material must take this level shifting into account. As a general rule, the higher the levels of organization and the stronger the energy charges, the greater the chances that the whole personality will be influenced and that more complexity will be needed from consciousness to deal with the issue.

In my dream groups, these are some of the levels of communication I differentiate between:

1   Socializing among group members during breaks and outside of the therapeutic setting: The work that has taken place on a higher level should be protected here – participants should not comment or interpret the work of others without clear permission from those who did the work.
2   Sharing experiences in a group without comment from other participants.
3   Communication between peers in structured exercises: The primary focus is on learning about specific aspects of dreamwork – not therapy. This may include exercises with various Core Qualities as well as in ways of communicating about dreams.
4   Participants' debriefings after structured exercises: In exercises with main characters (protagonists) and helpers, participants actively step into their roles with the words, "I want to be the main character," and "I am at your service as the helper." When the exercise comes to an end, a 'de-roling' takes place where the protagonist says, "I'm no longer the main character," and the helper, "I'm no longer your helper." The participants discuss what it was like to do the exercise and then return to their roles as peers in the group. These exercises are supervised and the participants will be able to share their experiences of resources and difficulties later in plenum.
5   Therapist and participant in a group: The therapist should be able to set up the work so a balance between the level of processing and the time allotted for it is achieved (see Good Dreamwork with Core Quality 5).
6   Participants will evaluate their own experiences during the course and also determine what they wish to continue working on.

Big Work: One-to-one in a Group

In my groups I shift between short dialogues with all participants and longer sessions with one participant. I am inspired by a concept I learned from analyst and psychodrama instructor Ethel Vogelsang during my three-year postgraduate psychodrama training at the Jung Institute in Zürich. Eighty minutes is set aside for this work. The various phases of the work relate to the many levels of communication found in human relations.

1   Choosing a protagonist: Participants wishing to work indicate this and also state their theme. If several people want to be protagonists, the therapist can facilitate a dialogue between the parties. Do the presented themes have anything in common? Could one person choose to witness another's work? If there is difficulty in determining who will be the protagonist, group participants can do monologues (soliloquies) about a common, active theme, or make a group drawing and find other creative ways to express their experiences of the process. Yet, in almost all cases, groups do manage to agree upon a protagonist through self-organizing processes.

2   One-to-one in a group: For this exercise, the therapist has the freedom to employ a combination of any or all tools available in the therapeutic process. The purpose is to demonstrate the method as a whole rather than practicing and exercising individual elements in the module. Laura (Core Quality 2), Paul (Core Quality 9) and Linda (Core Quality 10) were all experiencing this phase in a group setting.

3   Group participant sharing: Participants are provided with opportunities to share experiences from their own lives that have occurred in connection to their dreamwork. These debriefings are about associations, memories and feelings that have been awakened during the protagonist's work and do not include any evaluation of the work. The protagonist is 'off duty', thus 'protected' during this. The therapist ensures that participants remain mindful of their own experiences and do not refer directly to the protagonist.

4   Questions about the work: If the protagonist and time allow, participants get a chance to ask the therapist questions about the dreamwork. Questions and answers must remain respectful of the protagonist's dignity and sensitivity, and related to the general teaching points.

5   The protagonist's final state and perspectives for the future: The therapist ensures that the protagonist is in a grounded, emotionally balanced state and leaves from the dreamwork with resources and developmental potential in tow.

Together with individual therapy, this method is a learning process in group-dynamics. Conducted with the sufficient professional experience it demonstrates that people in a group – to everyone's benefit – can organize themselves around the sharp peaks in the energy landscape of the group, instead of succumbing to rivalry and competition.

(If the method in the second point above includes role-playing, then the participant involved should be instructed in the role of the protagonist with support from the therapist. Afterward, a de-roling should take place and the role-taker can talk about what it was like to portray the person concerned.)

GOOD DREAMWORK WITH CORE QUALITY 8: DREAMS ARE CONDENSED INFORMATION

Utilizing Dream Condensations in Creative Ways

Since dreams are condensed information, they also provide access to many possibilities of interpretation. If we have particular goals with our dreamwork, this may seem confusing and troublesome. However, if we acknowledge this multidimensionality as creative ways of processing information that can be educational, then it can be turned into an asset. Below, I will discuss various ways of constructively utilizing multidimensionality in dreams.

Monotony of Interpretations

One classic problem with dreamwork is that particular methods or approaches can lead to a 'monotony' of interpretation. Jung examined this issue in connection with Freud's sexual interpretations (Jung 1911–12, par. 9). Perls criticized both the psychoanalysts and the Jungians for intellectualizing. Further, he stated that, "my whole technique develops more and more into never, ever interpreting. Just back-feeding, providing an opportunity for the other person to discover himself" (Perls 1969, pp.143–4). Perls led the way to a method for processing emotions, yet he filled any theoretical holes in his own dreamwork with polemic observations and philosophical interpretations. Therefore, he overlooked important aspects of dreams that could have been enriched by psychoanalytical or Jungian perspectives (Vedfelt 2007). Medard Boss (1977), the leading pioneer in existential dream interpretation, posited sound arguments against over-interpretation, yet fell short of any real dream theory – his own was poorly conceived and burdened by idiosyncratic symbol interpretations (Vedfelt 2007).

In my experience, even if a dream can be interpreted, thematically categorized or understood in certain ways, details and contexts that may add new information will always be overlooked. If we look at dreams from new perspectives, or combine various theories and methodical approaches, stagnated dreamwork can be revitalized. I call this multidimensional dream interpretation (Vedfelt 1999).

According to network theory, we all interpret phenomena through certain inner patterns. This coincides with contemporary theory of interpretation expounded by Hans-Georg Gadamer in his book, *Truth and Method*. According to Gadamer, we always look at a text with "pre-understanding." We can make this bias our ally. We can choose to stick to a certain interpretation for practical reasons, yet we are still always able to make new inquiries (Gadamer 1975).

Finding New Perspectives in Dreams

Exercise 1

Always ask this question: Does this dream contain anything new or different from what I already know? The answer will be found if you view the dream through fresh eyes and make an effort to clarify or unfold the dream experience (Core Quality 2). If your dreamwork has a tendency to return to the same issues – such as bad childhood experiences – or, on the other hand, they are repeatedly interpreted as elevated spiritual experiences, then see what happens if you change perspective. If you always find yourself ending up in anger or sorrow – and overlooking all the other possible emotions – then see Good Work with Core Quality 9 and the variety of emotions described there for inspiration. Perhaps clarifying or unfolding the dream will reveal meaningful aspects that you have overlooked. Would a more thorough analysis of the narrative structure (Core Quality 4) bring new life to a stagnated process? This perspective on monotony can be applied to any aspect of dreamwork. (War veterans' monotonous PTSD nightmares that photographically recreate traumatic events have been shown to be waking memories that interrupt sleep and not dreams at all (Hartmann 1996)).

An example. When it came to Anders, the young doctor in Core Quality 7, I especially emphasized his relationship with male authority figures. This made sense and was of practical importance because Anders needed to improve at saying no in certain situations. Yet there were also some side-effects that were revealed when he provoked people on several occasions whom he did not wish to repel. When we discovered this – parallel to the sharp peak of his problem with authority – we realized that some other, softer patterns had also been sketched out in his dreams pertaining to how men and women relate. By shifting our focus to the female figures in his dreams, we discovered that his relationship with male authority figures was also affected by how the women in his life had perceived men. This was especially true of how his mother saw his father, and how she had affected Anders' experience of himself as a man. This led to a more nuanced attitude to male authority figures, both within him and in his relationships with others.

Creatively Combining Various Dream Perspectives

Exercise 2

Try combining three different perspectives of the same dream such as, for instance, past experiences, current life situations and future potentials, and see if all three can be useful. Perhaps a parent in your dream can also be a symbol for a therapist or an inner helper/judge. Are you able to see your dream on objective and subjective levels at the same time?

An example. Karen (Core Quality 8) dreamed that she forgot to pick up her daughter at school. Initially, we looked at this issue as a reflection of troubles in her everyday life – her daughter experienced separation anxiety (interpretation of the exterior level). Then we looked at her daughter as a personification of herself (interpretation of the interior level) and as a child (past experience context). This provided an emotional release (experiential dreamwork) that made her more aware of her own emotional state in situations where they experienced mother/daughter separation. Further, we viewed the daughter in her dream as a representative of a new opportunity within Karen – to finish her studies (future aspect of the context). We creatively played with these possibilities without problem solving or drawing any definite conclusions. However, during her group the following weekend, Karen recounted a dream where she, together with her husband, daughter and son, had reached a train on time. This seemed to demonstrate that her personality had become more collected and goal-oriented – suggesting the integration of a complementing masculine aspect. Simultaneously, on the exterior level, improvements had taken place in all the dimensions of her life that we had discussed.

Using Interpretation Bias in Creative Ways

Exercise 3

Is it possible to define the limits of your theoretical, methodological and practical dreamwork (see Chapter 1)? Would it be helpful to try to balance the use of experiential, existential, psychoanalytical, Jungian or cognitive behavioral methods in the dreamwork? In order to limit complexity for a period of time, can you employ focus-oriented dreamwork consciously and deliberately, and then return to a more flexible method if the dreams point in other directions?

These questions are useful in groups when supervising dreamwork. I utilize reflecting teams of peers working on the supervisee's material from various perspectives. Each team is encouraged to exhaust the possibilities contained in one aspect of dreams, and then compare and eventually synthesize the information with the other teams' work with other aspects (Vedfelt 1999).

GOOD DREAMWORK WITH CORE QUALITY 9: DREAMS ARE EXPERIENCES OF WHOLENESS

Dreams are a wholeness of images, body sensations, movements, thoughts and feelings. The central learning point in Core Quality 9 is that we can approach our dream experiences through various experiential modalities and switch between them by following the shifting intensity in our psychic energy landscapes.

Combining Experiential Modalities in Dreamwork

An example of this is the young woman Vera's dream of the German Shepherds (Core Quality 9). Her movement went from a basic mood of unpleasantness, to visualizing the dogs, on to a primary emotion of anxiety, then memories of conflict with a partner, role-playing a dog, sensing tightening stomach muscles, experiencing a primary emotion of fear, consciously feeling anger and, finally, a cognitive understanding of an overriding pattern of experience that could be changed in a positive way.

I have exemplified such supramodal transformations through dreamwork in greater detail, including Laura's symbol of closing doors that transformed to the image of an open bridge (Core Quality 2), and Linda's dream about the sad waiting room with her fragmented family that was replaced by a united holy family (Core Quality 10).

The Sequence of Image, Emotion and Body Reversed

Visualization is employed to gain control over the mind, body and emotional states in areas such as yoga, meditation, psychotherapy hypnosis and mental training of athletes. This is a key point in active imagination known from Jungian therapy. In his memoirs, Jung (1961) stated that the extent to which he managed to translate strong, disturbing emotions into images reflected the level of his reassurance and calmness.

This perception of the transformational powers of visualization harmonizes well with the theories described in Chapter 2 about the regulation of emotion through dreams, which suggests that dreams regulate strong emotions by turning them into visual narratives. In even greater detail, Ernest Hartmann (2011, p. 12) proposed that the dreams are guided by emotion and that, "the central image of the dream, pictures and measures the emotion."

Yet, from neuroscience we know that the so-called somatic marker system is very active in dreams and is also tied to the body-sensing modality. As described in Chapter 2, the somatic marker system includes brainstem nuclei in the PAG as well as the insula, the cingulate cortex, premotor cortex, and the ventromedial prefrontal cortex (Damasio 2003). Brainstem nuclei in the PAG sense, "the degrees of pleasure and displeasure which calibrate the basic qualitative range within the 'sense' of emotions." Further, this is equivalent to an inner sensing of "the body's homeostatic physiology" (Solms and Turnbull 2002, p. 108–9), and is a precondition for what Damasio calls "the feeling of emotions."

In dreams, the stream of information is generally understood to move from body to emotions to image. Thus, we can receive information from deeper, energy-charged layers by allowing consciousness to follow the reverse path from dream-imagery or the social emotions, to the primary emotions, to the background emotions and even further to the body sensations behind the background emotions.

In this section about Good Dreamwork with Core Quality 9, I will concentrate on supramodal dreamwork, particularly emphasizing dreamwork with emotions and bodywork, which are the modalities that people are least aware of experientially in dreams. The exercises I describe below provide dreamers with both insight and depth while increasing the helpers' abilities at all levels to empathize with and facilitate the dream experiences of others.

A Supramodal Exercise

The following exercise will provide a sense of the meaningfulness of the supramodal experience when working with dreams. Before starting you should think about what resource areas your dream might contain, rather than focusing on unpleasant portions.

You can start with a relaxation exercise such as sitting in a comfortable position with eyes closed. Turn your awareness to your breathing and try to focus on inhaling and exhaling. If thoughts arise that disturb you, identify them and then allow your attention to return to your breathing.

You might try counting your breaths from one to ten, for example – think 'one' when you inhale, 'and' when you exhale, 'two' inhale, 'and' exhale, etc. This classic mindfulness exercise is highly suitable for calming the mind. If you know other relaxation exercises, you can also use them. The important part is spending time disconnecting from everyday thoughts and opening your consciousness to your internal life.

Once you have created a relaxed state, you can examine your dream from beginning to end, paying attention to which dream elements make the greatest impression on you – the elements you find most interesting for further study.

Visualize the character, situation or object on which you have chosen to focus. Remain with this image a moment and notice what feeling it awakens. Choose a color you think fits the feeling.

How and where do you notice the feeling or color in your body? Describe the bodily sensations purely physically – size, form, consistency. Do not interpret the sensations in your body, nor translate them into psychological understanding. Just stay with the physical sensations. Then imagine that you reinforce these physical sensations. Do they go away? Do they grow stronger? Do they move? You will probably discover that new thoughts arise that you can also observe. Does this make new aspects of the dream more apparent?

If you experience the situation as pleasant, then stay with it and notice as many of its qualities as possible. If something pops up that you experience as unpleasant, then think about how you wish it were different. Should any of the characters act differently? Do you need help from outside? How would it feel if the situation turned into something positive? Give your feelings shapes, colors and/or symbols. Notice how they feel in your body.

Feel your arms and legs, and also the contact points between your body and the surface on which you are sitting. Close your eyes and turn your attention to the outer world while maintaining contact within. This exercise works particularly well as a guide inner journey, where the guidance helps you to be on the track.

Emotions in Dreams and Dreamwork

As described in Core Quality 3, one modality often overlooked in dreams is that of emotions. Tore Nielsen and his co-workers found that the number of emotions observed in dreams increased significantly if dreamers were provided with a list of the following 22 emotions: admiration, anger, disappointment, distress, fear, fear-confirmed, gloating, gratification, gratitude, happy-for, hate, hope, joy, love, pity, pride, relief, remorse, reproach, resentment, satisfaction, and shame (Nielsen *et al.* 1991). Some of these emotions correspond with Damasio's basic emotions (Core Quality 9); others are more complex social emotions. Ernest Hartmann's emotions, which are tied to especially intense dreams, are presented in Core Quality 10. Both lists can be inspiring when looking for emotions in dreams.

In educational contexts, I use a simpler model of the ten so-called categorical emotions compiled by psychologist and researcher Carroll Izard. I suggest you go through your dreams looking for the feelings listed here. These feelings are known in all cultures. They appear to be accompanied by the same inner experiences and facial expressions and are imbued with similar intentions all over the world. The ten categorical emotions are: interest, joy, surprise, sorrow, anger, disgust, contempt, shame, shyness and guilt.

Observing these emotions will sharpen your awareness of yourself and others while in waking states as well as while dreaming. Fully expressed emotions are typically found in children. For adults, these emotions may be more or less camouflaged by our acquired social facades. Emotions should be observed discreetly – direct comments about the body language of others can be experienced as invasive. The following list has been adapted from Caroll Izard's study of the psychology of emotions (Izard 1991):

1   Interest: Interest causes eyebrows to raise and narrow slightly, eyes to search, mouth to open a little or lips to purse. Slight forward movement with focused gaze.
2   Joy: A real smile makes the corners of the mouth turn up, wrinkles appear around the eyes. Willpower wanes. Enables psychological well-being and social bonding.
3   Surprise: Forehead rises creating horizontal wrinkles, making eyes look big and round. Mouth opens in an oval. Short-term feelings of pleasure.
4   Sorrow: Inner corners of the eyebrows are pulled up together at an angle while eyes narrow and mouth corners droop. For quiet sorrow: The face loses form and droops, eyes lose their luster, speech slows and decreases. The chin might pull up and tremble. Eyes potentially moisten or tear.
5   Anger: In full-blown anger, the eyebrows pull down and together, tightening the forehead. A fold of skin appears at the top of the nose. Eyes narrow becoming harsh, edgy and fixed. The mouth becomes square or rectangular, lips become thin exposing teeth.
6   Disgust: Disgust causes the eyebrows to pull down and together, nose wrinkles, upper lip lifts and the lower lip is pulled down. The tongue protrudes as if it is trying to escape a bad taste. The mouth forms somewhat of a rectangle.
7   Contempt: Contempt throws the head back as if looking down on someone. The corners of the mouth are forced together. One lifted eyebrow.

8   Fear: Eyebrows lift, slightly together which creates deeper furrows at the center of the forehead than the sides; 8a) eyes open wide, possibly with lifted eyelids so the whites are seen above the irises; 8b) the corners of the mouth pull way back with lips slightly parted.
9   Shyness: Darting eyes look down, face turns away. Body contracts, trying to be smaller, hiding body parts.
10 Guilt: A discrepancy appears between what is said and facial expression or movements. For instance, disgust appears when one says all is well, anger when one speaks of joy. A wry smile. Hand covering face.

It is vital not to pressure people, allowing their feelings to be expressed at a pace that can be integrated into their individual perceptions of themselves. I would like to point out a few of the countless examples of this: Anger can be difficult to express because it is often overshadowed by a fear of rejection or punishment. Acknowledgement of gloating is often suppressed by shame, which is then revealed if you are given the opportunity to unfold your emotions. Joy can be repressed if the childhood environment had difficulty relating to enthusiasm, or if the experience of joy became tied to disappointment – just to mention two of many possibilities. A general rule I adhere to is that feelings will be expressed when people are ready to do so. In courses and training groups I use observation of these emotions as a partner exercise.

Emotions Expressed through Color in Dreams and Drawings

Colors are connected to emotions and therefore have been used as expressions in all cultures through societal rituals, spiritual systems, art and architecture. Based on extensive literature studies and a questionnaire for dreamers, American dream researcher Bob Hoss found that we share a common human experience of the emotional qualities of colors in dreams (Hoss 2004). Hoss's discoveries harmonize well with the eastern descriptions of the Chakra systems, and also with my own experiences from my practice. Other good sources of studies of general color symbolism are Anni Ronnberg and Kathelin Martin (2010).

The following highly truncated description of color symbolism, which is based on many years of therapeutic experience with dreams, mediation and drawing therapy, can provide a sense of the connection between feelings and colors. The meaning of particular colors is, in practice, far more differentiated and dependent on context. It is important that the protagonists themselves are the ones to determine what their dream colors are expressing. Therefore, my intention with the following list is primarily to provide a sense of the spectrum of feelings and emotions that colors can express.

•   Red is experienced by many people as a warm color, and as a color that seems to repel us. In many languages the word 'red' is related to the word for blood and is associated with life and passion.

- Orange is a sparkling, warm, lively color connected to sunshine, light and joy. Many people experience this color as expansive and activating. In its more screeching shades it can also suggest restlessness and over-activity.
- Yellow is the color of the sun. Yellow can be radiant and shine like gold – as warm as an egg yolk symbolizing the beginnings of life. Yellow means optimism. It may be related to aging as with, for example, yellowing leaves, yellowing linen and yellowing paper. In English, yellow refers to anxiety, cowardice, jealousy and deceit.
- Green is the color of natural growth and self-development. Green vegetation appears in dreams when we are in touch with vital areas of ourselves. Hope is light green and reminds us of springtime. We get green with envy. Some nuances of green can be poisonous, or the shade of a stagnant pond.
- Blue often evokes feelings of calm and quiet satisfaction, and is generally introverted and alluring. This color is often associated with something spiritual. Dark blue represents the greater depths of the soul, both positively and more negatively when it comes to depression and aching hearts suffering 'the blues'.
- Purple and indigo symbolize spiritual and religious qualities – higher levels of consciousness and introversion. In Christianity, purple is the color of sorrow and fasting before the crucifixion holiday. When drawing dreams, purple is often associated with deep levels of grief.
- White ordinarily symbolizes purity, truth and goodness. Traditionally, girls wear white at their confirmations, as well as virgin brides at their weddings. Angels are white, and the dove of the Holy Spirit is white. White, radiating light is known from mystical experiences. Yet white may also symbolize colorlessness, lack of emotion and sterility.
- Brown associates to earth and tree trunks, and may refer to skin color. This color is typically used for clothing for manual labor and everyday dress, just like grey is often used by monks, who live humble, modest lives. Brown symbolizes everyday security and warmth, or boredom and stagnation. It is often associated with feces.
- Grey, in general, is the color of sadness and depression, mundanity and conventionality. More positively, this color might be an expression for modesty and humility. Combined with other colors, grey can have a dampening effect and provide elegance and class.
- Black is often highlighted for its negative associations in the form of a dark outlook, sorrow, death and depression. When drawing emotions, it is the most common color used to represent anger. Black also represents an array of the shadowy sides of sexuality, from sexy underwear to sadomasochistic equipment. Black can have a shiny and velvety-soft quality that is often described in mystic literature. It is the background for the night's stars, and can evoke cosmic experiences in dreams.

Movement and Body Position in Dreamwork

In role-playing there is usually a great deal of movement and certain kinds of body positions, such as when Tue experimented with being one of the birds in his dream (Core Quality 4); or the woman who pretended to be a dresser that had its drawers pulled out (Core Quality 5); or Anders who role-played being the characters from his dream about the tough biker and his boss (Core Quality 7).

Performed properly, role-playing is a powerful method. When using this technique, it is necessary to be vigilant to the waking self's integrative capacity of the characters and objects being role-played. It is also important to de-role and examine – in a more reflective state of conscious – how the individual feels.

Movement and body position have been employed as effective methods by various schools. In the initial phase of a psychodrama, the instructor and the protagonist work together in circles surrounded by the group. They inquire into the protagonist's associations to the dream. Moving slowly or quickly, and even pausing may indicate various levels of afterthought, contemplation or engagement. From my gestalt and art therapy training, I adopted a practice where I sometimes sit with the client on the floor doing, for instance, dynamic supramodal work with drawings. This inspires a more informal and playful approach that also affects associations. During my training in body psychotherapy, the influence of body positions on thoughts and feelings was further explored. Since then, I have used my knowledge of movement and body positions in an improvised way that adapts to the content of the dreams.

One exercise for a protagonist and helper, which, in a simple way, provides a sense of how associations are affected by body positions, is as follows:

1   Sit face-to-face in a chair opposite your partner with eyes open as if in ordinary conversational therapy. Talk about a dream theme relevant to your current process. This position aids in keeping associations relatively close to consciousness and promotes a more analytical or cognitive approach.
2   Shift position so the protagonist is lying on his/her back. Lying on your back usually provides a free flow of associations that can be both creative and regressive. Associations made in this position, if you remain too long, have a tendency to get a bit drowsy or stuck in certain ruminating patterns. The helper can ask questions from time to time about what is happening in the dreamer's mind and body, thus enabling the protagonist's observing ego to remain attentive. Changes in the protagonist's breathing, facial expressions or tiny, involuntary movements may indicate that the energy-charge is shifting from one way of experiencing to another. Usually, this would be a good moment for the helper to ask, "What's happening right now?"
3   Shift position so you are both standing up. This position may show whether you are prepared to carry through with the insights attained or decisions made while lying on your back. Language metaphors such as having a standpoint, standing up for someone or something or, on the contrary, weak knees, leaning back or forward, etc., can be experienced quite physically in this kind

of dreamwork and reveal a readiness to accept or withdraw the insights acquired in the lying position.

The psychic content tied to typical head positions, hand movements and body language can further be explored and utilized. An example of this is Alice (Core Quality 9) who sat with her eyes wide open with one hand in front of her face in a gesture of dismay. Staying with this gesture, and following a chain of associations put Alice in touch with her fear of not being able to be a good mother of her arriving newborn. This made good sense in relationship to her dream: her father and mother had kidnapped her child. Working with this dream turned Alice's fear into an experience of motherly competence and – purely physically – was followed by her baby moving into the optimal position for delivery.

Inner Body Sensations and Dreamwork

To feel the 'felt sense' – to sense how the body feels inside – feels foreign for most people to do without practice.

In the supramodal exercise above, I suggested that you should describe body sensations, yourself, in purely physical terms – size, shape, consistency, sensation. This can be further explored through the exercise below. At first it might be necessary to provide dreamers with a language for body sensations. It is also important that helpers encourage, acknowledge and mirror protagonists when they are ready to describe sensations in their bodies (Heller 2001). Some kinds of body sensations might create unforeseen associations to negative or traumatic experiences. Therefore, it is vital to go through the body at the outset to find out which areas feel safe and which feel unsafe at that particular point in time.

Exercise 1: Establishing a Safe Place in the Body

Sit or lie completely still, preferably guided by a helper. Move your attention slowly throughout your body from your feet to your head. Notice where there are pleasant, firm, calm, supportive feelings. Do not dwell on areas that feel unpleasant. Find the area that feels most resourceful. In connection to this, visualize a safe place where you know you have found good, positive experiences.

Exercise 2: Find the 'Peak' in your Body's Energy Landscape.

Sense your body. Move your attention throughout your body and pay attention to which body sensations are most intense. Describe them to yourself or your helper in physical terms – not feelings, images or thoughts. In this exercise you should not use movements such as pointing to communicate your experience as this will displace the experience to another modality (movement). Somatic experience explores the body and provides language for sensations:

1   Placement, shape and size. For instance, it is in my stomach, just under the navel. It is round. The size is similar to an orange.
2   How is the sensation noticed? What qualities does the perception have? Examples are tense, compelling, falling, jabbing, bubbly, trembling, soft, mushy, cold, warm, radiant, sucking, burning, icy, spinning, electric, tickling, dizzying, nauseating, expanding, contracting, fluid, blocked, etc.
3   The intensity of the sensation – vague, diffuse, weak, strong, intense, unbearable.
4   Does perception change when you know that you will stay with the sensations?
5   When body sensations have been felt and identified, the helper may ask the protagonist about associations, then connect to the meaning of the dream and, if necessary, reframe them in a positive way, as demonstrated in the supramodal exercise above.

In this exercise, you carefully find your way – less is more. Whenever something becomes too unpleasant, return to the safe place in your body instead of immersing yourself in emotions. When you have become more familiar with the 'felt sense', you will be able to remain with intense body sensations longer.

Drawing the Felt Sense

Employing the supramodal principle, you can amplify a body sensation by drawing it on a large sheet of paper with crayons. In these circumstances it is so surprisingly easy that most people are spontaneously able to find a color and abstract shape that, when combined, expressed the emotion(s) tied to the body sensation. In many cases, the body sensation changes or even vanishes. If it does not do so, I encourage the individual to draw it again, even several more times. To get the process flowing, it is important that the dreamer, helper or therapist has experience with and confidence that this kind of process works. A helper's trust in a method is contagious. Drawing on large paper involves movement and inspires spontaneity.

The typical meanings of the various colors have been discussed above. Shapes might have energetic or aggressive lines that move toward or away from the dreamer, or even zig-zagging patterns of movement. You might find spirals that move toward the center, or that develop as they move outward. In my experience, black is most commonly connected to anger – red comes in second. This work often develops through emotional release, from the darker, heavy end of the color scale toward the lighter airier end – from fewer colors to a broader spectrum; from hard lines to softer curves including transformational symbols, people in dialogue, or the dream self outlined and in color.

After emotional and body expression, I find it important to return to the dream as a whole, exploring how the emotional work connects to its overall wisdom. Can this be applied in everyday life or is it first and foremost a step in the inner process that must be allowed time and proved to be nurturing to mature?

Emotional Attunement through Body Language, Facial Expression and Tone of Voice

A major portion of our attitudes toward other people is built on an unconscious reading of their body language (Chapter 3, Core Quality 6). From the moment of birth, this kind of reading is a factor between infant and mother and/or other caregivers. This is called emotional attunement through body language, facial expression and tone of voice, and we use it constantly in our everyday life without thinking about it.

Emotional attunement can be practiced individually or in groups to ensure good, safe emotional and non-verbal contact. The exercise below is an extension of the mirroring exercise described in Good Dreamwork with Core Quality 2.

I have created this exercise for dreamers and helpers to train emotional attunement by employing three parameters: shape, intensity and timing. These are the same parameters described by Daniel Stern (1985) in the interaction between mothers and their infants.

Two participants step into the roles of main character and helper. The helper observes and mirrors according to the following characteristics:

1   Shape, i.e. attuning to body language:

    a   Symmetrical attunement. For instance, a smile is met by a smile.

    b   Asymmetrical attunement. For instance, moving forward in one's seat when a protagonist shows a facial expression of interest – or vice-versa. Lowering eyebrows when a client stamps on the floor – or vice-versa.

    c   Are there any particular patterns of movement repeated by the dreamer?

2   Intensity:

    a   How emotionally intense does the mirrored expression seem to be?

    b   How does body intensity match emotional intensity?

3   Timing:
    How often should feedback be given? When does the intensity rise and fall? Over time, does the way discernment takes place change? Does the frequency of discernment change in the various phases of the process?

Generally, the helper does not comment on body language, asking the dreamer instead, from time to time when typical patterns reappear and natural pauses occur, "What are you experiencing right now?" The dreamer's body language is especially useful in revealing whether the helper's feedback has been constructive. Such as if dreamers nod, smile or show interest when helpers mirror or, on the contrary, if dreamers seem to be emotionally unaffected, withdrawn, protecting themselves, looking away, etc.

Through practice and increased experience, emotional attunement becomes an increasingly fluid communication skill in the interaction between dreamer and helper.

GOOD DREAMWORK WITH CORE QUALITY 10: DREAMS ARE PSYCHOLOGICAL ENERGY LANDSCAPES

If you have unfolded a dream in a safe place and mastered the skills of appreciative dialogue and emotional attunement, then you may improvise employing the Core Qualities in secure ways that follow the energy fluctuations in dreamwork.

In dreamwork, creative factors take precedence over more instrumental principles. Utilizing this perception, the dreamer is supported in letting go of habitual thinking and encouraged to listen to creative impulses coming from within. Dreamers as well as helpers can learn to practice reflective attention of their experiences and learn to observe their creative impulses without reacting to them.

The Picasso Principle

Spanish painter Pablo Picasso has described how he consistently pushed aside any creative ideas that appeared while working. In his experience, these ideas were not lost or destroyed but rather reappeared later in more condensed forms that became the end products of creative processes (Evans 1937).

I have made a principle of this, and it can be transposed to dreamwork: we can let our ideas drift back and forth across the borderline of consciousness, allowing them to condense and further develop until they spontaneously let themselves be known again. This is different than the 'kill-your-darlings' principle from journalism where you extinguish your most cherished ideas instead of giving them time to gestate and form the beginnings of a new synthesis of creative dialogue.

The interaction between creativity and technique, between consciousness and unconscious intelligence, or between dreamer and helper, is reminiscent of jazz improvisation where melodic freedom is found within harmonic frameworks. Jazzmusicians have repertoires of well-practiced melodic figures and riffs that can be freely employed, combined, varied and developed in any way and at any time that serves the ensemble.

Working with Peak Experience Dreams

Exemplified in Core Quality 10, you will find there a complete list of the typical characteristics involved. In my experience, many people have experienced peak dreams but then lost contact with what these dreams mean to them, because these meanings do not fit into society's or their own understanding of what is relevant in our lives. To summarize, in your dreams explore if you have experienced:

1   numinous sensations of mystery, awe and wonder;
2   good fortune (the good fortune scale);

3   unknown territories and universal (archetypal) symbolism as opposed to everydayness;
4   symbols of transformation, such as death and rebirth;
5   lucidity and/or parapsychological phenomena.

You can revisit a dream by painting it, sharing it in a group, practicing active imagination, or doing supramodal exercises and asking the following questions:

1   What is it like to relive the dream and the dream's period of time?
2   Is your experience tied to a transitional phase in your life?
3   Does re-experiencing the dream invigorate you?
4   Does your dream provide a connection to something greater within you?
5   Does it open up opportunities and/or states that you still have time to realize?
6   Does it change your view of humanity as such?
7   Did the peak experience dream give you an opportunity to explore a state of lucidity?
8   Have you had any parapsychological experiences that altered your view of the world and/or made you feel a connectedness to something greater than yourself?

Working with Traumatic Nightmares and Bad Dreams

In Chapter 14 I examined and exemplified criteria and methods for working with traumatic dreams. In summary, the following questions are relevant when trying to distinguish a traumatic nightmare from an ordinary bad dream:

1   Does the dream contain any signs of consequences from traumatic events such as anxiety, feelings of being abandoned, victimization of the dream self, a sense of being drained of energy, memory problems tied to the dream, or the fear of going to sleep?
2   Is there any inkling or knowledge that the dream arose after some specific traumatic events, or that it might be the result of trauma to the character caused by abandonment, neglect or abuse in childhood?

I see traumatic dreams as a stage in a natural healing process that is attempting to create connections between inner, injured areas of the personality and areas that have not been damaged by trauma. Healing will often be tied to transitioning to new life phases and require a readjustment of the personality as a whole:

1   Is there anything in your general situation in life or actual external events that can be changed that causes the traumatic dream to recur?
2   Is your dream of such a nature that it requires special efforts to ensure a safe place and a good relationship (in therapy – individual or group) in order to process the dream?

3   Is there anything in your dreams that indicates a new view, phase in life or developmental opportunities?
4   Are there resources in the dreams that have been overlooked that need to be viewed with renewed focus? Can reframing, active imagination or cybernetic restructuring of the dream be employed?

Please see Chapter 14 about traumatic dreams.

Dream Series

Series of dreams can be utilized to explore energy movements between various networks in the psyche that create changes, promote new development and provide stable states. The Ten Core Qualities can be employed as a model for exploring these issues. I give three key points for each core quality.

Core Quality 1: Dealing with Important Matters

Initial dreams in your dream processes often take on rather cryptic, archetypal and impersonal forms with fewer associations to everyday life than subsequent dreams. They often provide dreamers with condensed central issues and new life opportunities that are better understood when viewed retrospectively. Keep your initial dream in the back of your mind while exploring any subsequent dreams in a series.

1   Do presupposed developments expressed abstractly on a high level appear in more tangible and everyday forms in the later dreams?
2   Have you maintained awareness of any positive qualities that your initial dream may have been indicating?
3   Can negatively experienced elements in your initial dream be retrospectively understood as a means to self-reorganization?

Core Quality 2: Dreams Symbolize

1   Have any changes taken place in the symbolism that might be viewed as progressive?
2   Can symbols in a dream originally understood as intuitive 'feelings of know-ing' be enriched by clarification of other aspects of the dream?
3   Does it make sense to utilize the knowledge gained from a dream series to amplify the symbols?

Core Quality 3: Dreams Personify

1   Does a dream series show changes in self-agency and mentalizing capability of the dream self?

2   What are the various dream characters' theories of mind and their relationships to each other?
3   Are there any changes in the variety of the characters that the dream self needs to relate to? Does it indicate more flexibility and requisite variety in dealing with complex challenges?

Core Quality 4: Trial Runs in a Safe Place

Looking at the dramatic structure:

1   Is there an increase in the frequency of dreams with problem solving and positive outcomes?
2   Is there a decrease in dreams that progress in a negative spiral, or do the coping strategies in the dream self continually improve in this type of dream?
3   Did dreams with cyclical processes change and then appear later on new levels?

Core Quality 5: Online to Unconscious Intelligence

1   Does the dream series suggest a focus on experiential work that has contributed to changes in the dream pattern?
2   How has analytical, self-reflecting work influenced the dream series?
3   On the cognitive behavioral level, did the dreamwork result in more integration of the self in the social reality?

Core Quality 6: Pattern Recognition

Examine the dream series in relationship to current, past and future aspects.

1   Is there any rhythm to how the dreams change during the work week as opposed to the weekends, or after seeing certain people, spending time with children, partner, parents, lover, etc.? Do your dreams change when it comes to memorable days, complicated relations and important, unforeseen events?
2   Did your dream series take you on a journey into the past, thus disclosing experiential patterns that are inhibiting your current life?
3   Does the dream series provide hints about the future for unfolding hitherto undeveloped potentials?

Core Quality 7: High-Level Communication

1   Do recurrent themes refer to higher, more general levels in your personality than you could see when you only looked at individual dreams?

2   On a meta-level, do the dreams refer to the dreamer's attitude to the dreamwork, or suggest a helper or therapist as the dreamer's own inner healer or spiritual quest guide?

3   Do reminiscences from an acute trauma or a character trauma diminish in the series, thus signaling an ongoing healing process?

Core Quality 8: Dreams are Condensed Information

1   Do you find material in the dream series that inspires new insights into older dreams?

2   Can various aspects of the dreams, for example, childhood memories, current experiences or aspects of the future, be synthesized?

3   Is a new interpretation of an earlier dream a result of the multidimensionality of dreams, rather than a fault in the first interpretation?

Core Quality 9: Experiences of Wholeness

1   In the dreamwork has there been a balance between thoughts, emotions, images, movement and inner body sensations?

2   Do you specifically prefer to work with some modalities over others?

3   What would happen if you gave other modalities priority in the dreamwork?

Core Quality 10: Psychological Energy Landscapes

1   Do any dreams have particularly sharp peaks in the psychological energy landscapes?

2   How did you work with these dreams?

3   Can you see a build-up to the peak experience in the dream series, and then a coming down to the low and soft hills again?

References

Boss, M. (1977) *I Dreamt Last Night.* (New York: Gardener Press)

Evans, M. (1937) *The Painter's Object: Conversations with Picasso* (London: G. Howe), s. 82

Damasio, A. (2003) *Looking for Spinoza: Joy, Sorrow, and the Feeling Brain.* (Boston, MA: Houghton Mifflin Harcourt), Kindle edition

Gadamer, H. G. (1975/2004) *Truth and Method.* (New York: Seabury Press), p. 236

Hartmann, E. (1996) 'Who develops PTSD nightmares and who doesn't' in D. Barrett, (Ed.), *Trauma and Dreams.* (Cambridge, MA: Harvard University Press), pp. 100–114

Hartmann, E. (2011) *The Nature and Functions of Dreaming.* (Oxford, UK: Oxford University Press), Kindle edition

Heller, D. P. (2001) *Crash Course: A Self-Healing Guide to Auto Accident Trauma & Recovery.* (Berkeley, CA: North Atlantic Books)

Hoss, R. (2004) *The Significance of Color in Dreams.* In collaboration with Hoffman, C., presented at the International Association for the Study of Dreams conference in Copenhagen, June

Izard, C. E. (1991) *The Psychology of Emotions.* (New York: Plenum Press)

Jung, C. G. (1911–12/1981) 'Symbols of transformation' in G. Adler, M. Fordham and Sir H. Read (Eds), *The Collected Works of C. G. Jung: Symbols of Transformation*, Vol. 5. (Abingdon, UK: Routledge and Kegan Paul)

Jung, C. G. (Author), Adler, G., Fordham, M. and Read, Sir H. (Eds) (1944) *The Collected Works of C.G. Jung: Psychology and Alchemy*, Vol. 12. (Abingdon, UK: Routledge and Kegan Paul)

Jung, C. G. (1961) *Memories, Dreams, Reflections.* (New York: Random House)

Nielsen, T. A. *et al.* (1991) 'Emotions in dream and waking event reports'. *Dreaming*, Vol. 1(4), s. 287–300

Perls, F. (1969/2013) *Gestalt Therapy Verbatim.* (Gouldsboro, ME: The Gestalt Journal Press), Kindle edition

Ronnberg, A. and Martin, K. (2010) *The Book of Symbols. The Archive for Research in Archetypal Symbolism.* (Cologne, Germany: Tachen)

Solms, M. and Turnbull, O. (2002) *The Brain and the Inner World.* (New York: Other Press)

Stern, D. (1985) *The Interpersonal World of the Infant: A View from Psychoanalysis and Developmental Psychology.* (London: Karnac Books), Kindle edition

Vedfelt, O. (1999) *The Dreams Many Faces.* Conference paper for The International Association for the Study of Dreams (Santa Cruz, CA: University of California)

Vedfelt, O. (2007) *The Dimensions of Dreams* (revised Danish edition). (Copenhagen: Gyldendal)

Vedfelt, O. (2009) 'Cultivating feelings through working with dreams'. *Jung Journal: Culture & Psyche*, Vol. 3(4), pp. 88–102

Epilogue

Good Dreamwork and the Future of Humankind

With the state of the world as it is today, skeptics may raise doubts as to whether we have any surplus energy left to use on dreams, which seem so introverted and removed from the thinking patterns of our waking consciousness. In this era – rife with financial crises, threats of ecological disaster and suffering brought on by the unfair distribution of world resources – should we not continue to just keep on acting?

Of course we must act. Yet, despite all the knowledge and experience we can muster through waking consciousness today, and despite all the resources we have at our disposal, we remain unable – or perhaps unmotivated – to do what often turns out to be obvious in the clear light of hindsight. Perhaps the ability contained in dreams – to shift focus away from superficiality and short-term gratification toward what is truly important – could give dreams a well-earned voice in those very considerations we have about the state of our world.

In all the examples I have described, dreamwork has proven to be beneficial to both dreamers and their surroundings. Working with dreams enables human beings of all ages to mature, to become more honest and empathic, to be better parents, partners, friends, colleagues and citizens.

The Ten Core Qualities of Dreams

The Ten Core Qualities of dreams I have elaborated in this work can contribute to the development of social competences in each of their own unique ways, thus stimulating innate, altruistic abilities and innovative skills that benefit society in its entirety.

Core Quality 1: Dreams Deal with Matters Important to Us – teaches us that dreamwork is not an individual way of passing time. Dreams are connected to motivating high-level dynamics of self-organization. Working with Core Quality 1 is about elevating conflict to a higher level than that on which it is being played out. This releases resources that underpin individual self-esteem, and develops a positive attitude toward other people, as well as to humankind as a whole.

Core Quality 2: Dreams Symbolize – highlights the symbols and metaphors in dreams that are a means of expressing influential, intuitive or unconscious experiences that cannot be represented verbally or through linear logic. Dreamwork unfolds these experiences so they become tangible and can be shared with others.

Core Quality 3: Dreams Personify – demonstrates that social skills such as understanding the thoughts and feelings of other people are more often present in dreams than in waking consciousness. Working with our dream characters helps us to differentiate our own expectations of and prejudices about others from our own qualities and potentials for development.

Core Quality 4: Dreams are Trial Runs in a Safe Place – clarifies how the imaginative narratives of dreams allow us to test-run problem-solving models in order to help keep us from harming ourselves and others while awake.

Core Quality 5: Dreams are Online to Unconscious Intelligence – shows how opening up in experiential and creative dreamwork releases energy and liberates our capacity for processing information when we get stuck and run in circles. Experiential dreamwork trains the use and the regulation of altered states of consciousness necessary for innovative work in society, as well as our individual lives.

Core Quality 6: Dreams are Pattern Recognition – reveals how the context-sensitivity of dreams makes it possible to discern to which life situations experiential or behavioral patterns belong. This helps us to apply our intentions in the right place and at the most fitting moment.

Core Quality 7: Dreams are High-Level Communication – emphasizes that our dreams are never-faltering friends who proactively tell us – night after night – if we are acting in accordance with our selves and our fundamental human values. The emphasis is that dreamwork – when it is as its best – is a mutual feedback process between the waking self and the creativity of other subsystems of the psyche and, likewise, the relationships we have to our fellow human beings – again at best – are creative dialogues.

Core Quality 8: Dreams are Condensed Information – deals with the ability of dreams to break with the routine thinking of everyday life, allowing us to see new, creative perspectives in seemingly dead-end situations. This core quality provides a surplus of requisite variety to waking consciousness. Condensed information can inspire complexity in thinking and respect for the diversity of individual human beings, as well as for cultural differences.

Core Quality 9: Dreams are Experiences of Wholeness – describes how dreams are always true to the wholeness of human experience. In doing so, our dreams compensate for the old biases of both individuals and society, and they may contribute to reshaping primitive emotions into cultivated feelings.

Core Quality 10: Dreams are Psychological Energy Landscapes – helps us to understand how dreamwork creates harmony between subsystems in our inner energy landscapes, thus aiding us in meeting our surroundings in the most mature and balanced manner. This applies to human growth at all ages in life, as well as enabling the healing of traumatic experience. Learning to maintain better balance in the ecological systems of our inner world will likely lead to more balance with our relational environment, and with the ecological systems of the world at large.

Our dreams are enormous resources. Globally, the 7.5 billion people that make up humankind dream for a total of 15 billion hours every night. Working with dreams can guide individual human beings to maturity, and may – potentially – contribute to the entirety of humankind growing out of the conflicts that bind our creativity and potential for creating a better world.

Index